SOCCERNOMICS

SOCCERNOMICS

Why England Loses, Why Germany and Brazil Win,

and Why the US, Japan, Australia, Turkey—

and Even Iraq—Are Destined to Become

the Kings of the World's Most Popular Sport

Simon Kuper and Stefan Szymanski

NATION
BOOKS

A Member of the Perseus Books Group
New York

Books published by Nation Books are available at special discounts for bulk
purchases in the United States by corporations, institutions, and other
organizations. For more information, please contact the Special Markets
Department at the Perseus Books Group, 2300 Chestnut Street, Suite 200,
Philadelphia, PA 19103, or call (800) 810-4145, ext. 5000, or e-mail
special.markets@perseusbooks.com.

Designed by Brent Wilcox

The Library of Congress has catalogued this book as follows:
Kuper, Simon.
    Soccernomics : why England loses, why Germany and Brazil win, and why the
U.S., Japan, Australia, Turkey and Even Iraq are destined to become the kings of
the world's most popular sport / by Simon Kuper and Stefan Szymanski.
        p.   cm.
    Includes bibliographical references and index.
    ISBN 978-1-56858-425-6 (alk. paper)
    1. Soccer—Social aspects.   I. Szymanski, Stefan.   II. Title.
GV943.9.S64K88 2009
796.334—dc22
                                                                    2009023502

From Simon:

To Pamela

(who doesn't know about football,
but knows about writing) for her astonishing tolerance.
And to Leila, Leo, and Joey, for all the smiles.

From Stefan:

To my father

We never saw eye to eye,
but he taught me to question everything.

CONTENTS

1 Driving with a Dashboard: In Search of New Truths
About Soccer   1

2 Why England Loses and Others Win   7

PART I The Clubs
Racism, Stupidity, Bad Transfers, Capital Cities,
the Mirage of the NFL, and What Actually Happened in
That Penalty Shoot-Out in Moscow

3 Gentlemen Prefer Blonds: How to Avoid
Silly Mistakes in the Transfer Market   47

4 The Worst Business in the World: Why Soccer Clubs
Don't (and Shouldn't) Make Money   75

5 Need Not Apply: Does English Soccer Discriminate
Against Black People?   97

6 The Economist's Fear of the Penalty Kick: Are Penalties
Cosmically Unfair, or Only If You Are Nicolas Anelka?   113

7 The Suburban Newsagents: City Sizes and Soccer Prizes   133

8 Football Versus Football   157

PART II The Fans
Loyalty, Suicides, Happiness, and
the Country with the Best Supporters

9 The Country That Loves Soccer Most 181

10 Are Soccer Fans Polygamists?
A Critique of the Nick Hornby Model of Fandom 203

11 A Fan's Suicide Notes: Do People Jump Off Buildings
When Their Teams Lose? 221

12 Happiness: Why Hosting a World Cup Is
Good for You 235

PART III Countries
Rich and Poor, Tom Thumb, Guus Ghiddink, Saddam,
and the Champions of the Future

13 The Curse of Poverty: Why Poor Countries
Are Poor at Sports 255

14 Tom Thumb: The Best Little Soccer
Country on Earth 275

15 Core to Periphery: The Future Map of Global Soccer 291

Acknowledgments 307
Select Bibliography 309
Index 313

1

DRIVING WITH A DASHBOARD
In Search of New Truths About Soccer

This book began in the Hilton in Istanbul. From the outside it's a squat and brutalist place, but once the security men have checked your car for bombs and waved you through, the hotel is so soothing you never want to go home again. Having escaped the 13-million-person city, the only stress is over what to do next: a Turkish bath, a game of tennis, or yet more overeating while the sun sets over the Bosporus? For aficionados, there's also a perfect view of the Besiktas soccer stadium right next door. And the staff are so friendly they are even friendlier than ordinary Turkish people.

The two authors of this book, Stefan Szymanski (a sports economist) and Simon Kuper (a journalist), met here. Fenerbahce soccer club was marking its centenary by staging the "100th Year Sports and Science Congress," and had flown them both in to give talks.

Simon's talk was first. He said he had good news for Turkish soccer: as the country's population mushroomed, and its economy grew, the national team was likely to keep getting better. Then it was Stefan's turn. He too had good news for Turkey: as the country's population mushroomed, and its economy grew, the national team was likely to

1

keep getting better. All of this may, incidentally, have been lost on the not-very-Anglophone audience.

The two of us had never met before Istanbul, but over beers in the Hilton bar we confirmed that we did indeed think much the same way about soccer. Stefan as an economist is trained to torture the data until they confess, while Simon as a reporter tends to go around interviewing people, but those are just surface differences. We both think that much in soccer can be explained, even predicted, by studying data—especially data found outside soccer.

For a very long time soccer escaped the Enlightenment. Soccer clubs are still mostly run by people who do what they do because they have always done it that way. These people used to "know" that black players "lacked bottle," and they therefore overpaid mediocre white players. Today they discriminate against black managers, buy the wrong players, and then let those players take penalties the wrong way. (We can, by the way, explain why Manchester United won the penalty shoot-out in the Champions League final in Moscow. It's a story involving a secret note, a Basque economist, and Edwin van der Sar's powers of detection.)

Entrepreneurs who dip into soccer also keep making the same mistakes. They buy clubs promising to run them "like a business," and disappear a few seasons later amid the same public derision as the previous owners. Fans and journalists aren't blameless, either. Many newspaper headlines rest on false premises: "Newcastle Lands World Cup Star" or "World Cup Will Be Economic Bonanza." The game is full of unexamined clichés: "Soccer is becoming boring because the big clubs always win," "Soccer is big business," and, perhaps the greatest myth in the English game, "The England team should do better." None of these shibboleths has been tested against the data.

Most male team sports are pervaded by the same overreliance on traditional beliefs. Baseball, too, was until very recently an old game stuffed with old lore. Since time immemorial, players had stolen bases, hit sacrifice bunts, and been judged on their batting averages. Everyone in baseball just *knew* that all this was right.

But that was before Bill James. Like Dorothy in *The Wizard of Oz*, James came from rural Kansas. He hadn't done much in life beyond keeping the stats in the local Little League and watching the furnaces in a pork-and-beans factory. However, in his spare time he had begun to study baseball statistics with a fresh eye and discovered that "a great portion of the sport's traditional knowledge is ridiculous hokum." James wrote that he wanted to approach the subject of baseball "with the same kind of intellectual rigor and discipline that is routinely applied, by scientists great and poor, to trying to unravel the mysteries of the universe, of society, of the human mind, or of the price of burlap in Des Moines."

In self-published mimeographs masquerading as books, the first of which sold seventy-five copies, James began demolishing the game's myths. He found, for instance, that the most important statistic in batting was the rarely mentioned "on-base percentage"—how often a player manages to get on base. James and his followers (statisticians of baseball who came to be known as sabermetricians) showed that good old sacrifice bunts and base stealing were terrible strategies.

His annual *Baseball Abstracts* turned into real books; eventually they reached the best-seller lists. One year, the cover picture showed an ape, posed as Rodin's *Thinker*, studying a baseball. As James wrote in one *Abstract*, "This is *outside* baseball. This is a book about what baseball looks like if you step back from it and study it intensely and minutely, but from a distance."

Some Jamesians started to penetrate professional baseball. One of them, Billy Beane, the bafflingly successful general manager of the little Oakland A's, is the hero of Michael Lewis's earthmoving book *Moneyball*. (We'll say more later about Beane's brilliant gaming of the transfer market and its lessons for soccer.)

Eventually, even the people inside baseball began to get curious about James. In 2002 the Boston Red Sox appointed him "senior baseball operations adviser." That same year, the Red Sox hired one of James's followers, the twenty-eight-year-old Theo Epstein, as the youngest general manager in the history of the major leagues. The "cursed" club quickly won two World Series.

Now soccer is due its own Jamesian revolution.

A NUMBERS GAME

It's strange that soccer has been so averse to studying data, because one thing that attracts many fans to the game is precisely a love of numbers.

The man to ask about that is Alex Bellos. He wrote the magnificent *Futebol: The Brazilian Way of Life*, but he also has a math degree, and his book on math for laypeople is expected out in 2010. "Numbers are incredibly satisfying," Bellos tells us. "The world has no order, and math is a way of seeing it in an order. League tables have an order. And the calculations you need to do for them are so simple: it's nothing more than your three-times table."

Though most fans would probably deny it, a love of soccer is often intertwined with a love of numbers. There are the match results, the famous dates, and the special joy of sitting in a pub with the newspaper on a Sunday morning "reading" the league table. Fantasy soccer leagues are, at bottom, numbers games.

In this book we want to introduce new numbers and new ideas to soccer: numbers on suicides, on wage spending, on countries' populations, on anything that helps to reveal new truths about the game. Though Stefan is a sports economist, this is not a book about money. The point of soccer clubs is not to turn a profit (which is fortunate, as almost none of them do), nor are we particularly interested in any profits they happen to make. Rather, we want to use an economist's skills (plus a little geography, psychology, and sociology) to understand the game on the field, and the fans off it.

Some people may not want their emotional relationship with soccer sullied by our rational calculations. On the other hand, the next time England loses a penalty shoot-out in a World Cup quarter-final these same people will probably be throwing their beer glasses at the TV, when instead they could be tempering their disappointment with some reflections on the nature of binomial probability theory.

We think it's a good time to be writing this book. For the first time ever in soccer, there are a lot of numbers to mine. Traditionally, the only data that existed in the game were goals and league tables. (Newspapers published attendance figures, but these were unreliable.) At the end of the 1980s, when Stefan went into sports economics, only about twenty or thirty academic articles on soccer had ever been published. Now there are countless. Many of the new truths they contain have not yet reached most fans.

The other new source of knowledge is the bulging library of soccer books. When Pete Davies published *All Played Out: The Full Story of Italia '90*, there were probably only about twenty or thirty good soccer books in existence. Now—thanks partly to Davies, who has been described as John the Baptist to Nick Hornby's Jesus—there are thousands. Many of these books (including Bellos's *Futebol*) contain truths about the game that we try to present here.

So unstoppable has the stream of data become that even people inside the game are finally starting to sift it. Michael Lewis, the author of *Moneyball*, wrote in the *New York Times* in February 2009, "The virus that infected professional baseball in the 1990s, the use of statistics to find new and better ways to value players and strategies, has found its way into every major sport. Not just basketball and football, but also soccer and cricket and rugby and, for all I know, snooker and darts— each one now supports a subculture of smart people who view it not just as a game to be played but as a problem to be solved."

In soccer, one of these smart men (it's part of the game's own "ridiculous hokum" that they have to be men) is Arsène Wenger. A trained economist, Wenger is practically addicted to statistics, like the number of kilometers run by each player in a game. What makes him one of the heroes of *Soccernomics* is his understanding that in soccer today, you need data to get ahead. If you study figures, you will see more and win more.

Slowly, Wenger's colleagues are also ceasing to rely on gut alone. Increasingly, they use computer programs like Prozone to analyze games and players. Another harbinger of the impending Jamesian takeover of soccer is the Milan Lab. Early on, AC Milan's in-house medical outfit found that just by studying a player's jump, it could predict with 70 percent accuracy whether he would get injured. It then collected millions of data on each of the team's players on computers, and in the process stumbled upon the secret of eternal youth. (It's still a secret: no other club has a Milan Lab, and the lab won't divulge its findings, which is why players at other clubs are generally finished by their early thirties.)

Most of Milan's starting eleven who beat Liverpool in the Champions League final of 2007 were thirty-one or older: Paolo Maldini, the captain, was thirty-eight, and Filippo Inzaghi, scorer of both of Milan's goals, was thirty-three. In large part, that trophy was won by the Milan Lab and its database. It is another version of the Triumph of the Geeks story.

As the two of us talked more and began to think harder about soccer and data, we buzzed around all sorts of questions. Could we find figures to show which country loved soccer the most? Might the game somehow deter people from killing themselves? And perhaps we could have a shot at predicting which clubs and countries—Turkey most likely, perhaps even Iraq—would dominate the soccer of the future. Stefan lives in London and Simon in Paris, so we spent a year firing figures, arguments, and anecdotes back and forth across the Channel.

All the while, we distrusted every bit of ancient soccer lore, and tested it against the numbers. As Jean-Pierre Meersseman, the Milan Lab's cigarette-puffing Belgian director, told us: "You can drive a car without a dashboard, without any information, and that's what's happening in soccer. There are excellent drivers, excellent cars, but if you have your dashboard, it makes it just a little bit easier. I wonder why people don't want more information." We do.

2

WHY ENGLAND
LOSES AND OTHERS WIN

BEATEN BY A DISHWASHER

When the England team flies to South Africa for the World Cup, an ancient ritual will start to unfold. Perfected over England's fourteen previous failures to win the World Cup away from home, it follows this pattern:

Phase 1: Pretournament—
Certainty That England Will Win the World Cup

Alf Ramsey, the only English manager to win the trophy, predicted the victory of 1966. However, his prescience becomes less impressive when you realize that almost every England manager thinks he will win the trophy, including Ramsey in the two campaigns he didn't. When his team was knocked out in 1970 he was stunned and said, "We must now look ahead to the next world cup in Munich where our chances of winning I would say are very good indeed." England didn't qualify for that one.

Glenn Hoddle, England's manager in 1998, revealed only after his team had been knocked out "my innermost thought, which was that England would win the World Cup." Another manager who went home early, Ron Greenwood, confessed, "I honestly thought we could have won the World Cup in 1982." A month before the World Cup of 2006, Sven Goran Eriksson said, "I think we will win it."

The deluded manager is never alone. As the England player Johnny Haynes remarked after elimination in 1958, "Everyone in England thinks we have a God-given right to win the World Cup." This belief in the face of all evidence was a hangover from empire: England is soccer's mother country and should therefore be the best today. The sociologist Stephen Wagg notes: "In reality, England is a country like many others and the England soccer team is a soccer team like many others." This truth is only slowly sinking in.

Phase 2: During the Tournament
England Meets a Former Wartime Enemy

In five of their last seven World Cups, England was knocked out by either Germany or Argentina. The matches fit seamlessly into the British tabloid view of history, except for the outcome. As Alan Ball summed up the mood in England's dressing room after the defeat to West Germany in 1970: "It was disbelief."

Even Joe Gaetjens, who scored the winning goal for the US against England in 1950, turns out to have been of German-Haitian origin, not Belgian-Haitian as is always said. And in any case, the US is another former wartime enemy.

Phase 3: The English Conclude That the Game Turned on One
Freakish Piece of Bad Luck That Could Happen Only to Them

Gaetjens, the accounting student and dishwasher in a Manhattan restaurant who didn't even have an American passport, must have scored his goal by accident. "Gaetjens went for the ball, but at the last moment, decided to duck," England's captain Billy Wright wrote later. "The ball bounced on the top of his head and slipped past the bewildered Williams."

In 1970 England's goalkeeper Gordon Banks got an upset stomach before the quarter-final against West Germany. He was okay on the morning of the game and was picked to play, but a little later was discovered on the toilet with everything "coming out both ends." His understudy, Peter Bonetti, let in three soft German goals.

There was more bad luck in 1973, when England failed to qualify for the next year's World Cup because Poland's "clown" of a goalkeeper, Jan Tomaszewski, unaccountably had a brilliant night at Wembley. "The simple truth is that on a normal day we would have beaten Poland 6–0," England's midfielder Martin Peters says in Niall Edworthy's book on England managers, *The Second Most Important Job in the Country*. Poland went on to reach the semifinals of the '74 World Cup.

In 1990 and 1998 England lost in what everyone knows is the lottery of the penalty shoot-out. In 2002 everyone knew that the obscure, bucktoothed Brazilian kid Ronaldinho must have lucked out with the free kick that sailed into England's net, because he couldn't have been good enough to place it deliberately. In 2006 Wayne Rooney would never have been sent off for stomping on Ricardo Carvalho's genitals if Cristiano Ronaldo hadn't tattled on him. These things just don't happen to other countries.

Phase 4: Moreover, Everyone Else Cheated

The Brazilian crowd in 1950 and the Mexican crowd in 1970 deliberately wasted time while England was losing by keeping the ball in the stands. The CIA (some say) drugged Banks. Diego Maradona's "hand of God" single-handedly defeated England in 1986. Diego Simeone playacted in 1998 to get David Beckham sent off, and Cristiano Ronaldo did the same for Rooney in 2006.

Every referee opposes England. Those of his decisions that support this thesis are analyzed darkly. Typically, the referee's nationality is mentioned to blacken him further. Billy Wright, England's captain in 1950, later recalled "Mr Dattilo of Italy, who seemed determined to let nothing so negligible as the laws of the game come between America and victory." The referee who didn't give England a penalty against West Germany in 1970 was, inevitably, an Argentine. The Tunisian referee of 1986 who, like most people watching the game, failed to spot the "hand of God" has become legendary.

Phase 5: England Is Knocked Out Without Getting Anywhere Near Lifting the Cup

The only exception was 1990, when they reached the semifinal. Otherwise, England has always been eliminated when still needing to defeat at least three excellent teams. Since 1970, Bulgaria, Sweden, and Poland have gotten as close to winning a World Cup as England has.

Perhaps England should be relieved that it doesn't finish second. As Jerry Seinfeld once said, who wants to be the greatest loser? The science writer Stefan Klein points out that winning bronze at the Olympics is not so bad, because that is a great achievement by any standards, but winning silver is awful, as you will always be tortured by the thought of what might have been.

England has never been at much risk of that. The team won only five of its eighteen matches at World Cups abroad from 1950 through 1970, and didn't qualify for the next two tournaments in 1974 and 1978, so at least it has been improving since. The general belief in decline from a golden age is mistaken.

Phase 6: The Day After Elimination, Normal Life Resumes

The one exception is 1970, when England's elimination may have caused Labour's surprise defeat in the general election four days later. But otherwise the elimination does not bring on a nationwide hangover. To the contrary, England's eliminations are celebrated, turned into national myths, or songs, or commercials for pizza chains.

Phase 7: A Scapegoat Is Found

The scapegoat is never an outfield player who has "battled" all match. Even if he directly caused the elimination by missing a penalty, he is a "hero."

Beckham was scapegoated for the defeat against Argentina in 1998 only because he got a red card after forty-six minutes. Writer Dave Hill explained that the press was simply pulling out its "two traditional responses to England's sporting failure: heralding a glorious defeat and mercilessly punishing those responsible for it, in this case Posh Spice's unfortunate fiancé."

Beckham wrote in one of his autobiographies that the abuse continued for years: "Every time I think it has disappeared, I know I will meet some idiot who will have a go at me. Sometimes it is at matches, sometimes just driving down the road." He added that he kept "a little book in which I've written down the names of those people who upset me the most. I don't want to name them because I want it to be a surprise when I get them back." One day they will all get upset stomachs.

Often the scapegoat is a management figure: Wright as captain in 1950, Joe Mears as chief selector in 1958, and many managers since. Sometimes it is a keeper, who by virtue of his position just stood around in goal rather than battling like a hero. Bonetti spent the rest of his career enduring chants of "You lost the World Cup." After retiring from soccer, he went into quasi exile as a mailman on a remote Scottish island.

In 2006 Cristiano Ronaldo was anointed scapegoat. Only after a defeat to Brazil is no scapegoat sought, because defeats to Brazil are considered acceptable.

Phase 8: England Enters the Next World Cup Thinking It Will Win It

The World Cup as ritual has a meaning beyond soccer. The elimination is usually the most watched British television program of the year. It therefore educates the English in two contradictory narratives about their country: one, that England has a manifest destiny to triumph, and, two, that it never does. The genius of the song "Three Lions," English soccer's unofficial anthem, is that it combines both narratives: "Thirty years of hurt / Never stopped me dreaming."

There is an alternative universe in which Beckham didn't get sent off, Banks's stomach held up, the referee spotted Maradona's handball, and so on. In that universe England has won about seven World Cups. Many English fans think they would have preferred that. But it would have deprived the English of a ritual that marks the passing of time much like Christmas or New Year's and celebrates a certain idea of England: a land of unlucky heroes that no longer rules the world, although it should.

A PERFECTLY DECENT TEAM

Any mathematician would say it's absurd to expect England to win the World Cup.

England wins two-thirds of its matches. To be precise, from 1970 to 2007 England played 411, won 217, tied 120, and lost 74. If we treat a tie as half a win, this translates into a winning percentage of 67.4 percent. If we then break this down into seven equal periods of just under four years each, England's winning percentage has never fallen below 62 percent or risen above 70 percent. In other words, the team's performance is very constant.

Yes, these statistics conceal some ghastly mishaps as well as some highs, but the statistics tell us that the difference between anguish and euphoria is a few percentage points.

On the face of it, winning two-thirds of the time—meaning bookies' odds of 1–2 on—is not too shabby in a two-horse race. Of course, some countries do even better. Brazil wins about 80 percent of its games. But against most teams, England is the deserved favorite. In the fairly typical period of 1980–2001, England's win percentage was tenth best in the world.

The problem comes when we try to translate this achievement into winning tournaments. England's failure to win anything since the holy year of 1966 is a cause of much embarrassment for British expatriates in bars on the Spanish coast.

It is tricky to calculate the exact probability of England qualifying for a tournament, because it requires an analysis of many permutations of events. However, we can reduce it to a simple problem of multiplicative probability if we adopt the "must-win" concept. For example, England failed to qualify for Euro 2008 by coming in third in its group behind Croatia and Russia. In doing so it won seven matches, lost three, and tied twice (for an average winning percentage of exactly 66.66 percent). It was narrowly beaten by Russia, which won seven, lost two, and tied three times (a winning percentage of 70.83 percent).

Suppose that to guarantee qualification you have to win eight games outright. Then the problem becomes one when you have to win eight out of twelve, where your winning probability in each game is 66 percent. Calculating this probability is a bit more complicated, since it involves combinatorics.

The answer is a probability of qualification of 63 percent. That means that England should qualify for fewer than two-thirds of the tournaments it enters. In fact, from 1970 through 2008 England qualified two-thirds of the time: for six out of nine World Cups and six out of nine European championships. Given that the number of qualifying matches has risen over time, England's performance is in line with what you might expect.

The sad fact is that England is a good team that does better than most. This means it is not likely to win many tournaments, and it doesn't.

The English tend to feel that England should do better. The team's usual status around the bottom of the world's top ten is not good enough. The national media, in particular, feel almost perpetually let down by the team. England is "known as perennial underachievers on the world stage," according to the tabloid the *Sun*; its history "has been a landscape sculpted from valleys of underachievement," says the *Independent* newspaper; the former England captain Terry Butcher grumbled in the *Sunday Mirror* in 2006 that "historical underachievement has somehow conspired to make England feel even more important."

"Why does England lose?" is perhaps the greatest question in English sports. In trying to answer it, we hear strange echoes from the field of development economics. The central question in that field is, "Why are some countries less productive than others?" The two main reasons England loses would sound familiar to any development economist. So would the most common reason *falsely* cited for why England loses. Here are those three reasons for England's eliminations—first the false one, then the correct ones.

BRITISH JOBS FOR BRITISH WORKERS? WHY THERE ARE TOO MANY ENGLISHMEN IN THE PREMIER LEAGUE

When pundits gather to explain why England loses, their favorite scapegoat of the moment is imports: the hundreds of foreigners who play in the Premier League (EPL). Here is England's midfielder Steven Gerrard speaking before England lost to Croatia and failed to qualify for Euro 2008: "I think there is a risk of too many foreign players coming over, which would affect our national team eventually if it's not already. It is important we keep producing players."

After all, if our boys can barely even get a game in their own league, how can they hope to mature into internationals? After England lost to Croatia, FIFA's president, Sepp Blatter; Manchester United's manager, Alex Ferguson; and UEFA's president, Michel Platini, all made versions of Gerrard's argument.

These men were effectively blaming imports for the English lack of skills. The reasoning is that our own workers don't get a chance because they are being displaced by foreign workers. Exactly the same argument is often made in development economics. Why are some countries not very productive? Partly because their inhabitants don't have enough skills. The best place to learn skills—such as making toothpaste, or teaching math, or playing soccer—is on the job. To learn how to make toothpaste, you have to actually make it, not just take a class to learn how to make it. But if you are always importing toothpaste, you will never learn.

That is why, for more than half a century, many development economists have called for "import substitution." Ban or tax certain imports so that the country can learn to make the stuff itself. Import substitution has worked for a few countries. Japan after the war, for instance, managed to teach itself from scratch how to make all sorts of high-quality cars and electrical gadgets.

The idea of "import substitution" in the Premier League has an emotional appeal to many English fans. Britons often complain about feeling overrun by immigrants, and few spots in the country are more foreign than a Premier League field on match day. Arsenal, in particular, has wisely dispensed with Englishmen almost altogether. All told, Englishmen accounted for only 37 percent of the minutes played by soccer players in the Premier League in the 2007–2008 season before Croatia's night at Wembley. To some degree, *English* soccer no longer exists.

"It is my philosophy to protect the identity of the clubs and country," said Platini. "Manchester United against Liverpool should be with players from Manchester and Liverpool, from that region. Robbie Fowler was from Liverpool. He grew up in that city, it was nice, but now you don't have the English players."

Imagine for a moment that Platini somehow managed to suspend EU law and force English soccer clubs to discriminate against players from other EU countries. If that happened, Platini and Gerrard would probably end up disappointed. If inferior English players were handed places in Premier League teams, they would have little incentive to improve. This is a classic problem with import substitution: it protects bad producers. What then tends to happen is that short-term protection becomes long-term protection.

But, in fact, Platini's entire premise is wrong. If people in soccer understood numbers better, they would grasp that the problem of the England team is not that there are too few Englishmen playing in the

Premier League. To the contrary: there are too *many*. England would do better if the country's best clubs fielded even fewer English players.

You could argue that English players accounted for "only" 37 percent of playing time in the Premier League. Or you could argue that they account for a massive 37 percent of playing time, more than any other nationality in what is now the world's toughest league.

This means that English players get a lot of regular experience in top-level club soccer. Even if we lump together the world's three toughest leagues—the Premier League, Spain's Primera Liga, and Italy's Serie A—then only Italians, Spaniards, and perhaps Brazilians and Frenchmen play more tough club soccer. But certainly English players get far more experience in top-level soccer than, say, Croatians or Russians do.

In fact, the English probably get too much of this kind of experience. The Premier League is becoming soccer's NBA, the first global league in this sport's history. So the players earn millions of dollars. So the league is all-consuming, particularly if you play for one of the "Big Four" clubs, as almost all regular English internationals do. The players have to give almost all their energy and concentration in every match. It's a little easier even in the Serie A or La Liga, where smaller teams like Siena, Catania, or Santander cannot afford to buy brilliant foreigners.

Clearly, an athlete can't peak in every match. If you are running in the Olympics, you plan your season so that you will peak only at the Olympics, and not before. If you play soccer for, say, Croatia and for a club in a smaller league (even the Bundesliga), you can husband your energy so as to peak in big international matches—for instance, when you are playing England at Wembley.

By contrast, English players have to try to peak every week for their clubs. In no other country do players face as many demanding games a season. No clubs in any other country play as many European games as the English do. Daniele Tognaccini, chief athletics coach at the "Milan Lab," probably the most sophisticated medical outfit in soccer, explains what happens when a player has to play sixty tough games a year: "The performance is not optimal. The risk of injury is very high. We can say the risk of injury during one game, after one week's training, is 10 percent. If you play after two days, the risk rises by 30 or 40 percent. If you are playing four or five games consecutively without the right recovery, the risk of injury is incredible. The probability of having one lesser performance is very high."

So when English players play internationally, they start tired, hurt, and without enough focus. Often they cannot raise their game. Harry Redknapp said when he was manager of Portsmouth, "I think England games get in the way of club soccer for the players now. Club soccer is so important, the Champions League and everything with it, that England games become a distraction to them." Moreover, players in the intense Premier League are always getting injured, and their clubs don't give them time to recover. That may be why half of England's regulars couldn't play against Croatia. For some of the same reasons, the US often disappoints in basketball world championships.

In short, if England wanted to do better in international matches, it should export English players to more relaxed leagues, like, for example, Croatia's.

England's former manager Eriksson understood the problem. When one of the authors of this book asked him why England lost in the quarter-finals in the World Cup 2002 and in Euro 2004, he said his players were tired after tough seasons. Was that really the only reason? "I would say so," Eriksson replied. "If you're not fit enough . . . In Japan, we never scored one goal the second half."

In any case, English fans *want* to see teams full of foreign players. Platini wonders whether Liverpudlians can identify with a Liverpool team full of foreigners. Well, they seem to manage. Judging by the Premiership's record crowds despite its record ticket prices, fans still identify enough. Arsenal's all-foreign team now draws sixty thousand fans weekly, the highest average crowd of any London team in history. England can have an excellent league, or it can have an English league, but it can't have both. Given the choice, fans seem to prefer excellence. In that sense, they are typical consumers. If you try to substitute imports, then, at least at first, consumers have to put up with worse products. They generally don't like that.

THE PROBLEM OF EXCLUSION: HOW ENGLISH SOCCER DRIVES OUT THE MIDDLE CLASSES

The Romans built their empire with an army drawn from every part of society. Only when the militia became an elite profession open just to particular families did the empire start to decline. When you limit your talent pool, you limit the development of skills. The bigger the group of people you draw from, the more new ideas that are likely to bubble up. That's why large networks like the City of London and Silicon Valley, which draw talent from around the world, are so creative. So is the Premier League.

The problem of English soccer is what happens *before* the best English players reach the Premier League. The Englishmen who make it to the top are drawn very largely from one single and shrinking social group: the traditional working class. The country's middle classes are mostly barred from professional soccer. That holds back the national team.

There are many ways to classify which social class someone was born into, but one good indicator is the profession of that person's father. Joe Boyle, with some help from Dan Kuper, researched for us the jobs of the fathers of England players who played at the World Cups of 1998, 2002, and 2006. Boyle ignored jobs the fathers might have been handed after their sons' rise to stardom. As much as possible, he tried to establish what the father did while the son was growing up. Using players' autobiographies and newspaper profiles, he came up with the following list. It doesn't include every player (asked, for instance, what Wayne Bridge's dad did for a living, we throw up our hands in despair), but most are here. Another caveat: some of the dads on the list were absent while their boys were growing up. That said, here are their professions:

Many of these job descriptions are imprecise. What exactly did Rob Lee's dad do at the shipping company, for instance? Still, it's possible to break down the list of thirty-four players into a few categories: Eighteen players, or more than half the total, were sons of skilled or unskilled

FIGURE 2.1 Employment of World Cup fathers

Player	Father's job
Tony Adams	Roofer
Darren Anderton	Ran moving company; later a taxi driver
David Batty	Sanitation worker
David Beckham	Heating engineer
Sol Campbell	Railway worker
Jamie Carragher	Pub landlord
Ashley Cole	None given, but in his autobiography describes "a grounded working-class upbringing in east London"
Joe Cole	Fruit and vegetable trader
Peter Crouch	Creative director at international advertising agency
Stewart Downing	Painter and decorator on oil rigs
Kieron Dyer	Manager of Caribbean social club
Rio Ferdinand	Tailor
Robbie Fowler	Laborer; later worked night shift at railway maintenance depot
Steven Gerrard	Laborer (bricklaying, paving, and so on)
Emile Heskey	Security worker at nightclub
Paul Ince	Railway worker
David James	Artist who runs gallery in Jamaica
Jermaine Jenas	Soccer coach in the United States
Frank Lampard	Soccer player
Rob Lee	"Involved in a shipping company"
Graeme Le Saux	Ran fruit and vegetable stall
Steve McManaman	Printer
Paul Merson	Coal worker
Danny Mills	Coach in Norwich City's youth academy
Michael Owen	Soccer player
Wayne Rooney	Laborer, mainly on building sites; often unemployed
Paul Scholes	Gas-pipe fitter
David Seaman	Garage mechanic, later ran sandwich shop, then worked at steelworks
Alan Shearer	Sheet-metal worker
Teddy Sheringham	Policeman
Gareth Southgate	Worked for IBM
John Terry	Forklift-truck operator
Darius Vassell	Factory worker
Theo Walcott	Royal Air Force administrator; later joined services company working for British Gas

manual laborers: Vassell, Terry, Shearer, Seaman, Scholes, Rooney, Merson, McManaman, Ince, Heskey, Gerrard, Fowler, Adams, Batty, Beckham, Campbell, Ferdinand, and Downing. Ashley Cole with his "working-class upbringing" is probably best assigned to this category, too. Four players (Jenas, Lampard, Mills, and Owen) had fathers who worked in soccer. Le Saux and Joe Cole were both sons of fruit and vegetable traders. Anderton's dad ran a moving company, which seems to have failed, before becoming a cab driver. Sheringham's father was a policeman. Carragher's and Dyer's dads ran a pub and a social club, respectively. That leaves only five players out of thirty-four—Crouch, James, Lee, Southgate, and Walcott—whose fathers seem to have worked in professions that required them to have had an education beyond the age of sixteen. If we define class by education, then only 15 percent of England players of recent years had "middle-class" origins.

The male population as a whole was much better educated. Of British men aged between thirty-five and fifty-four in 1996—the generation of most of these players' fathers—a little more than half had qualifications above the most basic level, according to the British Household Panel Study.

English soccer's reliance on an overwhelmingly working-class talent pool was only moderately damaging in the past, when most English people were working class. In the late 1980s, 70 percent of Britons still left school at the age of sixteen, often for manual jobs. But by then, the growth of the middle classes had already begun. In fact, middle-class values began to permeate the country, a process that sociologists call "embourgeoisement." It happened on what used to be the soccer terraces, which because of high ticket prices are now slightly more middle class than even the country at large.

Nowadays, more than 70 percent of Britons stay in school past the age of sixteen. More than 40 percent enter higher education. More and more, Britain is a middle-class nation. Yet because soccer still recruits overwhelmingly from the traditional working classes, it excludes an ever-growing swath of the population. That must be a brake on the England team.

The shrinking of the talent pool is only part of the problem. Until at least the late 1990s British soccer was suffused, without quite knowing it, by British working-class habits. Some of these were damaging, such as the sausages-and-chips diet, or the idea that binge drinking is a hobby. "Maybe in earlier generations the drinking culture carried over from the working-class origins of the players," wrote Manchester United's manager Alex Ferguson in his autobiography. "Most of them came from families where many of the men took the view that if they put in a hard shift in a factory or a coalmine they were entitled to relax with a few pints. Some footballers seem determined to cling to that shift-worker's mentality. . . . Also prevalent is the notion that Saturday night is the end of the working week and therefore a good time to get wrecked." Of course, "problem drinking" exists in the British middle classes, too. And of course most working-class people have no issues with alcohol. However, Ferguson is explicitly describing a traditional working-class attitude.

Another problem was that the British working classes tended to regard soccer as something you learned on the job, rather than from educationalists with diplomas. It was the attitude you would expect of an industry in which few people had much formal education. One British national soccer administrator, who worked for decades to introduce coaching courses, told us that clubs mocked his attempts as "some new-fangled thing got up by college boys—as if there was shame in being educated." He recalls that *coaching* and *tactics* became "shame words." "People would say, 'The trouble with soccer today is that there is too much coaching.' That's like saying, 'The trouble with school is that there's too much education.'"

It would be crazy to generalize too much about the working classes. There is a strong working-class tradition of self-education. Large numbers of postwar Britons became the first people in their families to go to college. Nonetheless, the anti-intellectual attitudes that the soccer administrator encountered do seem to be widespread in the English game.

These attitudes may help explain why English managers and English players are not known for thinking about soccer. When the Dutchman

Johan Cruijff said, "Soccer is a game you play with your head," he wasn't talking about headers.

Over the past decade these traditional working-class attitudes have begun to fade in British soccer. Foreign managers and players have arrived, importing the revolutionary notions that professional athletes should think about their game and look after their bodies. But one working-class custom still bars middle-class Britons from professional soccer: what you might call the "antieducational requirement."

Most British soccer players still leave school at sixteen. The belief persists that only thus can they concentrate fully on the game. The argument that many great foreign players—Ruud Gullit, Dennis Bergkamp, Tostao, Socrates, Osvaldo Ardiles, Jorge Valdano, Josep Guardiola, Fernando Redondo, Kaká, and others—stayed in school after that age, or even attended college, is ignored. This is probably because many British coaches and players are suspicious of educated people.

It is true that the clubs' new academies are meant to help players keep studying, but in practice this rarely happens. A few years ago one of us visited the academy of an English club. It's an academy of some note: two of its recent graduates first played for their countries while still teenagers. But all the boys we met there, bright or otherwise, were sent to do the same single lowly vocational course in leisure and tourism to fulfill the academy's minimum educational requirements. Together the boys caused such havoc in class that all the other students had dropped out of the course. It's not that soccer players are too busy to study; they rarely train more than a couple of hours a day. Rather, it's that being studious is frowned upon inside the English game.

English soccer consequently remains unwelcoming to middle-class teenagers. To cite just one example, Stuart Ford, who at seventeen played for England Schools, gave up on becoming a professional because he got tired of listening to rants from uneducated coaches. Being middle class, he always felt like an outsider. He recalled, "I was often goaded about my posh school or my gross misunderstanding of street fashion. That was just from the management." Instead, he became a Hollywood lawyer. Later, as a senior executive at one of the Hollywood studios, he was one of the people behind an unsuccessful bid to buy Liverpool FC.

If the working classes get little education, that is mainly the fault of the middle-class people who oversee the British school system. Nonetheless, the educational divide means that any middle-class person entering British soccer feels instantly out of place.

Many middle-class athletes drift to cricket or rugby instead. Often, this represents a direct loss to soccer. For most people, sporting talent is fairly transferable until they reach their late teens. Many English soccer players, like Phil Neville and Gary Lineker, were gifted cricketers, too. Some well-known rugby players took up rugby only as teenagers, when they realized they weren't going to make it in soccer. And in the past, several paragons represented England in more than one sport. Only a few sports demand very specific qualities that can't be transferred: it's hard to go from being a jockey to being a basketball player, for instance. But English soccer competes with other ball games for talent, and it scares away the educated middle classes.

This is particularly sad because there is growing evidence that sporting talent and academic talent are linked. The best athletes have fast mental reactions, and those reactions, if properly trained, would make for high-caliber intellects.

All this helps explain why even though the academies of English clubs are the richest in the world, England doesn't produce better players than poor nations. Instead of trying to exclude foreigners from English soccer, it would be smarter to include more middle-class English people. Only when there are England players with educated accents—as happens in Holland, Argentina, and even Brazil (Dunga and Kaká, for instance)—might the national team maximize its potential.

CLOSED TO INNOVATIONS:
ENGLISH SOCCER'S SMALL NETWORK

When the Internet arrived, many pundits predicted the decline of the city. After all, why live in a small apartment in East London when you could set up your laptop in an old farmhouse overlooking a sheep meadow?

The prediction turned out to be wrong. Cities have continued their growth of the past two hundred years, which is why apartments in East London became so expensive. Meanwhile, the countryside has turned into something of a desert, inhabited by a few farmers and old people, and used by the rest of us mostly for long walks. It turns out that people still want to live in dirty, overcrowded, overpriced cities. And the reason they do is the social networks. To be rural is to be isolated. Networks give you contacts.

Someone you meet at a party or at your kids' playground can give you a job or an idea. Just as the brain works by building new connections between huge bundles of neurons, with each connection producing a new thought, so we as individuals need to find ourselves in the center of the bundle in order to make more connections.

Networks are key to the latest thinking about economic development. Better networks are one reason that some countries are richer than others. As it happens, networks also help explain why some countries have done better at soccer than England. English soccer's biggest problem until very recently was probably geography. The country was too far from the networks of continental western Europe, where the best soccer was played.

Once upon a time, England was at the center of soccer's knowledge network. From the first official soccer international in 1872, until at least the First World War, and perhaps even until England's first home defeat against Hungary in 1953, you could argue that England was the dominant soccer nation. It was the country that exported soccer know-how to the world in the form of managers. The English expatriate manager became such a legendary figure that to this day in Spain and Italy a head coach is known as a "mister."

Many English people clung to the belief in England's supremacy long after it had ceased to be true. The astonishment each time England didn't win the World Cup ended only with the team's abject failures in the 1970s.

The gradual British decline in soccer echoes the decline in Britain's economic status. The country went from supreme economic power under Queen Victoria to having its hand held by the International Monetary Fund in the late 1970s. Admittedly, in soccer as in economics, most observers exaggerated Britain's slide. The country's position in the top ten of economies was never much in doubt. But in soccer it became clear by 1970 at the latest that dominance had shifted across the Channel to the core of western Europe. For the next thirty years, that part of the Continent was the most fertile network in soccer. And Britain was just outside it.

The German World Cup of 2006 demonstrated western Europe's grip on global soccer. The region has only about 400 million inhabitants, or 6 percent of the world's population, yet only once in the entire tournament did a western European team lose to a team from another region: Switzerland's insanely dull defeat on penalties to Ukraine.

That summer even Brazil couldn't match western Europe. Argentina continued its run of failing to beat a western European team in open play at a World Cup since the final against West Germany in 1986 (though it has won two of the eight subsequent encounters against Europeans on penalties). Big countries outside the region, like Mexico, Japan, the US, and Poland, could not match little western European countries like Portugal, Holland, or Sweden. If you understood the geographical rule of the last World Cup, you could sit in the stands for almost every match before the quarter-finals confident of knowing the outcome.

Western Europe excels at soccer for the same fundamental reason it had the scientific revolution and was for centuries the world's richest region. The region's secret is what historian Norman Davies calls its "user-friendly climate." Western Europe is mild and rainy. Because of that, the land is fertile. This allows hundreds of millions of people to inhabit a small space of land. That creates networks.

From the World Cup in Germany, you could have flown in two and a half hours to about twenty countries containing roughly 300 million people. That is the densest network on earth. There was nothing like that in Japan at the previous World Cup: the only foreign capital you can reach from Tokyo within that time is Seoul. South Africa, host of the next World Cup, is even more isolated.

For centuries now, the interconnected peoples of western Europe have exchanged ideas fast. The "scientific revolution" of the sixteenth and seventeenth centuries could happen in western Europe because its scientists were near each other, networking, holding a dialogue in their shared language: Latin. Copernicus, Polish son of a German merchant, wrote that the earth circled the sun. Galileo in Florence read Copernicus and confirmed his findings through a telescope. The Englishman Francis Bacon described their "scientific method": deductions based on data. England at the time was very much part of the European network.

A typical product of that network was the lens grinder, a crucial new machine in the development of the microscope in the early 1660s. Robert Hooke in London invented a new grinder, which made lenses so accurate that Hooke could publish a detailed engraving of a louse attached to a human hair. But meanwhile Sir Robert Moray, a Scot in London who knew what Hooke was up to, was sending letters in French about the new grinder to the Dutch scientist Christiaan Huygens. Thanks to Moray, Huygens had previously gotten hold of details of Hooke's balance-spring watch.

Moray and Huygens "sometimes wrote to each other several times a week," writes the historian Lisa Jardine. Their letters crossed the Channel in days, or about as quickly as mail does now. Meanwhile, the French astronomer Adrien Auzout in Paris was getting copies of some of their letters. So Hooke's breakthroughs were being spread to his European competitors almost instantly.

All this irritated Hooke. But the proximity of many thinkers in western Europe created an intellectual ferment. That is why so many of the great scientific discoveries were made there. These discoveries then helped make the region rich.

Centuries later, soccer spread the same way. In the nineteenth century the game infected western Europe first, because there it had the shortest distances to travel. Later the proximity of so many peoples brought the region two world wars. After 1945, western Europeans decided they could live crammed together only under a sort of single government: the European Union. Borders opened, and the region became the most integrated in the history of the world.

Again the best ideas spread fastest there, just as they had in the scientific revolution. The region's soccer benefited. One of the men who carried tactical ideas around Europe was Arrigo Sacchi. His father was a shoe manufacturer in Ravenna, Italy, and the young Sacchi used to accompany him on business trips. He saw a lot of games in Germany, Switzerland, France, and the Netherlands. "It opened my mind," he later said. As manager of AC Milan in the 1980s, he imported a version of Dutch soccer that revolutionized the Italian game.

Ideas spread even more quickly in European soccer than in other economic sectors, because soccer is the most integrated part of the Continent's economy. Only about 2 percent of all western Europeans live in a different European Union country, because few companies bother hiring bus drivers or office administrators from neighboring countries. In some professions, language barriers stop workers from moving abroad. But many soccer players do find work abroad, largely because television advertises their wares to employers across Europe. And so most of the EU's best players have gathered in the English, Spanish, and Italian leagues, and meet each other on weekday nights in the Champions League. This competition is the European single market come to life, a dense network of talent.

The teams in the Champions League can draw talent from anywhere in the world. Nonetheless, an overwhelming majority of their players are western Europeans. With the world's best players and coaches packed together, the world's best soccer is constantly being refined there.

The best soccer today is Champions League soccer, western European soccer. It's a rapid passing game played by athletes. Rarely does anyone dribble, or keep the ball for a second. You pass instantly. It's not the beautiful game—dribbles are prettier—but it works best. All good teams everywhere in the world now play this way. Even the Brazilians adopted the Champions League style in the 1990s. They still have more skill than the Europeans, but they now try to play at a European pace.

In other words, western Europe has discovered the secret of soccer. More precisely, a core group of western European countries has, namely, five of the six nations that in 1957 founded the European Economic Community, ancestor of the European Union. (We'll leave out the sixth founding nation, the hopeless minnow Luxembourg.) West Germany, France, Italy, Holland, and even Belgium don't all play exactly the same style. Holland and Italy, say, are rather different. But they all adhere to the basic tenets of rapid collectivized western European soccer. Here are some results from the past thirty years:

- The core five countries won twelve European championships and World Cups between them.
- The countries at the corners of Europe, the Brits, the former Soviet bloc, the Balkans, and Scandinavian nations north of the Baltic Sea between them won one: Greece's European championship of 2004, delivered by a German coach.
- Europe's only other trophy in these thirty years has gone to Denmark and Czechoslovakia. Denmark enjoys an utterly permeable border with the five core countries.

Countries separated from the core of the EU—either by great distance, by poverty, or by closed borders under dictatorships—often underperform in soccer. In the vast landmass running from Portugal in the west to Poland in the east, every country of more than 1 million inhabitants except Belgium qualified for Euro 2008. The nations that didn't make it are on Europe's margins: the Brits, most of Scandinavia, and most of Europe's eastern edge. The countries at great distance—and it can be a distance of the mind rather than geographical distance—are often out of touch with core European soccer. Many countries on the margins have traditionally had dysfunctional indigenous styles of soccer. The Greeks, for instance, dribbled too much. The Brits played mindless kick-and-rush.

Again, this is explained by theories of networks. If you are on the periphery, like the British were until recently in soccer, it's harder to make new connections, because you have to travel farther. Worse, those not on the periphery see you as only a second-best connection. You are the end of the line, not the gateway to a new set of connections. That's why foreign countries stopped hiring English coaches or even English players. As a result, the people on the periphery become more and more isolated and insular. The Ukrainian manager Valeri Lobanovski was a soccer genius, but during the days of the Soviet Union he was so isolated that when a Dutch journalist came to interview him in the mid-1980s, Lobanovski pumped him for information about Holland's players. Spain, to some degree, had the same problem under General Franco's dictatorship. "Europe ends at the Pyrenees" was the saying in those days.

Gradually, isolation becomes your mind-set: after a while you don't even *want* to adopt foreign ideas anymore. Anyone who has spent time in England—particularly before 1992—has witnessed this attitude. Isolation can lead you into your own blind alleys that nobody else appreciates. For instance, the long refusal of English players to dive may have been an admirable cultural norm, but they might have won more games if they had learned from continental Europeans how to buy the odd penalty.

Happily, the era of British isolationism is now over. This era began on Sunday, September 3, 1939, when the country's borders closed on the outbreak of the Second World War. In soccer, that isolation deepened when English clubs were banned from European competitions after the Heysel disaster of 1985. They lost what modest network they had.

But between 1990 and 1994, British isolation began to break down: English clubs were readmitted to European competitions, new laws enforced free movement of labor and capital within the EU, and Eurostar trains and budget airlines connected Britain to the Continent. London turned into a global city. Nowadays, southern England, at least, belongs to core Europe, just as it did during the scientific revolution.

The end of isolationism meant the end of English soccer managers managing England or the best English clubs. You wouldn't appoint a Frenchman to manage your baseball team, because the French don't have a history of thinking hard about baseball. And you wouldn't appoint an Englishman to manage your soccer team, because the English don't have a history of thinking hard about soccer. After various failures with the traditional British style of kick-and-rush, the English embraced European soccer. In 2000, England hired a manager with long experience in Italian soccer, Sven Goran Eriksson.

At this, the conservative *Daily Mail* newspaper lamented, "The mother country of soccer, birthplace of the greatest game, has finally gone from the cradle to the shame." It was a wonderful statement of "English exceptionalism": the belief that England is an exceptional soccer country that should rule the world playing the English way. However, the obvious statistical truth is that England is not exceptional. It is typical of the second-tier soccer countries outside the core of western Europe.

Other peripheral countries from Greece to Japan soon followed the English example. Importing know-how from the core of Europe turned out to be an excellent remedy for the problem of isolation, which makes it even odder that in 2006 England did an about-face and appointed the Englishman Steve McClaren. The English Football Association didn't realize that England, as a recovering isolationist, still needed foreign help.

Many of the countries that imported knowledge did very well indeed. Under Eriksson, England always reached the quarter-finals of major tournaments. Russia under Guus Hiddink got to the semifinals of Euro 2008, their best performance since the USSR collapsed. At the same tournament Turkey also reached the semifinals, in their case chiefly by importing fitness. Over Sunday lunch in a Lebanese restaurant in Geneva during the tournament, a Turkish official explained how the team kept coming back to win matches in the last few minutes. They had hired a fitness coach, Scott Piri, from the company Athletes' Performance in the United States. Despite Piri's American passport, he was really a borrowing from core Europe: in 2006 the German manager Jürgen Klinsmann had used Athletes' Performance to turn Germany into the fittest team at the World Cup. When Piri arrived in the Turkish camp, the official explained, the players had complained that he worked them too hard. They said he was causing them injuries. But soon they got used to the workload. They then became extremely fit, and achieved a string of last-ditch comebacks.

Spain in 2008 no longer needed much foreign help anymore. Spanish soccer had been opening to Europe since the early 1970s, when the Franco regime slowly began to give up on isolation and FC Barcelona imported the Dutch soccer thinkers Rinus Michels and Johan Cruijff. It also helped that Spain was then starting to grow richer. By now the country is fully networked with Europe. Its best players experience the Champions League every season. At Euro 2008, Spain won its first prize in forty-four years.

England now seems to have accepted the need for continental European know-how. The current England manager, the Italian Fabio Capello, is like one of the overpaid consultants so common in development economics, flying in on business class to tell the natives what to do. His job is to teach the English some of the virtues of western European soccer.

To cite just one of those virtues: *a game lasts ninety minutes.* Habitually, English players charge out of the gate, run around like lunatics, and exhaust themselves well before the match is over, even if they aren't hung over.

You see this in England's peculiar scoring record in big tournaments. In every World Cup ever played, most goals were scored in the second halves of matches. That is natural: in the second half players tire, teams start chasing goals, and gaps open up on the field. But England, in its last five big tournaments, scored twenty-two of its thirty-five goals in the first halves of matches. The team's record in crucial games is even starker: in the matches in which it was eliminated from tournaments, it scored seven of its eight goals before halftime. In other words, England performs like a cheap battery. This is partly because it plays in such an exhausting league, but also because it doesn't seem to have thought about pacing itself.

Italians know exactly how to measure out the ninety minutes. They take quiet periods, when they sit back and make sure nothing happens, because they know that the best chance of scoring is in the closing minutes, when exhausted opponents will leave holes. That's when you need to be sharpest. In the World Cup of 2006, typically, Italy knocked out Australia and Germany with goals in the final three minutes.

England has already bought Italian know-how. Now all it needs to do is include its own middle classes and stop worrying about foreigners in the Premier League, and it will finally stop underachieving and perform as well as it should. But hang on a moment: who says England underachieves?

SHOULD DO BETTER:
IS ENGLAND WORSE THAN IT OUGHT TO BE?

That England underachieves is usually taken for granted in the British media. After all, the team hasn't won anything since 1966, and sometimes doesn't even qualify for tournaments. Clearly, that is not good enough for "the mother country of soccer, birthplace of the greatest game."

But does England really underachieve? Or is it just that the English expect too much of their team? To answer this, we first need to work out how well England should do, *given its resources*.

Before we are accused of looking for excuses, let's consider what is and isn't possible. A five year old can't win the hundred-meter finals at the Olympics, and neither can a seventy year old. You aren't going to have a career in the NBA if you are only five feet tall, and you'll never ride the winner in the Kentucky Derby if you are six foot eight. It is very unlikely that you will have a career in show jumping if your parents earn less than forty thousand dollars per year, you probably won't win a boxing match if you've never had any training as a boxer, and you won't have a shot at being world chess champion unless you can persuade a team of grand masters to act as your seconds. Genetics are beyond our control; training depends partly on our own effort, but partly on the resources that other people give us.

What is true for the individual is also true for the nation. During his tenure an England soccer manager cannot easily (a) increase the size of the population from which he will have to draw the talent, (b) increase the national income so as to ensure a significant increase in the financial resources devoted to developing soccer, or (c) increase the accumulated experience of the national team by very much. (England has played more than eight hundred games since its first game in 1872, and currently plays around a dozen games per year, so each extra game doesn't add much to the history.)

Yet in any international match, these three factors—the size of the nation's population, the size of the national income, and the country's experience in international soccer—hugely affect the outcome. It's unfair to expect Belarus, say, to perform as well as much larger, more experienced, and richer Germany. It is fairer to assess how well each country *should* perform given its experience, income, and population and then measure that expected performance against reality. Countries like Belarus or Luxembourg will never win a World Cup. The only measure of performance that makes any sense for them is one based on how effectively they use their limited resources. The same exercise makes sense for England, too, if only as a check on tabloid hysteria: does England really underperform given what it has to work with?

In absolute terms England is about tenth in the world. But we want to know how well it does in relative terms—not relative to the expectations of the media but relative to English resources. Might it be that England in fact *overachieves*, given the country's experience, population, and income?

To work this out, we need to know the soccer results for all the national teams in the world. Luckily, we have them. There are a number of databases around of international matches, but one of the best is maintained by Russell Gerrard, a mathematics professor at Cass Business School in London. By day Russell worries about mathematical ways to represent the management problems of pension funds. For example, his most recent paper is snappily titled "Mean-Variance Optimization Problems for the Accumulation Phase in a Defined Benefit Plan." It concerns, among other things, Lévy diffusion financial markets, the Hamilton-Jacobi-Bellman equation, and the Feynman-Kac representation. As you might expect, Russell has been meticulous in accumulating the soccer data, which took him seven years. His database runs from 1872 through 2001, and includes 22,130 games.

RUSSELL GERRARD'S BRILLIANT SOCCER DATABASE

Later in the book, we will crunch Russell's data to discover which is the best soccer country on earth, and which punches most above its weight. But here, let's limit ourselves to a sneak preview of where England stands.

The distant past is of limited relevance. Let's therefore concentrate on the most recent period of Russell's database, 1980–2001. This was by no means a golden age for England. The country didn't even qualify for the European championship of 1984, or for the World Cup ten years later, and its best moments in these twenty-two years were two lost semifinals. Altogether in the period England played 228 matches. It won 49 percent of them and tied 32 percent, for a "win percentage" of 65 percent (remember that for these purposes we treat a tie as half a win). That is near the middle of the country's historical range.

We want to see how much of a team's success, match by match, can be explained by population, wealth, and experience. However, win percentage is not the best measure of success, because any two wins are not the same. We all know that a 1–5 away win against a certain someone is not the same as a tame 1–0. Put another way, if England plays Luxembourg and wins only 1–0, it's more likely that the Luxembourgian press will be in ecstasy than the British tabloids.

Instead, we chose goal difference as our measure, since for any match we expect that the greater the difference between the two teams' populations, wealth, and experience, the greater will be the disparity in scores. (Of course, a positive goal difference tends to be highly correlated with winning.)

We then analyzed Russell's database of matches using the technique of multiple regression. Quite simply, multiple regression is a mathematical formula (first identified by the mathematician Carl Friedrich Gauss in 1801) for finding the closest statistical fit between one thing (in this case success of the national team) and any other collection of things (here experience, population, and income per head). The idea is beautifully simple. The problem used to be the endless amount of computation required to find the closest fit. Luckily, modern computers have reduced this process to the press of a button (just look up "regression" on your spreadsheet package). For each international match you just input the population, income per head, and team experience of the two nations at that date, and in seconds you get a readout telling you how sensitive (on average) the team's performance is to each factor. We will also take into account home advantage for each match.

Collecting the data is usually the toughest part. We have assembled figures for the population, soccer experience, and income per capita of 189 countries. We will unveil our findings about the other 188 countries later in the book. Here, we will focus just on England and its supposed underperformance.

We ran our regression and immediately made several discoveries about international soccer. First, home-field advantage alone is worth a lead of about two-thirds of a goal. Obviously, that is nonsense if applied to a single game, but think of it this way: playing at home is like having a goal's head start in two out of every three games. Second, having twice as much international experience as your rival is worth just over half a goal. In fact, experience turns out to matter much more than the size of your population, which is why the Swedes, Dutch, and Czechs do better at World Cups than the very large but inexperienced US. Having twice your opponent's population is worth only about one-tenth of a goal. Having twice the gross domestic product (GDP) per head is worth about as little. In other words, although being large and rich helps a country win soccer matches, being experienced helps a lot more. That is not good news for the US.

It should be added that our estimates are statistically very reliable. Not only is there not much doubt that these factors matter, but there is little doubt about the size of the effects. It is these effects that make the first rounds of World Cups fairly predictable.

However, much still remains unexplained. Experience, population, and income per capita combined explain only just over a quarter of the variation in goal difference. That is good news: if we could predict outcomes perfectly by just these three factors, there would not be much point in watching World Cups at all. Nonetheless, the fact that these three factors explain so much tells us that, up to a point, soccer is rational and predictable.

For now, we are interested only in England. Are its resources so outstanding that it should do better than merely ranking around tenth in the world?

First let's look at experience. England is one of the most experienced countries in soccer. It played 790 internationals between 1872 and 2001. According to Russell's data, only Sweden played more (802). However, England's much vaunted history is not worth much against the other leading soccer nations, because most of them have now accumulated similar amounts of experience. Brazil, Argentina, and Germany had all played more than 700 internationals by 2001. When it comes to our second variable, national income, England scores high, too. It is usually one of the richest of the serious soccer countries. Where England falls short is in size. What often seems to go unnoticed is that England's population of 51 million puts it at a major disadvantage to the countries it likes to measure itself against in soccer. Not only is Germany much bigger, with 80 million inhabitants, but France and Italy have around 60 million each. Among the leading European nations, England is ahead only of that other "notorious underachiever," Spain (40 million). So in soccer terms, England is an experienced, rich, but medium-sized competitor.

Then we ran the numbers. We calculated that England, given its population, income, and experience, "should" score on average 0.63 goals per game more than its opponents. To get a feel for how this works, consider England's performance at the World Cup of 1998. England played Tunisia, Romania, Colombia, and Argentina, all on neutral ground, so there was no "home-field" effect. Facing Tunisia in its opening game, England had a population five times larger, a GDP per head four times larger, and two times more international experience than its opponent. That combination gave an expected goal difference of one goal in England's favor. In the event, England won 2–0 and so did better than expected.

Against Romania, England had the advantage of twice the population, five times the income per head, and a bit more experience (other countries have been playing soccer for longer than the English sometimes like to think). All this gave England an expected advantage of about half a goal. England's 1–0 defeat meant that it underperformed by one and a half goals.

Next England played Colombia, with a slight advantage in population, four times the income per head, and double the experience. The package was worth an advantage of almost an entire goal (you start to see how the Tom Thumb World Cup might be organized), but again England overperformed, winning 2–0.

Then came Argentina: as everyone in England knows, the English lost on penalties. Should England have done better? Well, it had a slight advantage in population over Argentina, double the income per head, but slightly less experience (Argentina plays a lot of games). Putting all that together, a fair score would have been a tie, which is exactly what happened after 120 minutes. Pity about the penalties, but more about those later in the book.

Our model allows us to reexamine every game ever played. The glorious uncertainty of soccer means that there are many deviations from expectations. However, if we average the difference between expectations and results for each country, we get a picture of whether any national team systematically outperforms or underperforms relative to its resources. Our finding: England in the 1980–2001 period outscored its opponents by 0.84 goals per game. That was 0.21 more than we had predicted based on the country's resources. In short, England was not underperforming at all. Contrary to popular opinion, it was overperforming.

As an example, take England's games against Poland. England played the Poles eleven times in the period, winning seven and tying four times, with a goal difference of plus sixteen. Over the period England's population was about 25 percent larger than Poland's, its income per head about three times greater, and its international experience about 20 percent more. These should have contributed for a positive goal difference of about one, three, and one goals, respectively, or a total of plus five. So England's goal difference of plus sixteen was eleven goals better than we might have expected. That is not too shabby.

Later in the book we will reveal our global table for relative performance from 1980 through 2001: a ranking of the teams that did best relative to their countries' experience, income, and populations. For now, we'll just say that England came in 67th out of 189 countries. That put them in a group of moderate overachievers, just below Russia, Azerbaijan, and Morocco and just above Ivory Coast and Mozambique. Like England, all these teams scored about a fifth of a goal per game more than they "should" have, given their populations, income, and experience.

However, England doesn't benchmark itself against Azerbaijan. It's more interesting to see whether England overperforms "more" than the teams it sees as its rivals: the best countries in the world. Here's a ranking of the game's giants, plus England, based on how many goals per game each scores above expectations:

Country	"Additional" Goals per Game Above Expectations
Brazil	0.67
France	0.35
West Germany	0.28
England	0.21
Italy	0.20
Germany (United)	0.18
Argentina	0.08

It turns out that England compares pretty well to the giants. Its "overperformance" is near the average for the world's leading nations, once we strip out the phenomenon that is Brazil.

Now let's look only at matches between European countries—the arena where England plays most of its soccer. The match results in Russell's database show that home advantage and experience count for a little less in Europe than in the world in general. On the other hand, population and GDP count for a bit more in Europe than in the world.

Taking all that into account, against European teams England over-performs very slightly. From 1980 through 2001 it scored a goal every twenty games more than expected given its experience, income, and population. That put England in 23rd place of the 49 European countries we ranked. It was just behind West Germany in 20th place, but ahead of France (25th) and Italy (31st), even though those countries won tournaments in this period and England didn't.

Our conclusion: England does just fine. The team actually performs better than expected, given what it has to start with. All it needs to bring home some trophies is better timing—it must win fewer friendlies and more World Cup semis—and a few million more inhabitants. Consider the England-Germany semifinal at Euro '96. Both countries had similar levels of experience, and by 1996 Germany's lead over Britain in income per capita had slipped to only about 7 percent. However, according to our analysis, England's home advantage (worth just under half a goal in a game between Europeans) was largely wiped out by Germany's much larger population. That made the expected goal difference only 0.26 in favor of the English home team, not far short of the tie that materialized in open play. In the end Gareth Southgate missed his penalty, and England lost.

Overall in the 1980–2001 period, England played Germany ten times. Taking the results at the end of normal time, England won two, tied three, and lost five. Its goal difference over the ten games was minus 2. Given Germany's slight lead in GDP per head in these years, but particularly given England's shortage of people, that is almost exactly the goal difference we would have predicted. The "thirty years of hurt" shouldn't be a mystery.

PHASE 8: ENGLAND ENTERS THE NEXT WORLD CUP THINKING IT WILL WIN IT

Famously, there is a manic-depressive quality to supporting England. The nation tends to feel either very high or very low about the team. The night of that home defeat to Croatia in November 2007 was a low. As we write, in summer 2009, most English fans feel high again. Capello's team is eating up its qualifying group. People are starting to daydream about July 11, 2010, when a certain side might just be walking out for the World Cup final in Soccer City outside Johannesburg.

It sounds reasonable to presume that a good qualifying performance presages a good tournament. But is this belief backed up by the facts? When England qualifies in style, is it really more likely to excel at the final tournament? We checked the data.

England has tried to qualify for fourteen World Cups and Euros since 1980 (it didn't have to qualify for Euro '96, because it was the host). Of those fourteen tournaments, it failed to qualify for three, and got knocked out in the first round four times. That means that half the England teams in this period can be considered failures. Collectively, we'll label these teams "Bad England." Of the remaining seven tournaments, England reached the round of sixteen twice, the quarterfinals four times, and the semifinal once, in 1990. We'll label these seven teams "Good England."

You would assume that Good England did much better in qualifying matches than Bad England. After all, Bad England regularly failed even to qualify. Yet the data show otherwise: in qualifiers, Good England and Bad England were much of a muchness.

The England team at Euro '88, for instance, was unmistakably Bad England. It lost all three games in West Germany before going home with the hooligans. Yet it had qualified gloriously: five wins, one tie, no losses, and a goal difference of nineteen for and just one against. By contrast, the Good England team of 1990 had muddled through qualifying, winning three and tying three.

Even more curiously, England often performed just as well in qualifiers when it failed to make the tournament as when it succeeded. For example, in missing Euro 2008, England got exactly the same percentage of the available qualifying points (namely 66 percent) as when it managed to qualify for Euro 2000 or for the World Cup of 1982.

Figure 2.2 shows a comparison of the qualifying records of Good England (teams that made at least the round of sixteen) versus Bad England (teams that either missed the final tournament or went home after the first round). The figure shows that Good England and Bad England had almost indistinguishable win-loss records in qualifying. Indeed, Bad England scored many more goals than Good England while conceding only slightly more. The lesson of history: England's performance at specific World Cups and European championships is almost entirely unpredictable.

FIGURE 2.2 **England's qualifying record since 1980**

Team	Played	Won	Tied	Lost	For	Against
Bad England	60	36	16	8	140	33
Good England	56	36	13	7	106	28

What we see here is partly the enormous role of luck in history. We tend to think with hindsight that a team that did well in a particular tournament was somehow always going to do well, and a team that lost was doomed to do so. The winner's victory comes to seem inevitable. This is a common flaw in the writing of any kind of history.

But in fact, inevitable victories hardly ever happen in soccer tournaments. Perhaps the only recent case was Brazil at the World Cup of 2002. Just how dominant that team was dawned on a leading European club manager a few months after the final. This manager was trying to sign Brazil's goalkeeper, Marcos. After all, Marcos was a world champion. Marcos visited the club and did some physical tests, in which he didn't perform particularly well. Never mind, thought the manager, the guy won the World Cup. So he offered Marcos a contract. At two o'clock the next morning, the manager was awoken at home by a phone call. It was Marcos's agent.

The agent said, "I'm sorry, but Marcos won't sign for you."

The sleepy manager said, "All right, but why not?"

Then the agent confessed. A couple of years before the World Cup, Marcos had broken his wrist. It had never healed properly. But his old club manager, Luiz Felipe Scolari, became manager of Brazil and put Marcos on the team. Suddenly, Marcos was going to a World Cup. Every day at the tournament, the agent explained, Marcos was in pain. He could barely even train. In matches he could barely catch a ball. Every day Marcos told himself, "I really must tell Scolari about my wrist." But he could never quite bring himself to. So he went on, day after day, until he found that he had won the World Cup. Brazil was so superior that it became world champion with a crocked goalkeeper.

However, such dominance is very rare. Normally, the differences between teams in the final stages of a World Cup are tiny. The difference between an England team being considered legendary or a failure is two to three games, each generally decided by a single goal, over two years. After all, the difference between making a World Cup and spending the summer on the beach can be just a point. Sometimes it's a point that you lost by hitting the post. Sometimes it's a point garnered by a rival in a match you didn't even play in.

Once you're at the World Cup, the difference between going home ignominiously in the first round and making the semifinals is often a matter of a few inches here or there on a couple of shots. The greatest prize in the sport hinges on a very few moments. It's the same in baseball, notes Michael Lewis in *Moneyball*: "The season ends in a giant crapshoot. The play-offs frustrate rational management because, unlike the long regular season, they suffer from the sample size problem." Lewis means that because there are so few games in the play-offs—because the "sample size" is so small—random factors play an outsize role in determining the winner. It's the same in soccer World Cups, and even more so in European championships. "Euros" last only three weeks, and as Arsène Wenger notes, any team in a league can be top of the table after three weeks.

Most fans understand that luck matters, even if they construct a postfact story about the tournament that makes either victory or humiliation seem fated from the start. But our data point to an even scarier truth than the existence of fluke: namely, there is barely any difference between "brilliant" and "terrible" England teams. It looks suspiciously as if England is always more or less equally good.

This may sound hard to believe. Fans feel strongly about the qualities of managers and players. There are periods of national optimism and national pessimism, associated with the view that the England team is either strong or disgraceful.

But in fact, watching England play resembles watching a coin-tossing competition. If we focus on outright victories, then England on average wins just over 50 percent of its games; the rest it either ties or loses. So just as a coin has half a chance of landing heads up and half tails up, England in the average game has about half a chance of winning and half of not winning.

We assigned a "1" for each win and a "0" for a loss or a tie, and examined the sequence of England's four hundred games since 1980. Before we discuss this sequence, let's look at coin tossing. If you tossed a coin four hundred times, you would expect on average to get two hundred heads and two hundred tails. However, there is no reason to think that the outcomes would alternate (heads, tails, heads, tails . . .). Sometimes you will get sequences of a few heads, sometimes a few tails. Crucially, though, there would be no relationship at all between the current coin toss and the last one. If you toss a fair coin there is always a fifty-fifty chance of heads, whatever sequence has occurred up to this point. There is no statistical correlation between current coin tosses and past coin tosses, even if the average of any sequence is always around 50 percent.

Here is our finding: England's win sequence over the four hundred games is indistinguishable from a random series of coin tosses. There is no predictive value in the outcome of England's last game, or indeed in any combination of England's recent games. Whatever happened in one match appears to have no bearing on what will happen in the next one. The only thing you can predict is that over the medium to long term, England will win about half its games outright. We have seen that the outcome of matches can be largely predicted by a country's population, income, and experience. However, this explains only the *average* outcome.

In other words, if England were smaller, poorer, or less experienced, it would have a lower percentage of wins, but the sequence of those wins would still be unpredictable.

To make sure that our finding was right, we constructed a few random sequences of 1s and 0s to see if they looked like England's results. Often we found more apparent correlation in our random sequences than in England's results.

Contrary to popular opinion, it may be that the strength of the England team barely ever changes (which would make the entire apparatus of punditry attached to the team instantly redundant). A star player might fade or retire, but in a country of 51 million people, there is always someone coming up who is near enough his level to make almost no difference. Over the long term, the three key factors that determine a country's performance are very stable. The British economy boomed in the 1990s and is now dropping down the global wealth rankings, but measured over the last century Britain has always been one of wealthiest nations in the world. Equally, its share of the soccer population changes only glacially. And while the England team gains experience, so do its main rivals. The only key factor that changes is home advantage. Given that playing at home is worth a lead of two-thirds of a goal per game in global soccer, it's little wonder that England won the World Cup in England in 1966.

Otherwise, England's performances in good or bad times are much the same. It's just that fans and the media seek to see patterns where none exist. Nick Taleb, the financial investor who wrote *The Black Swan: The Impact of the Highly Improbable*, famously explained that we are constantly fooled by randomness. In neuroscientific terms, our rational brains are egged on by our emotional brains to find patterns even if there aren't any. In the end, the best explanation for the short-term ups and downs of the England team is randomness.

PART I
The Clubs

Racism, Stupidity, Bad Transfers,
Capital Cities, the Mirage of the NFL,
and What Actually Happened in
That Penalty Shoot-Out in Moscow

3

GENTLEMEN PREFER BLONDS

How to Avoid Silly Mistakes in
the Transfer Market

In 1983 AC Milan spotted a talented young black forward playing for Watford. The word is that the player Milan liked was John Barnes, and that it then confused him with his fellow black teammate Luther Blissett. Whatever the truth, the Italians ended up paying Watford a "transfer fee" of $1.4 million for Blissett.

As a player Blissett became such a joke in Italy that the name "Luther Blissett" is now used as a pseudonym by groups of Italian anarchist writers. He spent one unhappy year in Milan, before the club sold him back to Watford for just over half the sum it had paid for him. At least that year gave soccer one of its best quotes: "No matter how much money you have here," Blissett lamented, "you can't seem to get Rice Krispies." More on Rice Krispies later.

Transfers in soccer are very different from trades in American sports. In soccer, when a good player moves, his new club usually pays a "transfer fee" to his old club. Moreover, the player's old contract is torn up, and he negotiates a new deal with his new club. Each year European clubs pay each other a total of between $1 billion and $2 billion in transfer fees. (The record is the $130 million that Real Madrid paid Manchester United for Cristiano Ronaldo in 2009.)

But much of this money is wasted on the wrong transfers. In fact, the amount that almost any club spends on transfer fees bears little relation to where it finishes in the league. We studied the spending of forty English clubs between 1978 and 1997, and found that their outlay on transfers explained only 16 percent of their total variation in league position. By contrast, their spending on salaries explained a massive 92 percent of that variation. In the 1998–2007 period, spending on salaries by clubs in the Premier League and the Championship (the second tier of English soccer) still explained 89 percent of the variation in league position. It seems that high wages help a club much more than do spectacular transfers.

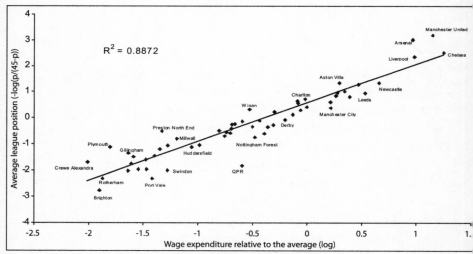

FIGURE 3.1 Premier League and Championship teams, 1998–2007

In short, the more you pay your players in wages, the higher you will finish; but what you pay *for* them in transfer fees doesn't seem to make much difference. (This suggests that, in general, it may be better to raise your players' pay than risk losing a couple of them and have to go out and buy replacements.)

FIGURE 3.2 The more you pay your players, the higher you finish, 1998–2007

Club	Average league position	Wage spending relative to the average spending of all clubs			
Manchester United	2	3.16	Coventry City	27	0.70
Arsenal	2	2.63	Sheffield United	27	0.50
Chelsea	3	3.50	Barnsley	28	0.45
Liverpool	4	2.68	Preston North End	28	0.26
Newcastle United	9	1.93	Watford	29	0.48
Aston Villa	9	1.34	Norwich City	29	0.50
Tottenham Hotspur	10	1.60	Sheffield Wednesday	29	0.68
Everton	12	1.41	Crystal Palace	30	0.47
Middlesbrough	12	1.32	Nottingham Forest	31	0.62
Leeds United	13	1.70	Millwall	31	0.30
West Ham United	14	1.31	Cardiff City	33	0.37
Blackburn Rovers	14	1.48	Burnley	33	0.28
Charlton Athletic	15	0.98	Huddersfield Town	34	0.35
Bolton Wanderers	16	0.92	Plymouth Argyle	34	0.16
Fulham	16	1.24	Stoke City	35	0.26
Southampton	16	0.92	Gillingham	36	0.19
Sunderland	18	1.00	Tranmere Rovers	37	0.25
Manchester City	18	1.24	Stockport County	37	0.20
Wigan Athletic	19	0.59	Oxford United	38	0.23
Wimbledon	19	0.94	Crewe Alexandra	38	0.13
Birmingham City	20	0.74	Grimsby Town	38	0.20
Leicester City	21	0.88	Queen's Park Rangers	39	0.55
Derby County	23	0.82	Hull City	40	0.23
Ipswich Town	24	0.65	Bury	40	0.21
Bradford City	24	0.55	Swindon Town	40	0.28
West Bromwich Albion	25	0.52	Walsall	40	0.19
Reading	26	0.50	Port Vale	41	0.24
Portsmouth	26	0.73	Rotherham United	41	0.15
Wolverhampton Wanderers	26	0.61	Brighton & Hove Albion	42	0.15

While the market for players' wages is pretty efficient—the better a player is, the more he earns—the transfer market is inefficient. Much of the time, clubs buy the wrong players. Even now that they have brigades of international scouts, they still waste fortunes on flops like Blissett. (The transfer market is also of dubious legality—do clubs really have a right to "buy" and "sell" employees?—but that's another matter.)

Any inefficient market is an opportunity for somebody. If most clubs are wasting most of their transfer money, then a club that spends wisely is going to outperform. In fact, a few wise buyers have consistently outperformed the transfer market: Brian Clough and his assistant-cum-soul mate Peter Taylor in their years at Nottingham Forest, Arsène Wenger during his first decade at Arsenal, and, most mysteriously of all, Olympique Lyon, which has progressed from an obscure provincial club to a dictatorial rule over French soccer. From 2002 through 2008, Lyon won the French league seven times running. The usual way to win things in soccer is to pay high salaries. These clubs have found a different route: they have worked out the secrets of the transfer market.

There is a fourth master of the transfer market who is worth a look, even if he works in a different sport across an ocean: Billy Beane, general manager of the Oakland A's baseball team. In his book *Moneyball*, Michael Lewis explains how Beane turned one of the poorest teams in baseball into one of the best by the simple method of rejecting what everyone in the sport had always "known" to be true about the transfer market. Lewis writes, "Understanding that he would never have a Yankee-sized checkbook, Beane had set about looking for inefficiencies in the game." It's odd how many of the same inefficiencies exist in soccer, too.

MARKET INEFFICIENCIES

If we study these masters of transfers, it will help us uncover the secrets of the market that all the other clubs are missing. First of all, though, we present a few of the most obvious inefficiencies in the market. Although it doesn't take a Wenger or a Beane to identify these, they continue to exist.

A New Manager Wastes Money

Typically, the new manager wants to put his mark on his new team. So he buys his own players. He then has to "clear out" some of his predecessor's purchases, usually at a discount.

Strangely, it's Alan Sugar's tightfisted Tottenham that provides the worst example. In May 2000 the club's manager, George Graham, paid Dynamo Kiev $16.5 million—nearly twice Spurs's previous record fee—for the Ukrainian striker Sergei Rebrov. Clearly, Rebrov was meant to be a long-term investment.

But nine months later, Sugar, the club chairman, sold his stake in Tottenham, whereupon the new owners sacked Graham and replaced him with Glenn Hoddle. Hoddle didn't appreciate Rebrov. The record signing ended up on the bench, was sent on loan to a Turkish team, and in 2004 moved to West Ham on a free transfer.

A few years later Spurs discovered a new method for short-term money burning: sell and then buy back exactly the same players. In January 2008, they transferred Jermain Defoe to Portsmouth for nearly $15 million, and six months later sent Robbie Keane to Liverpool for $38 million. Then, in January 2009, under their new manager, Harry Redknapp, they bought both players back again. They shelled out about the same total sum that they had received for the duo the year before, though their outlay could rise by about another $11 million depending on how often Keane plays. If you add in agents' fees, taxes, the loss of a year of Defoe's services and six months of Keane's, plus the twofold disruption to the team, this sort of waste helps explain why Spurs got left behind by Wenger's Arsenal.

Yet Spurs and Newcastle are only marginally sillier than most clubs. This form of waste is common across soccer: a new manager is allowed to buy and sell on the pretense that he is reshaping the club for many years to come, even though in practice he almost always leaves pretty rapidly. He doesn't care how much his wheeler-dealing costs: he doesn't get a bonus if the club makes a profit.

Stars of Recent World Cups or European Championships Are Overvalued

The worst time to buy a player is in the summer when he's just done well at a big tournament. Everyone in the transfer market has seen how good the player is, but he is exhausted and quite likely sated with success. Overpaying for these shooting stars fits what *Moneyball* calls "a tendency to be overly influenced by a guy's most recent performance: what he did last was not necessarily what he would do next."

Newcastle is, of course, the supreme sucker for shooting stars. This is largely because its fans demand it. Newcastle (or Spurs, or Marseille in France) probably isn't even trying to be "rational" in the transfer market. Its aim is not to buy the best results for as little money as possible. Rather, its big signings (like buying fragile Michael Owen for $30 million) are best understood as marketing gifts to their fans. Buying a big name is a way of saying, "Yes, we are a big club." It gives the supporters the thrill of expectation, a sense that their club is going somewhere, which may be as much fun as actually winning things. Buying big names is how these clubs keep their customers satisfied during the three-month summer shutdown.

So addicted is Newcastle to buying big names that even its high spending on salaries doesn't bring it the high league position you would expect. When Francisco Pérez Cutiño analyzed data for the Premier League for the 2006–2007 season, for an unpublished MBA paper at Judge Business School in Cambridge, he found that "only Newcastle United seemed to significantly underperform taking into account its wage expenditure."

Certain Nationalities Are Overvalued

Clubs will pay more for a player from a "fashionable" soccer country. American goalkeeper Kasey Keller says that in the transfer market, it's good to be Dutch. "Giovanni van Bronckhorst is the best example," Keller told the German journalist Christoph Biermann. "He went from Rangers to Arsenal, failed there, and then where did he go? To Barcelona! You have to be a Dutchman to do that. An American would have been sent straight back to DC United."

The most fashionable nationality of all in the transfer market is Brazilian. As Alex Bellos writes in *Futebol: The Brazilian Way of Life*:

"The phrase 'Brazilian soccer player' is like the phrases 'French chef' or 'Tibetan monk.' The nationality expresses an authority, an innate vocation for the job—whatever the natural ability." A Brazilian agent who had exported very humble Brazilian players to the Faeroe Islands and Iceland told Bellos, "It's sad to say, but it is much easier selling, for example, a crap Brazilian than a brilliant Mexican. The Brazilian gets across the image of happiness, party, carnival. Irrespective of talent, it is very seductive to have a Brazilian in your team."

A wise club will buy unfashionable nationalities—Bolivians, say, or Belorussians—at discounts.

Gentlemen Prefer Blonds

At least one big English club noticed that its scouts kept recommending blond players. The likely reason: when you are scanning a field of twenty-two similar-looking players, the blonds tend to stand out (except, presumably, in Scandinavia). The color catches the eye. So the scout notices the blond player without understanding why. The club in question began to take this distortion into account when judging scouting reports.

Similarly, Beane at the Oakland A's noticed that baseball scouts had all sorts of "sight-based prejudices." They were suspicious of fat guys or skinny little guys or "short right-handed pitchers," and they overvalued handsome, strapping athletes of the type that Beane himself had been at age seventeen. Scouts look for players who *look* the part. Perhaps in soccer, blonds are thought to look more like superstars.

This taste for blonds is an example of the "availability heuristic": the more available a piece of information is to the memory, the more likely it is to influence your decision, even when the information is irrelevant. Blonds stick in the memory.

| |

The inefficiencies we have cited so far are so-called "systemic failures": more than just individual mistakes, they are deviations from rationality.

All this is what you might call Transfer Market 101. To learn more about how to play the market, we need to study the masters.

DRUNKS, GAMBLERS, AND BARGAINS: CLOUGH AND TAYLOR AT FOREST

"Cloughie likes a bung," Alan Sugar told the High Court in 1993. Sugar's former manager at Spurs, Terry Venables, had told him so.

A "bung" is British slang for an illegal under-the-table payment to sweeten a deal. The court heard that when Clough bought or sold a player for Nottingham Forest, he expected to get a "bung." In a perfect world, he liked it to be handed over at a highway rest stop. Clough denied everything—"A bung? Isn't that something you get from a plumber to stop up the bath?"—and was never prosecuted. Yet what seems likely is this: "Old Big Head" (as Clough called himself) was so good at transfers, making profits even while turning a little provincial club into European champions, that he felt he deserved the odd bonus. More than anyone else in his day, Clough and his right-hand man, Peter Taylor, had succeeded in gaming the transfer market.

Clough and Taylor met while playing in a "Probables versus Possibles" reserve game at Middlesbrough in 1955. They seem to have fallen in love at first sight. Pretty soon they were using their free time to travel around the North of England watching soccer and coaching children together. Taylor never became more than a journeyman keeper, but Clough scored the fastest two hundred goals ever notched in English soccer until, at the age of twenty-seven, he wrecked his right knee skidding on a frozen field on Boxing Day in 1962. Three years later he phoned Taylor and said, "I've been offered the managership of Hartlepools and I don't fancy it. But if you'll come, I'll consider it." He then immediately hung up. Taylor took the bait, though to get in he had to double as Hartlepools' medical department, running onto the field with the sponge on match days. It was the prelude to their legendary years together at Derby and Nottingham Forest.

David Peace's novel *The Damned United*—and Tom Hooper's film of it—is in large part the love story of Clough and Taylor. The men's wives have only walk-on parts. As in all good couples, each partner has his assigned role. As Peace's fictional Clough tells himself, "Peter has the eyes and the ears, but you have the stomach and the balls." Taylor found the players, and Clough led them to glory.

The relationship ended in "divorce" in 1982, with Taylor's resignation from Forest. It seems that the rift had opened two years before, when Taylor published his excellent but now forgotten memoir, *With Clough by Taylor*. More of this in a moment, because it is the closest thing we have to a handbook to the transfer market.

But clearly the couple had other problems besides literature. Perhaps Clough resented his partner because he needed him so badly—not the sort of relationship Clough liked. Indeed, the film *The Damned United* depicts him failing at Leeds partly because Taylor is not there to scout players, and finally driving down to Brighton with his young sons to beg his partner's forgiveness. He finds Taylor doing the gardening. At Taylor's insistence, he gets down on his knees in the driveway and recites: "I'm nothing without you. Please, please, baby, take me back." And Taylor takes him back, and buys him the cut-price Forest team that wins two European Cups. For whatever their precise relationship, the duo certainly knew how to sign players. Here are a few of their coups:

- Buying Gary Birtles from the nonleague club Long Eaton for $3,500 in 1976, and selling him to Manchester United four years later for $2.9 million. A measure of what a good deal this was worth to Forest: United forked out about $500,000 more for Birtles than they would pay to sign Eric Cantona from Leeds twelve years later, in 1992. Birtles ended up costing United about $175,000 a goal, and after two years was sold back to Forest for a quarter of the initial fee.
- Buying Roy Keane from an Irish club called Cobh Ramblers for $80,000 in 1990 and selling him to Manchester United three years later for $5.6 million, then a British record fee.

- Buying Kenny Burns from Birmingham City for $250,000 in 1977. Taylor writes in *With Clough by Taylor* that Burns was then regarded as "a fighting, hard-drinking gambler . . . a stone [fourteen pounds] overweight." In 1978, English soccer writers voted Burns the league's player of the year.
- Twice buying Archie Gemmill cheaply. In 1970, when Gemmill was playing for Preston, Clough drove to his house and asked him to come to Derby. Gemmill refused. Clough said that in that case he would sleep outside in his car. Gemmill's wife invited him to sleep in the house instead. The next morning at breakfast Clough persuaded Gemmill to sign. The fee was $145,000, and Gemmill quickly won two league titles at Derby. In 1977 Clough paid Derby $35,000 and the forgotten goalkeeper John Middleton to bring Gemmill to his new club Forest, where the player won another league title.

If there is one club where almost every penny spent on transfers bought results, it was Forest under Clough. In the 1970s the correlation must have been off the charts: they won two European Cups with a team assembled largely for peanuts. Sadly, there are no good financial data for that period, but we do know that even from 1982 to 1992, in Clough's declining years, after Taylor had left him, Forest performed as well on the field as clubs that were spending twice as much on wages. Clough had broken the usually iron link between salaries and league position.

It's hard to identify all of the duo's transfer secrets, and if their rivals at the time had understood what they were up to, everyone would simply have imitated them. Taylor's book makes it clear that he spent a lot of time trying to identify players (like Burns) whom others had wrongly undervalued due to surface characteristics, but then everyone tries to do that. Sometimes Forest did splurge on a player who was rated by everybody, like Trevor Francis, the first "million-pound man," or Peter Shilton, whom they made the most expensive goalkeeper in British history.

Yet thanks to *With Clough by Taylor* we can identify three of the duo's rules. First, be as eager to sell good players as to buy them. "It's as important in soccer as in the stock market to sell at the right time," wrote Taylor. "A manager should always be looking for signs of disintegration in a winning side and then sell the players responsible before their deterioration is noticed by possible buyers." (Or in Billy Beane's words: "You have to always be upgrading. Otherwise you're fucked.")

The moment when a player reaches the top of his particular hill is like the moment when a stock market peaks. Clough and Taylor were always trying to gauge that moment, and sell. Each time they signed a player, they would give him a set speech, which Taylor recorded in his book: "Son, the first time we can replace you with a better player, we'll do it without blinking an eyelid. That's what we're paid to do—to produce the best side and to win as many things as we can. If we see a better player than you but don't sign him then we're frauds. But we're not frauds." In 1981, just after Kenny Burns had won everything with Forest, the club offloaded him to Leeds for $800,000.

Second, older players are overrated. "I've noticed over the years how often Liverpool sell players as they near or pass their thirtieth birthday," notes Taylor in his book. "Bob Paisley [Liverpool's then manager] believes the average First Division footballer is beginning to burn out at thirty." Taylor added, rather snottily, that that was true of a "running side like Liverpool," but less so of a passing one like Forest. Nonetheless, he agreed with the principle of selling older players.

The master of that trade today is Wenger. Arsenal's manager is one of the few people in soccer who can view the game from the outside. In part, this is because he has a degree in economic sciences from the University of Strasbourg in France. As a trained economist, he is inclined to trust data rather than the game's received wisdom. Wenger sees that in the transfer market, clubs tend to overvalue a player's past performance. That prompts them to pay fortunes for players who have just passed their peak. Probably because Wenger was one of the first managers to use statistics to assess players, he spotted that older players declined sooner than was conventionally realized. When Dennis Bergkamp was in his early thirties, Wenger began to substitute him late in games. If Bergkamp complained about it afterward, Wenger would simply produce the match statistics:

"Look, Dennis, after seventy minutes you started to run less. And your speed decreased."

Wenger often lets defenders carry on until their midthirties, but he usually gets rid of his midfielders and forwards much younger. He sold Patrick Vieira for $25 million (age twenty-nine), Thierry Henry for $30 million (age twenty-nine), Emmanuel Petit for $10.5 million (age twenty-nine), and Marc Overmars for $37 million (age twenty-seven), and none of them ever did as well again after leaving Arsenal.

Curiously, precisely the same overvaluation of older players exists in baseball, too. The conventional wisdom in the game had always been that players peak in their early thirties. Then along came Bill James from his tiny town in Kansas. In his mimeographs, the father of sabermetrics showed that the average player peaked not in his early thirties, but at just twenty-seven years old.

Finally, Clough and Taylor's third rule: buy players with personal problems (like Burns, or the gambler Stan Bowles) at a discount. Then help them deal with their problems.

Clough, a drinker, and Taylor, a gambler, had empathy with troubled players. While negotiating with a new player they would ask him a stock question, "to which we usually know the answer," wrote Taylor. It was: "Let's hear your vice before you sign. Is it women, booze, drugs or gambling?"

Clough and Taylor thought that once they knew the vice, they could help the player manage it. Taylor says he told Bowles, who joined Forest in 1979 (and, as it happens, failed there): "Any problem in your private life must be brought to us; you may not like that but we'll prove to you that our way of management is good for all of us." After a player confided a problem, wrote Taylor, "if we couldn't find an answer, we would turn to experts: we have sought advice for our players from clergymen, doctors and local councilors." Taking much the same approach, Wenger helped Tony Adams and Paul Merson combat their addictions.

All this might sound obvious, but the usual attitude in soccer is, "We paid a lot of money for you, now get on with it," as if mental illness, addictions, or homesickness should not exist above a certain level of income.

RELOCATION, RELOCATION, RELOCATION:
THE RICE KRISPIES PROBLEM

Clough and Taylor understood that many transfers failed because of a player's problems off the field. In a surprising number of cases, these problems are the product of the transfer itself.

Moving to a job in another city is always stressful; moving to another country is even more so. The challenge of moving from Rio de Janeiro to Manchester involves cultural adjustments that just don't compare with moving from Springfield, Missouri, to Springfield, Ohio. Yet European clubs that pay millions of dollars for foreign players are often unwilling to spend a few thousand more to help the players settle in their new homes. Instead, the clubs typically tell them: "Here's a plane ticket, come over, and play brilliantly from day 1." The player fails to adjust to the new country, underperforms, and his transfer fee is wasted. "Relocation," as the industry of relocation consultants calls it, is one of the biggest inefficiencies in the transfer market.

All the inefficiencies surrounding relocation could be assuaged. Most big businesses know how difficult relocation is, and do their best to smooth the passage. When a senior Microsoft executive moves between countries, a "relocation consultant" helps his or her family find schools and a house and learn the social rules of the new country. If Luther Blissett had been working for Microsoft, a relocation consultant could have found him Rice Krispies. An expensive relocation might cost $25,000, or 0.1 percent of a large transfer fee. But in soccer, the most globalized industry of all, spending anything at all on relocation is regarded as a waste of money.

Boudewijn Zenden, who has played in four countries, for clubs including Liverpool and Barcelona, told us at his latest stop, Marseille:

> It's the weirdest thing ever that you can actually buy a player for 20 mil, and you don't do anything to make him feel at home. I think the first thing you should do is get him a mobile phone and a house. Get him a school for the kids, get something for his missus, get a

teacher in for both of them straight away, because obviously everything goes with the language. Do they need anything for other family members, do they need a driving license, do they need a visa, do
they need a new passport? Sometimes even at the biggest clubs it's
really badly organized.

Milan: best club ever. AC Milan is organized in a way you can't
believe. Anything is done for you: you arrive, you get your house,
it's fully furnished, you get five cars to choose from, you know the
sky's the limit. They really say: we'll take care of everything else;
you make sure you play really well. Whereas unfortunately in a lot
of clubs, you have to get after it yourself. . . . Sometimes you get to
a club, and you've got people actually at the club who take profit
from players.

In soccer, bad relocations are the norm, like Chelsea signing cosmopolitan Ruud Gullit in 1996 and sticking him in a hotel in Slough, or
Ian Rush coming back from two bad years in Italy marveling, "It was
like another country." Many players down the decades would have understood that phrase. But perhaps the great failed relocation, one that a
Spanish relocation consultant still cites in her presentations, was Nicolas Anelka's to Real Madrid in 1999.

A half hour of conversation with Anelka is enough to confirm that
he is self-absorbed, scared of other people, and not someone who makes
contact easily. Nor does he appear to be good at languages, because after
a decade in England he still speaks very mediocre English. Anelka is
the sort of expatriate who really needs a relocation consultant.

Real had spent $35 million buying him from Arsenal. It then spent
nothing on helping him adjust. On day 1 the shy, awkward twenty year
old reported at the club, and found that there was nobody to show him
around. He hadn't even been assigned a locker in the dressing room.
Several times that first morning, he would take a locker that seemed to
be unused, only for another player to walk in and claim it.

Anelka doesn't seem to have talked about his problems to anyone at
Real. Nor did anyone at the club ask him. Instead, he talked to *France*

Football, a magazine that he treated as his newspaper of record, like a 1950s prime minister talking to *The Times*. "I am alone against the rest of the team," he revealed midway through the season. He claimed to possess a video showing his teammates looking gloomy after he had scored his first goal for Real after six months at the club. He had tried to give this video to the coach, but the coach hadn't wanted to see it. Also, the other black Francophone players had told Anelka that the other players wouldn't pass to him. Real ended up giving him a forty-five-day ban, essentially for being maladjusted.

Paranoid though Anelka may have been, he had a point. The other players really didn't like him. And they never got to know him, because nobody at the club ever seems to have bothered to introduce him to anyone. As he said later, all Real had told him was, "Look after yourself." The club seems to have taken the strangely materialistic view that Anelka's salary should determine his behavior. But even in materialistic terms, that was foolish. If you pay $35 million for an immature young employee, it is bad management to make him look after himself. Wenger at Arsenal knew that, and he had Anelka on the field scoring goals.

Even a player with a normal personality can find emigration tricky. Tyrone Mears, an English defender who moved to Marseille, where his best relocation consultant was his teammate Zenden, says, "Sometimes it's not a problem of the player adapting. A lot of the times it's the family adapting." Perhaps the player's girlfriend is unhappy because she can't find a job in the new town. Or perhaps she's pregnant and doesn't know how to negotiate the local hospital, or perhaps she can't find Rice Krispies ("or beans on toast," adds Zenden, when told about the Blissett drama). The club doesn't care. It is paying her boyfriend well. He simply has to perform.

There may never have been a soccer club with an HR department. There are a few relocation consultants in soccer, but they are never called that, and they usually aren't hired by clubs. Instead, they work either for players' agents or for sportswear companies. If Nike or Adidas is paying a player to wear its boots, it needs him to succeed. If the player moves to a foreign club, the sportswear company—knowing that the club probably won't bother—sometimes sends a minder to live in that town and look after him.

The minder gives the player occasional presents, acts as his secretary, friend, and shrink, and remembers his wife's birthday. The minder of a young midfielder who was struggling in his first weeks at Milan said that his main task, when the player came home from training frustrated, lonely, and confused by Italy, was to take him out to dinner. At dinner the player would grumble and say, "Tomorrow I'm going to tell the coach what I really think of him," and the minder would say, "That might not be such a brilliant idea. Here, have some more *linguine alle vongole*." To most players, this sort of thing comes as a bonus in a stressful life. To a few, it is essential.

However, these minders are clearly not enough. Too many players still flop abroad. Clubs often anticipate this by avoiding players who seem particularly ill-equipped to adjust. For instance, on average Brazilians are the world's best players. Yet historically English clubs rarely buy them, because Brazilians don't speak English, don't like cold weather, and don't tend to understand the core traditions of English soccer, like drinking twenty pints of beer in a night. Few Brazilians adjust easily to English soccer.

English clubs have traditionally bought Scandinavians instead. On average, Scandinavians are worse soccer players than Brazilians, but they are very familiar with English, cold weather, and twenty pints of beer. Scandinavians adapted to England, and so the clubs bought them. But the clubs were missing an opportunity. Anyone who bought a great Brazilian player and hired a good relocation consultant to help him adjust would be onto a winner. Yet few clubs did. Years used to go by without any English club buying a Brazilian.

Gradually, the soccer business is becoming less stupid. A few years ago Ajax Amsterdam hired a woman to help foreign players settle in. She found that some of their problems were absurdly easy to solve. When Steven Pienaar and another young South African player joined Ajax, they were teenagers, had never lived on their own before, and suddenly found themselves sharing an apartment in a cold country at the other end of the earth. Inevitably, they put their music speakers on the bare floor and turned the music on. Inevitably, the neighbors complained. The South Africans had a miserable time in their building, until the woman from Ajax came around to see what was wrong and suggested they put their speakers on a table instead. They did. The noise diminished, their lives got easier, and that might just have helped their soccer. Ajax has since appointed a full-time employee to help with relocation. Zenden says of clubs in general: "For any foreign player, or even a player who comes in new, they could get one man who's actually there to take care of everything. But then again, sometimes players are a bit—I don't want to say abusive, but they might take profit of the situation. They might call in the middle of the night, just to say there's no milk in the fridge. You know how they are sometimes."

Most clubs still don't believe in relocation. Didier Drogba in his autobiography recounts joining Chelsea from Olympique Marseille in 2004 for $44 million. He writes, "I plunged into problems linked to my situation as an expatriate. Chelsea didn't necessarily help me." Nobody at the club could help him find a school for his children. All Chelsea did to get him a house was put him in touch with a real estate agent who tried to sell him one for $18 million. For "weeks of irritation" the Drogba family lived in a hotel while Drogba, who at that point barely spoke English, went house hunting after practice.

All Chelsea's expensive foreign signings had much the same experience, Drogba writes. "We often laughed about it with Gallas, Makelele, Kezman, Geremi. 'You too, you're still living in a hotel?' After all these worries, I didn't feel like integrating [at Chelsea] or multiplying my efforts."

At a recent conference in Rome, relocation consultants literally lined up to tell their horror stories about soccer. Almost all of them had tried to get into the sport and been rebuffed. A Danish relocator had been told by FC Copenhagen that her services weren't required because the players' wives always helped each other settle. Many clubs had never even heard of relocation. Moreover, they had never hired relocation consultants before, so given the logic of soccer, not hiring relocation consultants must be the right thing to do. One Swedish relocator surmised, "I guess it comes down to the fact that they see the players as merchandise."

The only relocation consultants who had penetrated soccer happened to have a friend inside a club, or, in the case of one Greek woman, had married a club owner. She had told her husband, "All these guys would be happier if you find out what their needs are, and address their needs."

Another relocator had entered a German club as a language teacher and worked her way up. She said, "I was their mother, their nurse, their real estate agent, their cleaning lady, their everything. They didn't have a car; they didn't speak the language." Did her work help the players play better? "Absolutely." The club was happy for her to work as an amateur, but as soon as she founded a relocation company, it didn't want her anymore. She had become threatening.

THE NICEST TOWN IN EUROPE:
HOW TO BUY AND SELL LIKE OLYMPIQUE LYON

If you had to locate the middle-class European dream anywhere, it would be in Lyon. It's a town the size of Oakland, about two-thirds of the way down France, nestled between rivers just west of the Alps. On a warm January afternoon, drinking coffee outside in the eighteenth-century Place Bellecour where the buildings are as pretty as the women, you think: nice. Here's a wealthy town where you can have a good job, nice weather, and a big house near the mountains.

Lyon also has some of the best restaurants in Europe, known locally as *bouchons,* or "corks." Even at the town's soccer stadium you can have a wonderful three-course pregame meal consisting largely of intestines or head cheese, unless you prefer to eat at local boy Paul Bocuse's brasserie across the road and totter into the grounds just before kickoff. And then you can watch some of the best soccer in Europe, too.

Until about 2000 Lyon was known as the birthplace of cinema and nouvelle cuisine, but not as a soccer town. It was just too bourgeois. If for some reason you wanted soccer, you drove thirty-five miles down the highway to gritty proletarian Saint-Étienne. In 1987, Olympique Lyon, or "OL," or *"les Gones"* (the Kids), was playing in France's second division on an annual budget of about $3 million. It was any old backwater provincial club in Europe. Today it rules French soccer, and proclaims that it is only a matter of time before it wins the Champions League. Its ascent is in large part a story of the international transfer market. Better than any other club in Europe today, Lyon has worked out how to play the market.

In 1987 Jean-Michel Aulas, a local software entrepreneur with the stark, grooved features of a Roman emperor, became club president. Aulas had played fairly good handball as a young man and had a season ticket at OL.

"I didn't know the world of soccer well," he admits over a bottle of "OL" mineral water in his office beside the stadium (which he aims to tear down and replace with a bigger one). Had he expected the transformation that he wrought? "No."

Aulas set out to improve the club step by step. "We tried to abstract the factor 'time,'" he explains. "Each year we fix as an aim to have sporting progress, and progress of our financial resources. It's like a cyclist riding: you can overtake the people in front of you." Others in France prefer to liken Aulas to *"un bulldozer."*

In 1987 even the local *Lyonnais* didn't care much about *les Gones*. You could live in Lyon without knowing that soccer existed. The club barely had a personality, whereas Saint-Étienne were the "miners' club" that had suffered tragic defeats on great European nights in the 1970s. Saint-Étienne's president at the time said that when it came to soccer, Lyon was a suburb of Saint-Étienne, a remark that still rankles. At one derby after Lyon's domination began, *les Gones'* fans unfurled a banner that told the Saint-Étienne supporters: "We invented cinema when your fathers were dying in the mines."

Aulas appointed local boy Raymond Domenech as his first coach. In Domenech's first season, OL finished top of the second division without losing a game. Right after that it qualified for Europe. Aulas says, "At a stroke the credibility was total. The project was en route."

It turned out that the second city in France, even if it was a bit bourgeois, was just hungry enough for a decent soccer club. The *Lyonnais* were willing to buy match tickets if things went well, but if things went badly, they weren't immediately waving white handkerchiefs in the stands and demanding that the president or manager or half the team be gotten rid of. Nor did the French press track the club's doings hour by hour. It's much easier to build for the long term in a place like that than in a "soccer city" like Marseille or Newcastle. Moreover, players were happy to move to a town that is hardly a hardship posting. Almost nothing they get into in Lyon makes it into the gossip press. Another of Lyon's advantages: the locals have money. "It allowed us to have not just a 'popular clientele,' but also a 'business clientele,'" says Aulas.

Talking about money is something of a taboo in France. It is considered a grubby and private topic. Socially, you're never supposed to ask anyone a question that might reveal how much somebody has. Soccer, to most French fans, is not supposed to be about money. They find the notion of a well-run soccer club humorless, practically American.

It therefore irritates them that Aulas talks about it so unabashedly. He might have invented the word *moneyball.* Aulas's theme is that over time, the more money a club makes, the more matches it will win, and the more matches it wins, the more money it will make. In the short term you can lose a match, but in the long term there is a rationality even to soccer. (And to baseball. As *Moneyball* describes it, Beane believes that winning "is simply a matter of figuring out the odds, and exploiting the laws of probability. . . . To get worked up over plays, or even games, is as unproductive as a casino manager worrying over the outcomes of individual pulls of the slot machines.")

Aulas thinks that rationality in soccer works more or less like this: If you buy good players for less than they are worth, you will win more games. You will then have more money to buy better players for less than they are worth. The better players will win you more matches, and that will attract more fans (and thus more money), because Aulas spotted early that most soccer fans everywhere are much more like shoppers than like religious believers: if they can get a better experience somewhere new, they will go there. He told us, "We sold 110,000 replica shirts last season. This season we are already at 200,000. I think Olympique Lyon has become by far the most beloved club in France."

Polls suggest he is right: in Sport+Markt's survey of European supporters in 2008, Lyon emerged as the country's most popular club just ahead of Olympique Marseille. This popularity was a new phenomenon. In 2002, when Lyon first became champion of France, the overriding French emotion toward the club had still been: "Whatever." The editor of *France Football* magazine complained around that time that when Lyon won the title, his magazine didn't sell. But from 2002 to 2008 the club won the title every year—the longest period of domination of any club in any of Europe's five biggest national leagues ever—and many French fans began to care about it.

With more fans, Lyon makes more money. On match days now you can get a haircut at an official OL salon, drink an OL Beaujolais at an OL café, book your holiday at an OL travel agency, and take an OL taxi to the game—and many people do. Lyon uses that money to buy better players.

The club now survives the winter in the Champions League almost every season, which makes Lyon one of the sixteen best clubs in Europe. Aulas says it is only a matter of time before it wins the Champions League. "We know it will happen; we don't know *when* it will happen. It's a necessary step to achieve a growth in merchandising."

The cup with the big ears would cap perhaps the most remarkable rise in soccer history. And for all Aulas's "OL mineral water," what made it possible was the transfer market. On that warm winter's afternoon in Lyon, Aulas told us, "We will invest better than Chelsea, Arsenal, or Real Madrid. We will make different strategic choices. For instance, we won't try to have the best team on paper in terms of brand. We will have the best team relative to our investment." Here are Lyon's rules of the transfer market:

Use the wisdom of crowds. When Lyon is thinking of signing a player, a group of men sits down to debate the transfer. Aulas is there, and so is Bernard Lacombe, once a bull-like center forward for Lyon and

France, and for most of the past twenty years the club's "technical director." Lacombe is known for having the best pair of eyes in French soccer. He coached Lyon from 1996 to 2000, but Aulas clearly figured out that if you have someone with his knack for spotting the right transfer, you want to keep him at the club forever rather than make his job contingent on four lost matches. The same went for Peter Taylor at Forest.

Whoever happens to be Lyon's head coach at the moment sits in on the meeting too, and so will four or five other coaches. "We have a group that gives its advice," Aulas explains. "In England the manager often does it alone. In France it's often the technical director."

Like Lyon, the Oakland A's sidelined their manager, too. Like Lyon, the A's understood that he was merely "a middle manager" obsessed with the very short term. The A's let him watch baseball's annual draft. They didn't let him say a word about it.

Lyon's method for choosing players is so obvious and smart that it's surprising all clubs don't use it. The theory of the "wisdom of crowds" says that if you aggregate many different opinions from a diverse group of people, you are much more likely to arrive at the best opinion than if you just listen to one specialist. For instance, if you ask a diverse crowd to guess the weight of an ox, the average of their guesses will be very nearly right. If you ask a diverse set of gamblers to bet on, say, the outcome of a presidential election, the average of their bets is likely to be right, too. (Gambling markets have proved excellent predictors of all sorts of outcomes.) The wisdom of crowds fails when the components of the crowd are not diverse enough. This is often the case in American sports. But in European soccer, opinions tend to come from many different countries, and that helps ensure diversity.

Clough and Taylor at least were a crowd of two. However, the typical decision-making model in English soccer is not "wisdom of crowds," but short-term dictatorship. At most clubs the manager is treated as a sort of divinely inspired monarch who gets to decide everything until he is sacked. Then the next manager clears out his predecessor's signings at a discount. Lyon, notes a rival French club president with envy, never has expensive signings rotting on the bench. It never has revolutions at all. It understands that the coach is only a "temp." OL won its seven consecutive titles with four different coaches—Jacques Santini, Paul Le Guen, Gerard Houllier, and Alain Perrin—none of whom, judging by their subsequent records, is exactly a Hegelian world-historical individual. When a coach leaves Lyon, not much changes. No matter who happens to be sitting on the bench, the team always plays much the same brand of attacking soccer (by French standards).

Emmanuel Hembert grew up in Lyon supporting OL when it was still in the second division. Now, as head of the London sports practice of the management consultancy A. T. Kearney, he is always citing the club as an example to his clients in soccer. "A big secret of a successful club is stability," explains Hembert over coffee in Paris. "In Lyon, the stability is not with the coach, but with the sports director, Lacombe."

Another Lyon rule: *the best time to buy a player is when he is in his early twenties.* Aulas says, "We buy young players with potential who are considered the best in their country, between twenty and twenty-two years old." It's almost as if he had read *Moneyball*. The book keeps banging away about a truth discovered by Bill James, who wrote, "College players are a better investment than high school players by a huge, huge, laughably huge margin."

Baseball clubs traditionally preferred to draft high school players. But how good you are at seventeen or eighteen is a poor predictor of how good you will become as an adult. By definition, when a player is that young there is still too little information to judge him. Beane himself had been probably the hottest baseball prospect in the United States at seventeen, but he was already declining in his senior year at high school, and he then failed in the major leagues. Watching the 2002 draft as the A's general manager, he "punches his fist in the air" each time rival teams draft schoolboys.

It's the same in soccer, where brilliant teenagers tend to disappear soon afterward. Here are a few recent winners of the Golden Ball for best player at the under-seventeen World Cup: Philip Osundo of Nigeria, William de Oliveira of Brazil, Nii Lamptey of Ghana, Scottish goalkeeper James Will, and Mohammed al-Kathiri of Oman. Once upon a time they must have all been brilliant, but none of them made it as adults. (Will ended up a policeman in the Scottish Highlands playing for his village team.) The most famous case of a teenager who flamed out is American Freddy Adu, who at fourteen was the next Pelé and Maradona.

Only a handful of world-class players in each generation, most of them creators—Pelé, Maradona, Wayne Rooney—reach the top before they are eighteen. Most players get there considerably later. You can be confident of their potential only when they are more mature.

Beane knows that by the time players are in college—which tends to put them in Lyon's magical age range of twenty to twenty-two—you have a pretty good idea of what they will become. There is a lot of information about them. They are old enough to be nearly fully formed, but too young to be expensive stars.

Lyon always tries to avoid paying a premium for a star player's "name." Here, again, it is lucky to be a club from a quiet town. Its placid supporters and local media don't demand stars. By contrast, the former chairman of a club in a much more raucous French city recalls, "I ran [the club] with the mission to create a spectacle. It wasn't to build a project for twenty years to come." A team from a big city tends to need big stars.

Soccer being barely distinguishable from baseball, the same split between big and small towns operates in that sport, too. "Big-market teams," like the Boston Red Sox and the New York Yankees, hunt players with names. Their media and fans demand it. In *Moneyball*, Lewis calls this the pathology of "many foolish teams that thought all their questions could be answered by a single player." (It's a pathology that may sound strangely familiar to European soccer fans.) By contrast, the Oakland A's, as a small-market team, were free to forgo stars. As Lewis writes, "Billy may not care for the Oakland press but it is really very tame next to the Boston press, and it certainly has no effect on his behavior, other than to infuriate him once a week or so. Oakland A's fans, too, were apathetic compared to the maniacs in Fenway Park or Yankee Stadium."

Happy is the club that has no need of heroes. Lyon was free to buy young unknowns like Michael Essien or Mahamadou Diarra just because they were good. And unknowns accept modest salaries. According to the French sports newspaper *L'Equipe,* in the 2007–2008 season Lyon spent only 31 percent of its budget on players' pay. The average in the English Premier League was about double that. Like Clough's Forest, Lyon performs the magic trick of winning things without paying silly salaries.

Here are a few more of Lyon's secrets. First, *try not to buy center forwards.* Center forward is the most overpriced position in the transfer market. (Goalkeeper is the most underpriced, even though keepers have longer careers than outfield players; in baseball, the most overpriced position is pitcher.) Admittedly Lyon "announced" itself to soccer by buying the Brazilian center forward Sonny Anderson for $19 million in 1999, but the club has scrimped on the position since. Houllier left OL in 2007 grumbling that even after the club sold Florent Malouda and Eric Abidal for a combined total of $45 million, Aulas still wouldn't buy him a center forward.

Second, *help your foreign signings relocate.* All sorts of great Brazilians have passed through Lyon: Sonny Anderson; the current club captain, Cris; the future internationals Juninho and Fred; and the world champion Edmilson. Most were barely known when they joined the club. Aulas explains the secret: "Ten years ago we sent one of our old players, Marcelo, to Brazil. He was an extraordinary man, because he was both an engineer and a professional soccer player. He was captain of Lyon for five years. Then he became an agent, but he works quasi exclusively for OL. He indicates all market opportunities to us." As a judge of players, Marcelo is clearly in the Lacombe or Peter Taylor class.

Marcelo says he scouts only "serious boys." Or as the former president of a rival French club puts it, "They don't select players just for their quality but for their ability to adapt. I can't see Lyon recruiting an Anelka or a Ronaldinho."

After Lyon signs the serious boys, it makes sure they settle. Drogba notes enviously, "At Lyon, a translator takes care of the Brazilians, helps them to find a house, get their bearings, tries to reduce as much as possible the negative effects of moving. . . . Even at a place of the calibre of Chelsea, that didn't exist."

Lyon's "translator," who works full-time for the club, sorts out the players' homesickness, bank accounts, nouvelle cuisine, and whatever else. Other people at the club teach the newcomers Lyon's culture: no stars or showoffs. By concentrating on Brazilians, the club can offer them a tailor-made relocation service. Almost all the other foreign players Lyon buys are French speakers.

Finally, sell any player if another club offers more than he is worth. This is what Aulas means when he says, "Buying and selling players is not an activity for improving the soccer performance. It's a trading activity, in which we produce gross margin. If an offer for a player is greatly superior to his market value, you must not keep him." The ghost of Peter Taylor would approve.

Like Clough and Taylor, and like Billy Beane, Lyon never gets sentimental about players. In the club's annual accounts, it books each player for a certain transfer value. (Beane says, "Know exactly what every player in baseball is worth to you. You can put a dollar figure on it.")

Lyon knows that sooner or later its best players will attract somebody else's attention. Because the club expects to sell them, it replaces them even before they go. That avoids a transition period or a panic purchase after the player's departure. Aulas explains, "We will replace the player in the squad six months or a year before. So when Michael Essien goes [to Chelsea for $43 million], we already have a certain number of players who are ready to replace him. Then, when the opportunity to buy Tiago arises, for 25 percent of the price of Essien, you take him."

Before Essien's transfer, Aulas spent weeks proclaiming that the Ghanaian was "untransferable." He always says that when he is about to transfer a player, because it drives up the price. In his words, "Every international at Lyon is untransferable. Until the offer surpasses by far the amount we had expected."

As a free service to clubs, here are the twelve main secrets of the transfer market in full:

A new manager wastes money on transfers; don't let him.
Use the wisdom of crowds.
Stars of recent World Cups or European championships are overvalued; ignore them.
Certain nationalities are overvalued.
Older players are overvalued.
Center forwards are overvalued; goalkeepers are undervalued.
Gentlemen prefer blonds: identify and abandon "sight-based prejudices."
The best time to buy a player is when he is in his early twenties.
Sell any player when another club offers more than he is worth.
Replace your best players even before you sell them.
Buy players with personal problems, and then help them deal with their problems.
Help your players relocate.

Alternatively, clubs could just stick with the conventional wisdom.

4

THE WORST BUSINESS IN THE WORLD

Why Soccer Clubs Don't (and Shouldn't) Make Money

A man we know once tried to do business with a revered institution of English soccer. "I can do business with stupid people," he said afterward, "and I can do business with crooks. But I can't do business with stupid people who want to be crooks."

It was a decent summary of the soccer business, if you can call soccer a business. People often do. William McGregor, the Scottish draper who founded the English Football League in 1888, was probably the first person to describe soccer as "big business," but the phrase has since become one of the game's great clichés. In fact, McGregor was wrong. Soccer is neither big business nor good business. It arguably isn't even business at all.

"BIG BUSINESS"

Few people have heard of the corporation Titanium Metals. It was founded in 1950, chiefly to produce titanium for the airplanes, submarines, rockets, and missiles that the United States needed for the cold war. TIMET now mostly supplies the aerospace industry. This is pretty unglamorous work, and TIMET is an unglamorous corporation. It's the smallest of the five hundred publicly traded American companies that make up the S&P 500. In 2008 it had revenues of $1.15 billion and operating income of $220 million. TIMET, whose headquarters is on the LBJ Freeway in Dallas, is not big business. For comparison: in 2008 the biggest company in the S&P 500, the oil giant Exxon, had revenues that were more than four hundred times bigger.

But compared to any soccer club, Titanium Metals is a behemoth. Every year business adviser Deloitte ranks the richest clubs on earth in its "Soccer Money League." In 2009 Real Madrid led the league with revenues of about $475 million. That's a tidy sum, but less than half of TIMET's revenues, and less than one-thousandth the size of Exxon's. Second in the Soccer Money League was Manchester United with a paltry $422 million.

It's worth noting that the Money League ranks clubs based on how much they sell. When business analysts judge normal companies they usually focus on profits, or the company's value if it were sold on the market. However, neither of those methods works with soccer clubs. Because almost no clubs are quoted on the stock market anymore, for extremely good reasons, it is hard to work out their value. We can certainly say that not even Real or United would get anywhere near the S&P 500.

And if Deloitte ranked clubs by their profits, the results would be embarrassing. Not only do most clubs make losses and fail to pay any dividends to their shareholders, but many of the "bigger" clubs would rank near the bottom of the list. Deloitte reported in 2008 that the three most profitable clubs in the Premier League were Watford, Reading, and Arsenal, while the three least profitable were Chelsea, Manchester United, and Newcastle.

Whichever way you measure it, no soccer club is a big business. Real and United are dwarfed by Titanium Metals. As for all the rest, the author Alex Fynn noted in the 1990s that the average Premier League club had about the same turnover as a British supermarket—not a chain of supermarkets, but one single out-of-town Tesco supermarket. True, soccer clubs have grown since then: by 2008 the average club in the Premier League had a turnover of about $150 million, compared with $100 million for the average British Tesco supermarket. However, since Tesco has six hundred supermarkets or superstores in Britain, the average take of the twenty largest is probably still much larger than that of the average club. And unlike most clubs, Tesco actually makes a profit.

A good way to visualize the size of the soccer industry is to visit UEFA's headquarters in the Swiss town of Nyon. The building has a lovely view of Lake Geneva, but it looks like the offices of a small insurance company. Soccer is small business.

This feels like a contradiction. We all know that soccer is huge. Some of the most famous people on earth are soccer players, and the most watched television program in history is generally the most recent World Cup final. Nonetheless, soccer clubs are puny businesses. This is partly a problem of what economists call appropriability: soccer clubs can't make money out of (can't appropriate) more than a tiny share of our love of soccer.

It may be that season tickets are expensive and replica shirts overpriced, but buying these things once a year represents the extravagant extreme of soccer fanaticism. Most soccer is watched not from $1,500 seats in the stadium but on TV—sometimes at the price of a subscription, often at the price of watching a few commercials, or for the price of a couple of beers in the pub. Compare the cost of watching a game in a pub with the cost of eating out, or watching a movie, let alone going on vacation.

Worse still, soccer generates little income from reruns of matches or transfers to DVD. And watching soccer (even on TV) is only a tiny part of the fan's engagement with the game. There are newspaper reports to be read, Internet sites trawled, and a growing array of computer games to keep up with. Then there is the soccer banter that passes time at the dinner table, work, or the office. All this entertainment is made possible by soccer clubs, but they cannot appropriate a penny of the value we attach to it. Chelsea cannot charge us for talking or reading or thinking about Chelsea. As the Dutch international Demy de Zeeuw says, "There are complaints that we [players] earn too much, but the whole world earns money from your success as a player: newspapers, television, companies." In fact, the world earns more from soccer than the soccer industry itself does.

BAD BUSINESS

Soccer is not merely a small business. It's also a bad one. Anyone who spends any time inside soccer soon discovers that just as oil is part of the oil business, stupidity is part of the soccer business.

This becomes obvious when people in soccer encounter people in other industries. Generally, the soccer people get exploited because people in other industries understand business better. In 1997 Peter Kenyon, then chief executive of the sportswear company Umbro, invited a few guests to watch a European game at Chelsea, the club he would end up running a few years later. After the game, Kenyon took his guests out for dinner. Over curry he reminisced about how the sportswear industry used to treat soccer clubs. In the 1970s, he said, big English clubs used to *pay* companies like Umbro to supply their clothing. It was obviously great advertising for the gear makers to have some of England's best players running around in their clothes, but the clubs had not yet figured that out. And so sportswear companies used to get paid to advertise themselves.

Ricky George saw the ignorance of soccer in those days from point-blank range. In 1972, when George scored the legendary goal for non-league Hereford that knocked Newcastle out of the FA Cup, he was working for Adidas as a "soccer PR." His job was to represent Adidas to England players, former world champions like Bobby Moore, Bobby Charlton, and Gordon Banks. There was little need to persuade them to choose Adidas. Most of them wore the three stripes for free anyway. George says, "It is quite a fascinating thing if you compare it with today. There were no great sponsorship deals going on. All that happened is that you would give the players boots. But even then, at the beginning of every season the clubs would go to their local sports retailer and just buy twenty, thirty pairs of boots and hand them out. For a company like Adidas, it was the cheapest type of PR you could imagine."

Only on special occasions did George have to pay players. "When it came to a big international, and the game was going to be televised, my job was to go to the team hotel, hang around there, make myself known, and a couple of hours before the game I would go into the players' rooms and paint the white stripes on their boots with luminous paint so it was more visible. My bosses used to be keenly watching the television to make sure the stripes were visible, and if they weren't I would be in for bollocking."

For this service, an England player would receive seventy-five pounds per match, which was then about two hundred dollars—not a princely sum even in 1972. George recalls, "Bobby [Moore], the most charming of people, didn't take the money on the day of the game. He just used to say to me, 'Let it build up for a few games, and I'll ring you when I need it.' And that's what he did." Then the most famous defender of the era would pocket a cumulative few hundred dollars for having advertised an international brand to a cumulative audience of tens of millions.

Only in the late 1980s did English soccer clubs discover that some people were willing to buy replicas of their team shirts. That made it plain even to them that their gear must have some value. They had already stopped paying sportswear companies for the stuff; now they started to charge them.

Gradually over time, soccer clubs have found new ways of making money. However, the ideas almost never came from the clubs themselves. Whether it was branded clothing, or the gambling "pools," or television, it was usually people in other industries who first saw there might be profits to be made. It was Rupert Murdoch who went to English clubs and suggested putting them on satellite TV; the clubs would never have thought of going to him. In fact, the clubs often fought against new moneymaking schemes. Until 1982 they refused to allow any league games to be shown live on TV, fearing that it might deter fans from coming to the stadium. It took another decade for clubs to grasp that games on television meant both free money and free advertising.

It took them even longer to realize how much soccer was worth to people like Murdoch. In 1992 he began paying about $115 million a season for the television rights to the new Premier League. Now the league gets about ten times as much a season from television. "I've been screwed by television," admitted Sir John Hall, then the Newcastle chairman, one rowdy night at Trinity College Dublin in 1995. "But I'll tell you one thing: I won't be screwed again."

Or take the renovation of English stadiums in the early 1990s. It was an obvious business idea. Tesco doesn't receive customers in sheds built in the Victorian era and gone to seed since. It is forever renovating its stores. Yet soccer clubs never seem to have thought of spending money on their grounds until the Taylor Report of 1990 forced them to. They did up their stadiums, and bingo: more customers came.

All this proves how much like consumers soccer fans are. It's not that they come running when a team does well. Rather, it seems that soccer can quickly become popular across a whole country. All teams then benefit, but particularly those that build nice new stadiums where spectators feel comfortable and safe. That would explain why the three English clubs whose crowds grew fastest over the nineties were Manchester United, Sunderland, and Newcastle. In other leagues, clubs such as Ajax and Celtic also drew huge new crowds to their new grounds— in Ajax's case, even though its soccer spontaneously combusted. There is such a close link between building a nice stadium and drawing more spectators that the traditional fans' chant of "Where were you when you were shit?" should be revised to "Where were you when your stadium was shit?"

Yet like almost all good business ideas in soccer, the Taylor Report was imposed on the game from outside. Soccer clubs are classic late adopters of new ideas. Several years after the Internet emerged, Liverpool, a club with millions of fans around the world, still did not have a Web site. It's no wonder that from 1992 through May 2008, even before the financial crisis struck, forty of England's ninety-two professional clubs had been involved in insolvency proceedings, some of them more than once.

HOW THE TRIBE CHOOSES ITS CHIEFS

Rather than stack up endless examples of the dimness of soccer clubs, let's take one contemporary case study: how clubs hire their key employee, the manager. English fans are still asking themselves how Steve McClaren ever got to be appointed England manager, but in fact it is unfair to single him out. The profusion of fantasy soccer leagues, in which office workers masquerade as coaches, indicates the widely held suspicion that any fool could do as well as the people who actually get the jobs. The incompetence of soccer managers may have something to do with the nonsensical and illegal methods by which they are typically recruited.

Soccer "is a sad business," says Bjørn Johansson, who runs a headhunting firm in Zurich. Like his colleagues in headhunting, Johansson is never consulted by clubs seeking managers. Instead, a club typically chooses its man based on the following factors.

The New Manager Is Hired in a Mad Rush

In a panel at the International Football Arena conference in Zurich in 2006, Johansson explained that in "normal" business, "an average search process takes four to five months." In soccer, a club usually finds a coach within a couple of days of sacking his predecessor. "Hesitation is regarded as weak leadership," explained another panelist in Zurich, Ilja Kaenzig, then general manager of the German club Hannover 96. Brian Barwick, the English Football Association's former chief executive, has noted that McClaren's recruitment "took from beginning to end nine weeks," yet the media accused the FA of being "sluggish." If only it had been more sluggish.

A rare slow hire in soccer became perhaps the most inspired choice of the past two decades: Arsenal's appointment of Arsène Wenger in 1996. Wenger, working in Japan, was not free immediately. Arsenal waited for him, operating under caretaker managers for weeks, and was inevitably accused of being sluggish. Similarly, in 1990 Manchester United's chairman, Martin Edwards, was derided as sluggish when he refused to sack his losing manager, Alex Ferguson. Edwards thought that in the long term, Ferguson might improve.

The New Manager Is Interviewed Only Very Cursorily

In "normal" business, a wannabe chief executive writes a business plan, gives a presentation, and undergoes several interviews. In soccer, a club calls an agent's cell phone and offers the job.

The New Manager Is Always a Man

The entire industry discriminates illegally against women. He is also almost always white, with a conservative haircut, aged between thirty-five and sixty, and a former professional player. Clubs know that if they choose someone with that profile, then even if the appointment turns out to be terrible they won't be blamed too much, because at least they will have failed in the traditional way. As the old business saying goes, "Nobody ever got fired for buying IBM."

There is no evidence that having been a good player (or being white and of conservative appearance) is an advantage for a soccer manager. Arrigo Sacchi, coach of the great Milan from 1987 to 1991, who couldn't play soccer himself, explained, "You don't have to have been a horse to be a jockey."

Playing and coaching are different skill sets. Match for match, the most successful coach in soccer's history is probably Jose Mourinho, who barely ever kicked a ball for money. When Milan's coach Carlo Ancelotti noted Mourinho's modest record as a player, the Portuguese replied, "I don't see the connection. My dentist is the best in the world, and yet he's never had a particularly bad toothache." Asked why failed players often become good coaches, Mourinho said, "More time to study."

The problem with ex-pros may be precisely their experience. Having been steeped in the game for decades, they just *know* what to do: how to train, who to buy, how to talk to their players. They don't need to investigate whether these inherited prejudices are in fact correct. Rare is the ex-pro who realizes, like Billy Beane at the Oakland A's, that he needs to jettison what he learned along the way. Michael Lewis writes in *Moneyball*, "Billy had played pro ball, and regarded it as an experience he needed to overcome if he wanted to do his job well. 'A reformed alcoholic,' is how he described himself."

Managers Don't Need Professional Qualifications

Only in 2003 did UEFA insist that new managers in the Premier League have passed the "Pro Licence" course. In England's lower divisions this remains unnecessary. Yet Sue Bridgewater, an associate professor at Warwick Business School, showed that managers with the Pro Licence won significantly more matches than managers without it. She also showed that experienced managers outperformed novices. That qualifications and experience are useful is understood in every industry except soccer, where a manager is expected to work the magic he acquired as a superhero player.

The New Manager Is Often Underqualified
Even If He Has Qualifications

Chris Brady, a business school professor, teaches finance and accounting in the Pro Licence course. He says his entire module takes half a day. No wonder some English managers mismanage money: they don't understand it. Clubs are ceasing to entrust their finances to managers, giving them instead to more qualified executives like Kaenzig, who guarantee stability by staying longer than the club manager's average two-year tenure. That at least is the theory: the week after that conference in Zurich, Hannover released Kaenzig.

Immediate Availability

The new manager is appointed either because he is able to start work immediately (often as a result of having just been sacked), or because he has achieved good results over his career, or, failing that, because he achieved good results in the weeks preceding the appointment. Mc-Claren became England manager only because his team, Middlesbrough, reached the UEFA Cup final in 2006 and avoided relegation just as the FA was deciding who to pick. By the time Middlesbrough was waxed 4–0 by Seville in the final, McClaren already had the job.

His period under review was so short as to be a random walk. The same went for the main candidates to manage England in 1996: Bryan Robson, Frank Clark, Gerry Francis, and the eventual choice, Glenn Hoddle. Today none of them works as a manager (Francis and Clark haven't for many years), none had his last job in the Premier League, and none will probably work that high again. They were in the frame in 1996 because they had had good results recently and were English—another illegal consideration in hiring.

Star Power

The new manager is generally chosen not for his alleged managerial skills but because his name, appearance, and skills at public relations are expected to impress the club's fans, players, and the media. That is why no club hires a woman—stupid fans and players would object—and why it was so brave of Milan to appoint the unknown Sacchi, and Arsenal the unknown Wenger. Tony Adams, Arsenal's then captain, doubted the obscure foreigner on first sight. In his autobiography, *Addicted*, the player recalls thinking, "What does this Frenchman know about soccer? He wears glasses and looks more like a schoolteacher. He's not going to be as good as George. Does he even speak English properly?"

A manager must above all look like a manager. Clubs would rather use traditional methods to appoint incompetents than risk doing anything that looks odd.

BAD STAFF

The most obvious reason soccer is such an incompetent business is that soccer clubs tend to hire incompetent staff. The manager is only the start of it. Years ago one of us requested an interview with the chairman of an English club quoted on the stock market. The press officer asked me to send a fax (a 1980s technology revered by soccer clubs). I sent it. She said she never got it. On request I sent three more faxes to different officials. She said none arrived. This is quite a common experience for soccer journalists. Because soccer clubs are the only businesses that get daily publicity without trying to, they treat journalists as humble supplicants instead of as unpaid marketers of the clubs' brands. The media often retaliate by being mean. This is not very clever of the clubs, because almost all their fans follow them through the media rather than by going to the stadiums.

A month after all the faxes, I was granted permission to send my request by e-mail. When I arrived at the club for the interview, I met the press officer. She was beautiful. Of course she was. Traditionally, soccer clubs recruit the women on their office staff for their looks, and the men because they played professional soccer or are somebody's friend.

If soccer clubs wanted to, they could recruit excellent executives. Professors at business schools report that many of their MBA students, who pay about forty thousand dollars a year in tuition fees, dream of working in soccer for a pitiful salary. Often the students beg clubs to let them work for free as summer interns. The clubs seldom want them. If you work for a soccer club, your goal is to keep working there, not to be shown up by some overeducated young thing who has actually learned something about business.

In part this is because much of the traditionally working-class soccer industry distrusts education. In part, says Emmanuel Hembert of A. T. Kearney, it is because many clubs are dominated by a vain owner-manager: "Lots of them invested for ego reasons, which is never a good thing in business. They prefer not to have strong people around them, except the coach. They really pay low salaries."

Historically, only Manchester United recruited respected executives from normal industries (such as Peter Kenyon from Umbro), though now a few other big clubs like Barcelona are starting to do so, too.

Baseball appears to be just as incompetent. In *Moneyball* Lewis asks why, among baseball executives and scouts, "there really is no level of incompetence that won't be tolerated." He thinks the main reason "is that baseball has structured itself less as a business than as a social club. . . . There are many ways to embarrass the Club, but being bad at your job isn't one of them. The greatest offense a Club member can commit is not ineptitude but disloyalty." Club members—and this applies in soccer as much as in baseball—are selected for clubbability. Clever outsiders are not clubbable, because they talk funny, and go around pointing out the things that people inside the Club are doing wrong. "It wasn't as simple as the unease of jocks in the presence of nerds," writes Lewis—but that unease does have a lot to do with it.

The staff of soccer clubs tends not merely to be incompetent. They are also often novices. This is because staff turnover is rapid. Whenever a new owner arrives, he generally brings in his cronies. The departing staff rarely joins a new club, because that is considered disloyal (Kenyon, an exception, was persecuted for moving from United to Chelsea), even though players change clubs all the time. So soccer executives are always having to reinvent the wheel.

Worse, the media and fans often make it impossible for clubs to make sensible decisions. They are always hassling the club to do something immediately. If the team loses three games, fans start chanting for the club to sack the coach or buy a new player, in short to tear up the plans it might have made a month ago. "Consumer activism in this industry is extreme," warns A. T. Kearney in its report *Playing for Profits*. Hembert says, "The business plan—as soon as you sign a player for £10 million, you blow up your business plan. Commercial employees have to fight for £100,000 of spending here or there, but then suddenly the club spends £10 million."

Or more. Sven Goran Eriksson once flew into Zurich to tell the International Football Arena a "good story" about his time managing Lazio. "The chairman I had was very good," Eriksson recalled for an audience of mostly Swiss businessmen. "If I wanted a player, he would try to get that player. One day I phoned him up and I said: 'Vieri.'"

Christian Vieri was then playing for Atletico Madrid. Eriksson and Lazio's chairman, Sergio Cragnotti, flew to Spain to bid for him.

Atletico told them Vieri would cost 50 billion Italian lire. At the time, in 1998, that was nearly $29 million. Eriksson reminisced, "That was the biggest sum in the world. No player had been involved for that." He says the talks then went more or less as follows:

CRAGNOTTI: "That's a lot of money."
ERIKSSON: "I know."

At this point Atletico mentioned that it might accept some Lazio players in part payment for Vieri.

CRAGNOTTI: "Can we do that?"
ERIKSSON: "No, we can't give away these players."
CRAGNOTTI: "What shall we do then?"
ERIKSSON: "Buy him."
CRAGNOTTI: "Okay."

Eriksson recalled in Zurich: "He didn't even try to pay 49. He just paid 50."

Nine months after Vieri joined Lazio, Inter Milan wanted to buy him. Once again, Eriksson reports the conversation:

CRAGNOTTI: "What shall I ask for him?"
ERIKSSON: "Ask for double. Ask 100."
CRAGNOTTI: "I can't do that."

Eriksson recalled: "So he asked 90. And he got 90. That's good business." (Or the ultimate example of the greater-fool principle.)

Someone in the audience in Zurich asked Eriksson whether such behavior was healthy. After all, Lazio ran out of money in 2002 when Cragnotti's food company, Cirio, went belly-up. Cragnotti later spent time in prison, which even by the standards of Italian soccer is going a bit far.

Eriksson replied, "It's not healthy. And if you see Lazio, it was not healthy. But we won the league. And we won the Cupwinners Cup. We won everything."

The point is that soccer clubs, prompted by media and fans, are always making financially irrational decisions in an instant. They would like to think long term, but because they are in the news every day they end up fixating on the short term. An executive with an American entertainment company tells a story about his long-arranged business meeting with Real Madrid. His company was hoping to build a relationship with the club. But on the day of the meeting, Real ritually sacked its manager. The usual chaos ensued. Two of the club officials scheduled to attend the meeting with the American executive did not show up. That's soccer.

SAFER THAN THE BANK OF ENGLAND: WHY SOCCER CLUBS ALMOST NEVER DISAPPEAR

On September 15, 2008, the investment bank Lehman Brothers collapsed, followed almost immediately by the world's stock markets.

Any soccer club on earth was a midget next to Lehman. In the year to September 2007, the bank had income of $59 billion (148 times Manchester United's at the time) and profits of $6 billion (50 times Manchester United's), and was valued by the stock market at $34 billion. If United's shares had still been traded on the market, they would probably have been worth less than 5 percent of Lehman's. Yet Lehman no longer exists while United very much does.

Over the past decade, people worried a lot more about the survival of soccer clubs than of banks. Yet it was many of the world's largest banks that disappeared. The public perception that soccer clubs are inherently unstable businesses is wrong. Despite being incompetently run, they are some of the most stable businesses on earth.

First, some facts. In 1923 England's Football League consisted of eighty-eight teams spread over four divisions. In the 2007–2008 season, eighty-five of these clubs still existed (97 percent), and seventy-five remained in the top four divisions (85 percent). An actual majority, forty-eight clubs, were in the same division as they had been in 1923. And only nine teams still in the top four divisions were two or more divisions away from where they had been in 1923 (poor Notts County had sunk from first to fourth tier).

So almost every professional club in England had survived the Great Depression, the Second World War, recessions, corrupt chairmen, and appalling managers. It is a history of remarkable stability. By comparison, economic historian Les Hannah made a list of the top one hundred British companies in 1912, and researched what had become of them by 1995. Nearly half the companies—forty-nine—had ceased to exist. Five of these had gone bankrupt, six were nationalized, and thirty-seven were taken over by other firms. Even among the businesses that survived, many had gone into new sectors or moved to new locations.

What made these nonsoccer businesses so unstable was, above all, competition. There is such a thing as brand loyalty, but when a better product turns up, most people will switch sooner or later. So normal businesses keep having to innovate or die. They face endless pitfalls: competitors pull ahead, consumers' tastes change, new technologies make entire industries obsolete, cheap goods arrive from abroad, the government interferes, recessions hit, companies overinvest and go bust or simply get unlucky.

By contrast, soccer clubs are immune from almost all these effects: a club that fails to keep up with the competition might get relegated, but it can always survive at a lower level. Some fans lose interest, but clubs have geographical roots. A bad team might find its catchment area shrinking, but not disappearing completely. The "technology" of soccer can never become obsolete because the technology is the game itself. At worst soccer might become less popular.

Foreign rivals cannot enter the market and supply soccer at a lower price. The rules of soccer protect domestic clubs by forbidding foreign competitors from joining their league. English clubs as a whole could fall behind foreign competitors and lose their best players, but foreign clubs have financial problems and incompetent management of their own.

The government is not about to nationalize soccer.

Clubs often overinvest, but this almost never destroys the club, only the wealth of the investor. At worst, the club gets relegated.

A club's income might decline in a recession, but it can always live with a lower income.

In most industries a bad business goes bankrupt, but soccer clubs almost never do. The forty English clubs that entered insolvency proceedings through May 2008 cut deals with their creditors (usually the players and the tax man) and moved on. Yes, Aldershot FC went bankrupt in 1992, but supporters simply started a new club almost identical to the old one. The "new" Aldershot Town AFC has a badge that shows a phoenix rising from the ashes. In Italy Fiorentina went bust in 2002 and got relegated to the Italian fourth division, but within a couple of years it was back at the top, the bankruptcy forgotten. No big soccer club disappears under its debts. If West Ham or (imagine) Liverpool fell into administration, they too would be guaranteed to be reborn under new ownership. No matter how much money clubs waste, someone will always bail them out. This is what is known in finance as "moral hazard": when you know you will be saved however much money you lose, you are free to lose money. Soccer clubs are incompetent because they can be. The professional investors who briefly bought club shares in the 1990s got out as soon as they discovered this.

Even the current economic crisis is unlikely to destroy any clubs. A glance at past crises shows how resilient they are. You would have expected the Great Depression to pose something of a threat to English clubs. After all, the Depression bit deepest in the North of England, where most professional clubs were based, and all romantic rhetoric aside, you would have thought that when people cannot afford to buy bread they would stop going to soccer matches.

Crowds in the English Football League did indeed fall 12 percent between 1929 and 1931. However, by 1932 they were growing again, even though the British economy was not. And clubs helped each other through the hard times. When Orient hit trouble in 1931, Arsenal wrote its tiny neighbor a check for £3,450 to tide it over. Clubs know they cannot operate without opponents, and so unlike in most businesses, the collapse of a rival is not a cause for celebration.

The Depression culled only a couple of clubs. Merthyr Town, after failing to be reelected to the league in 1930, folded a few years later, the victim of economic hardship in the Welsh valleys (as well as competition from the far more popular rugby union). Wigan Borough went bankrupt a few games into the 1931–1932 season. It left the league, and its remaining fixtures were never played. Aldershot was elected to replace it, and sixty years later, in another recession, it became only the second English club in history to withdraw from the league with fixtures unplayed.

During the "Thatcher recession," crowds in the English Football League fell by nearly a quarter between 1979–1980 and 1982–1983. Many clubs struggled, and several survived only thanks to a "sub"—financial support—from the players' union, which didn't want to see employers go bust. Charlton and Bristol Rovers had to move grounds because they could not pay the rent. However, nobody "did an Accrington Stanley" and resigned from the league.

Most stricken clubs instead "do a Leeds": cut their wages, get relegated, and compete at a lower level. Imagine if other businesses could do this. Suppose that Ford could sack skilled workers and hire unskilled ones to produce worse cars, or that American Airlines could replace all their pilots with people who weren't as well qualified to fly planes. Governments would stop it, and in any case, consumers would not put up with terrible products. Soccer clubs, unlike most businesses, survive crises because some of their customers stick with them no matter how lousy the product. Calling this brand loyalty is not quite respectful enough of the sentiment involved. To quote Rogan Taylor, a Liverpool fan and Liverpool University professor: "Soccer is more than just a business. No one has their ashes scattered down the aisle at Tesco."

NOT BUSINESSES AT ALL

When businesspeople look at soccer, they are often astonished at how unbusinesslike the clubs are. Every now and then one of them takes over a club and promises to run it "like a business." Alan Sugar, who had made his money in computers, became chairman of Tottenham Hotspur in 1991. His brilliant wheeze was to make Spurs live within its means. Never would he fork out 50 billion lire for a Vieri. After Newcastle bought Alan Shearer for $23 million in 1996, Sugar remarked, "I've slapped myself around the face a couple of times, but I still can't believe it."

He more or less kept his word. In the ten years that he ran Spurs, the team lived within its means. But most of the fans hated it. The only thing Spurs won in that decade was a solitary League Cup. It spent most of its time midtable of the Premier League, falling far behind Arsenal. Nor did it even make much money: about $3 million a year in profits in Sugar's first six years, which was much less than Arsenal and not very good for a company its size. Sugar's Spurs disappointed both on and off the field, and it also illustrated a paradox: when businesspeople try to run a soccer club as a business, then not only does the soccer suffer, but so does the business.

Other businessmen pursue a different strategy than Sugar's. They assume that if they can get their clubs to win prizes, profits will inevitably follow. But they too are wrong. Even the best teams seldom generate profits. We plotted the league positions and profits of all the clubs that have played in the Premier League from its inaugural season of 1992–1993 until the 2006–2007 season in figure 4.1.

The figure shows how spectacularly unprofitable the soccer business is. Each point on the chart represents the combination of profit and position for a club in a particular year. One obvious point to note is that most of the dots fall below zero on the profit axis: these clubs were making losses. But the figure also shows that there was barely any connection between finishing high and making money. Although there is some suggestion that a few clubs at the top of the table make more money than other clubs, the chart also shows that other clubs in these positions can make huge losses. Manchester United's profitability is clearly the exception. In the thirty years before being taken over by the Glazer family the club generated more than £250 million

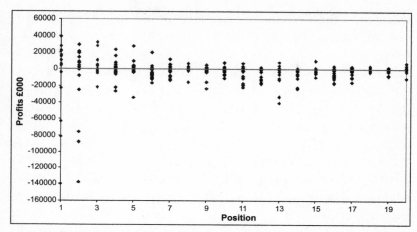

FIGURE 4.1 Premier League pretax profits and position, 1992–1993 to 2006–2007

($400 million) in pretax profits while also winning eight league titles. Indeed, other American owners might never have bothered buying into English soccer without United's example. But no other club could replicate its success.

For most English clubs, our graph shows that there is not even a connection between changing league position and changing profits. In 45 percent of all cases, when a club changed its league position, its profits moved in the opposite direction: higher position, lower profits or lower position, higher profits. Only 55 percent of the time did profits and position move in the same direction. Had there been no correlation at all between winning and making profits, that figure would have been much the same, namely, 50 percent. Clearly, winning games is not the route to making money. As Francisco Pérez Cutiño notes in his MBA thesis, it's not that winning matches can help a club make profits. Rather, the effect works the other way around: if a club finds new revenues, that can help it win matches.

It is in fact almost impossible to run a soccer club like a profit-making business. This is because there will always be rival owners—the Cragnottis, the Abramoviches, or the Gaddhafis who own a chunk of Juventus—who don't care about profits and will spend whatever it takes in the hope of winning prizes. All other club owners are forced to keep up with them. If one owner won't pay large transfer fees and salaries, somebody else will, and that somebody else will get the best players and win prizes. The consequence is that the biggest slice of money that soccer makes gets handed over to the best players. As A. T. Kearney says, you could even argue that soccer clubs are nothing more than vessels for transporting soccer's income to players. "The players are completely free to move," explains Hembert. "They are a key factor in winning, and also in the ego, in pleasing the fans. And they all have pretty savvy agents who are able to maximize their bargaining power."

It means that even the cautious Sugar type cannot make decent profits in soccer. In fact, because his team will win fewer matches than its free-spending rivals, some fans will desert him. That will eat further into his profits. From 1991 to 1998 average attendance in the Premier League rose 29 percent, but Tottenham's crowds fell 5 percent.

Running a soccer club to make money looks like a lost cause. Nor, it might be argued, should anyone attempt it. Most of a club's customers (its fans) and employees (its players and coaches) and even usually its owners would say that the club exists to play good soccer and win things, not to turn profits. That's why a report by the British Commission on Industrial Relations in 1974 quoted an anonymous club chairman as saying, "Any club management which allows the club to make a profit is behaving foolishly." In the not-so-distant past the FA used to forbid club owners to profit from their investment. Traditionally, soccer clubs have behaved more like charitable trusts than like businesses.

Making profits deprives a club of money that it could spend on the team. One reason Bundesliga clubs rarely do well in the Champions League anymore is precisely that they make profits. In the 2006–2007 season, they spent an average of just 45 percent of their revenues on players' salaries. That's not the way to win things, unless you happen to be Olympique Lyon.

The business of soccer is soccer. Almost all soccer clubs that are not Manchester United should ditch the fantasy of making profits. But that doesn't mean that they should continue to be badly run. The weight of money that now washes through soccer demands a more businesslike approach to managing cash. Bungs might have been no big deal when transfer fees were measured in the hundred of thousands of dollars but become a problem when they run into the tens of millions.

Soccer clubs need to know what they are. They shouldn't kid themselves that they are Titanium Metals. Rather, they are like museums: public-spirited organizations that aim to serve the community while remaining reasonably solvent. It sounds like a modest goal, but few of them achieve even that.

5

NEED NOT APPLY

Does English Soccer Discriminate Against Black People?

In 1991 Ron Noades, chairman of Crystal Palace, popped up on British TV talking about blacks. "The problem with black players," explained Noades, whose heavily black team had just finished third in the country, "is they've great pace, great athletes, love to play with the ball in front of them. . . . When it's behind them it's chaos. I don't think too many of them can read the game. When you're getting into the midwinter you need a few of the hard white men to carry the athletic black players through."

Noades's interview was one of the last flourishes of unashamed overt racism in British soccer. Through the 1980s racism had been more or less taken for granted in the game. Fans threw bananas at black players. Pundits like Emlyn Hughes explained the curious absence of black players at Liverpool and Everton by saying, "They haven't got the bottle." The writer Dave Hill summed up the stereotypes: "'No bottle' is a particular favorite, lack of concentration another. 'You don't want too many of them in your defence,' one backroom bod told me, 'they cave in under pressure.' Then there is the curious conviction that blacks are susceptible to the cold and won't go out when it rains."

It's clear that English soccer in those days was shot through with racism: prejudice based on skin color. But what we want to know is whether that racism translated into discrimination: unfair *treatment* of people. People like Noades may have been prejudiced against black players, but did they make it harder for these players to get jobs in soccer? The '80s black striker Garth Crooks thought they did: "I always felt I had to be 15 percent better than the white person to get the same chance," he said. Of course, there was never an explicit color bar in English soccer, but was there and implicit one?

Yet the notion of discrimination against blacks clashes with something we think we know about soccer: that on the field at least, the game is ruthlessly fair. In soccer good players of whatever color perform better than bad ones. People in the game may walk around with Noadesesque fantasies in their heads, but when a black player plays well, everyone can see it. Nick Hornby writes in *Fever Pitch*: "One of the great things about sport is its cruel clarity; there is no such thing, for example, as a bad one-hundred-metre runner, or a hopeless center-half who got lucky; in sport, you get found out. Nor is there such a thing as an unknown genius striker starving in a garret somewhere."

In short, it would seem that in soccer there is no room for ideologies. You have to be right, and results on the field will tell you very quickly if you are. So would clubs really discriminate against blacks at the cost of winning matches? After all, even Ron Noades employed black players. (He knew something about soccer, too: after leaving Palace he bought Brentford, appointed himself manager, won promotion, and was voted manager of the year in Division 2.) In fact, the very success of blacks on the field might be taken as evidence that the opportunities were there.

It's also often hard to prove objectively that discrimination exists. How can you show that you failed to get the job because of prejudice rather than just because you weren't good enough? Liverpool and Everton might argue that they employed white players in the 1980s simply because the whites were better.

Luckily, there is no need to get into a "he said, she said" argument. We have data to prove that English soccer discriminated against black players. We can show when this particular kind of discrimination ended. And we can predict that the new forms of discrimination that pervade English soccer today will be harder to shift.

| |

The first black person to set foot in the British Isles was probably a soldier in Julius Caesar's invading army, in 55 BC. The "indigenous" English themselves only arrived about four hundred years later, during the collapse of the Roman Empire.

Much later, under Victoria, Britain's own empire ruled a large share of the world's black people. A few of the better-educated or entrepreneurial ones made their way from the Raj, the Caribbean, or Africa to Britain. Arthur Wharton, born in 1865 in the Gold Coast (now Ghana), became the world's first black professional soccer player. As well as keeping goal for Preston, he set the world record of ten seconds for the one-hundred-yard sprint.

But until the 1950s most Britons had probably never seen a black person. Unlike Americans, they never developed any kind of relationship with blacks, whether positive or negative. Then, after the Second World War, hundreds of thousands of colonial immigrants began arriving. The influx was small enough—less than 5 percent of Britain's total population, spread over a quarter of a century—to pose little threat to the concepts of Englishness, Scottishness, or Welshness. Nonetheless, the signs went up in the windows of apartment houses: "No Coloureds."

One of the authors of this book, Stefan Szymanski, is the son of an immigrant from Poland who had escaped to London in 1940 and joined the British army to fight the Nazis. Stefan remembers his father telling him about looking for lodging in London in the early 1950s, and finding signs in the windows saying, "Rooms to let—no Poles, no Hungarians." Not only was this kind of discrimination legal, but Stefan's father accepted it. In his mind, he was the immigrant, and it was his job to fit in. Luckily for him (and for Stefan), he was an educated man, able to find a reasonable job and make a reasonable living. He was also a racist. This might sound harsh, the British equivalent of Archie Bunker, but by today's standards most British adults seemed to be racist in the 1970s, when Stefan was growing up. In the popular comedy series of the time, *'Till Death Us Do Part*, the hero, Alf Garnett, was a ludicrously prejudiced Londoner who favored labels like "Coon," "Nig-nog," "Darky," "Paki," and "the Jews up at Spurs" (Garnett supported West Ham). Not only were these words used on the BBC, but they were accompanied by canned laughter. Admittedly, the joke of the series was ultimately on Garnett, who was regularly exposed to the falsity of his own prejudices. But Stefan used to argue that these labels were offensive. His father took this as evidence of a lack of a sense of humor.

It was against this 1970s background of instinctive racism that black players began arriving in English soccer. Most were the British-born children of immigrants. That didn't stop them from being treated to monkey noises and bananas. (As Hornby notes in *Fever Pitch*, "There may well be attractive, articulate and elegant racists, but they certainly never come to soccer matches.") For a while, neo-Nazi parties even imagined that they could lead a revolution from the soccer terraces.

Given the abuse the early black players received, it would have been easy for them to give up on soccer. It was thinkable that they would be driven out of the game. Instead, they stayed, played, and triumphed. In 1978, Viv Anderson became the first black player to play for England. Still, even after the black winger John Barnes scored his solo goal to beat Brazil in Rio in 1984, the Football Association's chairman was harangued by England fans on the flight back home: "You fucking wanker, you prefer sambos to us."

As late as 1993 you could still witness the following scene: A crowd of people in a pub in the City of London is watching England-Holland on TV. Every time Barnes gets the ball, one man—in shirtsleeves and a tie, just out of his City office—makes monkey noises. Every time, his coworkers laugh. If anyone had complained, let alone gone off to find a policeman and asked him to arrest the man, the response would have been: "Where's your sense of humor?" (Hornby's line on this sort of problem: "I wish I were enormous and of a violent disposition, so that I could deal with any problem that arises near me in a fashion commensurate with the anger I feel.")

Whenever people reminisce about the good old days, when ordinary working people could afford to go to soccer matches, it's worth scanning the photographs of the cloth-capped masses standing on the terraces for the faces you *don't* see: blacks, Asians, women. It's true that today's all-seaters in the Premier League exclude poor people. However, the terraces before the 1990s probably excluded rather more varieties of people. In the 1970s and 1980s, when soccer grew scary, the violence forced out even many older white men.

| |

In the late 1980s Stefan Szymanski began thinking about the economics of soccer. He was then working for the Centre for Business Strategy at London Business School. Everyone in the center was an economist, and therefore tempted to think that markets, more or less, "worked." The theory was that any businessperson who came up with a brilliant innovation—inventing the telephone, say—would not keep his advantage for long, because others would imitate him and compete.

But the economists were interested in the few companies that stayed successful despite competition. Clearly, there must be something to learn from them. Stefan suggested looking for these paragons in soccer. It was clearly a highly competitive industry, yet some clubs managed to dominate for years on end. How did they manage to stay ahead for so long?

Stefan enlisted the support of Ron Smith, who had taught him when he was writing his Ph.D. Smith, as well as being an expert on Marxist economics and the economics of defense, is a well-known econometrician. Econometrics is essentially the art of finding statistical methods to extract information from data—or, as a lawyer friend of Stefan's likes to put it, taking the data down into the basement and torturing them until they confess. Studying the accounts of soccer clubs, Stefan and Ron could see how much each club spent on salaries. The two discovered that this spending alone explained almost all the variation in positions in the English Football League. We've already seen that when Stefan analyzed the accounts of forty clubs for the period 1978–1997, he found that their wage spending accounted for 92 percent of the variation in their league positions.

Clearly, the market in players' pay was highly efficient: the better a player was, the more he earned. And this made sense, because soccer is one of the few markets that indisputably meets the conditions in which competition can work efficiently: there are large numbers of buyers and sellers, all of whom have plenty of information about the quality of the players being bought and sold. If a player got paid less than he was worth, he could move to another club. If he got paid more, he would soon find himself being sold off again.

But what about the variation in league position that remained unexplained after adjusting for players' pay? If buying talent was generally enough to win titles—as rich club chairmen like Jack Walker at Blackburn Rovers and Roman Abramovich at Chelsea would soon demonstrate—what else accounted for a team's success? If it was something that was easy to copy—a new tactic, for instance—then other teams would copy it, and the advantage would disappear. That got Stefan thinking about discrimination. What if owners were simply not willing to copy the secret of others' success, because they didn't want to hire the kinds of players that brought that success? He began to search for discrimination against black players.

In most industries, there is a way to demonstrate that discrimination exists. Suppose you could construct a sample of all applicants for a job, and also of all their relevant qualifications. If you then found that a much larger proportion of relevantly qualified white applicants received job offers than relevantly qualified black applicants, you could reasonably infer the presence of discrimination. For example, if 50 percent of whites with doctorates in philosophy got job offers from university philosophy departments, but only ten percent of their black equivalents did, then you should suspect discrimination.

This is essentially how economists have tried to identify job discrimination. The method also works for wage discrimination. If equivalently qualified blacks (or women, or left-handers, or whoever) get lower wages for equivalent jobs, then there is probably discrimination going on. Researchers have put together databases of thousands of workers, each identified by dozens of relevant qualifications, to test whether discrimination exists. When it comes to ethnic minorities and women, the evidence usually shows that it does.

The problem is that there are few measurable qualifications that make someone a great soccer player. When a company is accused of racism, it often says that while the black (or purple, or female) candidates may possess some of the relevant characteristics, there are other, less quantifiable, characteristics that they don't have. Intellectually, this point is hard to overturn. Hundreds of cases of racial discrimination have been fought in American courts, and evidence based on the kinds of studies we have mentioned has often run into trouble.

Happily, there is another way to test for discrimination in soccer. Once again, it relies on evidence from the market. As a general rule, the best way to find out what people are up to is to see how they behave when faced with a price. Don't know if you prefer Coke to Pepsi? Well, let's see what you choose when they both cost the same. (Most people choose Coke.) Do managers prefer white players to blacks? Well, let's see how they spend their clubs' money.

If clubs discriminate, then they will prefer to hire a white player instead of an equivalently talented black player. If they do that, then blacks will find it harder to get jobs as professional soccer players. The blacks will then be willing to accept lower wages than equivalently talented whites. After all, when demand for what we sell is lower, we tend to lower our asking price. So black players become cheaper than white players. If there is discrimination, we would expect to find black players earning less than equally talented whites.

If black players are being discriminated against, that creates an economic opportunity for unprejudiced clubs. By hiring black players they can do just as well in the league as an equivalently talented (but more expensive) team of whites. That means that a simple experiment will reveal whether discrimination exists: *if teams with more black players achieve higher average league positions for a given sum of wage spending, then the teams with fewer black players must have been discriminating.* Otherwise, the "whiter" teams would have seen that black players were good value for the money, and would have tried to hire them. Then black players' wages would have risen due to increased competition for their services, and the relative advantage of hiring black players would have disappeared.

Note that the argument is not that some teams hire more black players than others. That could happen for many reasons. Rather, we can infer discrimination if (a) some teams have more black players than others and (b) those same teams outperform their competitors for a given level of wage spending.

After Stefan figured this out, he had the luck of running into just the right person. Around that time, he was also researching the relationship between the pay of senior executives in the biggest British companies and the performance of their companies. (Very unlike soccer players' wages, there turned out to be almost no correlation between the pay of senior executives and the performance of a company's share price, until share options became common in the 1990s.) Stefan was interviewed for a BBC program by the political journalist Michael Crick. Over time he and Crick got to talking about soccer.

Crick is a famously thorough researcher. Book reviewers delight in finding errors, no matter how trivial, but they never succeed with Crick's political biographies. And as it happens, Crick supports Manchester United. In 1989 he wrote a fascinating history of the club with David Smith, describing how United packaged its legend for commercial gain. About this time Crick became interested in whether soccer clubs discriminated in their hiring. Everyone knew of the suspicious cases of the day, chiefly Liverpool and Everton.

Crick began collecting data from the 1970s onward to see which clubs had hired black players. This was no easy task. How do you decide who is "black"? Crick took a commonsense approach. He started with the old Rothmans Soccer Yearbooks, which published a photograph of every English league team. From this he made a judgment as to which players "looked black." He then followed up by asking clubs and supporters' clubs to fill in any gaps. It took him months to come up with a list of players who, to most fans, would have appeared to be black. This sounds arbitrary, but it is precisely what was required. Prejudice is based on appearance. For example, several years after Crick did his research, it emerged that Ryan Giggs's father was black. Giggs even spoke publicly about his pride in his Caribbean ancestry. However, until that point, most people would not have considered Giggs a black player. He didn't *look* black, and for that reason he would have been unlikely to face discrimination. So Crick was right not to count Giggs as black.

When Crick told Stefan about his list of black players, it was a cinch to create a test for discrimination. All that was necessary was to count how many times each black player had played for his club in a given season. It would then be clear which teams hired a larger proportion of black players.

Stefan then matched these data with figures on each team's league position, and its spending on wages. If there were no discrimination in the market, then wages alone would almost entirely explain league performance. Everything else would just be random noise—"luck." But if black players were systematically being paid less than equally talented white players, then logically the teams that hired an above-average proportion of black players would do systematically better than their wage bill alone would predict.

Back in the 1970s, there were very few black players in English soccer. Combining our data on wages with Crick's database had given us a sample of thirty-nine out of the ninety-two professional league teams. In the 1973–1974 season only two of these clubs had fielded any black players at all. By 1983–1984 there were still twenty teams in our sample that did not a field a black player all season. However, at this point there seems to have been a major breakthrough. By 1989 every team in the sample had fielded at least one black player at some point. By 1992, when the Premier League was founded, only five teams in the sample did not field a black player that season. This implied that about 90 percent of clubs were putting blacks in the first team. Attitudes were changing. Bananas left the game. When Noades voiced his theories on black players in 1991, he was widely mocked.

It is interesting to look at the characteristics of the black players in the English game in these years. For purposes of comparison, Stefan constructed a random sample of an equal number of white players with similar age profiles. Almost all the black players (89 percent) were born in Britain, not very different from the white players (95 percent). Most of the black players were strikers (58 percent) compared to only 33 percent of white players. There were no black goalkeepers at the time. Noades would have noted the fact that black players seemed underrepresented in defense. But then strikers always carry a premium to defenders in the market: it takes more talent to score than to stop other people from scoring.

Certain facts about the sample stood out: The careers of the black players averaged more than six years, compared to less than four for the whites. And 36 percent of the blacks had played for their countries compared to only 23 percent of the whites. On this evidence, it looked suspiciously as if the black players were better than the whites.

The proof came when Stefan deployed the economist's favorite tool, regression analysis. He used it to isolate the distinct effects of wages and the share of black players on each club's league performance. What he found was discrimination. The data showed that clubs with more black players really did have a better record in the league than clubs with fewer blacks, after allowing for wage spending. If two teams had identical annual wage budgets, the team with more blacks would finish higher in the league. The test implied that black players were systematically better value for money than whites. Certain teams of the 1980s like Arsenal, Noades's Palace, and Ron Atkinson's West Bromwich Albion (this was years before Atkinson called Marcel Desailly "a fucking lazy thick nigger" on air) benefited from fielding blacks.

The clubs with fewer blacks were not suffering from a lack of information. Anyone who knew soccer could judge fairly easily how good a player was just by watching him play. So the only credible reason clubs would deny themselves the opportunity to hire these players was prejudice. Clubs didn't like the look of black players, or they thought their fans wouldn't, either simply because of skin hue or because they perceived weaknesses that were just not there. By testing the behavior of managers against the market, it proved possible to uncover evidence of discrimination.

In soccer, you can judge someone's performance only against other competitors. This means that I lose nothing by being inefficient if my competitors are inefficient in the same way as I am. I can go on hiring mediocre players as long as other clubs do, too. As long as all clubs refused to hire talented black players, the cost of discriminating was low. What the data showed was that by the beginning of the 1980s, so many teams were hiring talented blacks that the cost of discriminating had become quite high. Teams that refused to field black players were overpaying for white players and losing more matches as a consequence. Yet some level of discrimination persisted. Even by the end of the 1980s, an all-white team like Everton would cost around 5 percent more than an equally good team that fielded merely an average proportion of black players. As Dave Hill wrote in the fanzine *When Saturday Comes* in 1989, "Half a century after Jesse Owens, a quarter of a century after Martin Luther King, and 21 years after two American sprinters gave the Black Power salute from the Olympic medal rostrum, some of these dickheads don't even know what a black person is." But by the time Hill wrote that, precisely because soccer is so competitive, more and more clubs had begun to hire black players. In 1995 even Everton signed the Nigerian Daniel Amokachi. The economic forces of competition drove white men to ditch their prejudices.

Quite soon, enough clubs were hiring blacks that black players came to be statistically overrepresented in soccer. Only about 1.6 percent of people in the British census of 1991 described themselves as black. Yet in the early 1990s, about 10 percent of all players in English professional soccer were black. By the end of the decade, after the influx of foreign players, the share was nearer 20 percent.

So did clubs learn to overcome their prejudices? A few years after Stefan ran his first test for discrimination, he badgered some students who were looking for undergraduate projects into compiling a list of black players for another six seasons. That took the data set up to the 1998–1999 season. Once again, Stefan merged the data with figures on wages and league performances. Now he could run the regression to the end of the 1990s. For these six additional years, there was no evidence that the share of black players in a team had any effect on team performance, after allowing for the team's wage bill. In other words, by then black players were on average paid what they were worth to a team.

Perhaps the best witness to the acceptance of blacks in soccer is Lilian Thuram. A black man born on the Caribbean island of Guadeloupe, and raised in a poor suburb of Paris, Thuram played professionally from 1991 to 2008 and became France's most capped player. He is also a French intellectual, possibly the only soccer player ever to have spoken the words, "There's an interesting young ethnographer at the Musée de l'Homme . . ."

Thuram is acutely sensitive to racism. He now runs an antiracism foundation. Nonetheless, he feels soccer is innocent of the sin. Over late-night pasta in an Italian restaurant in Barcelona, he explained, "In soccer it's harder to have discrimination, because we are judged on very specific performances. There are not really subjective criteria. Sincerely, I've never met a racist person in soccer. Maybe they were there, but I didn't see it." In fact, he added, "In sport, prejudices favor the blacks. In the popular imagination, the black is in his place in sport. For example, recently in Barcelona, the fitness coach said about Abidal [a black French defender]: 'He's an athlete of the black race.' It's not because he stays behind after training to run. No, it's because he's black."

So by the 1990s, discrimination against black players had disappeared. Gradually, they came to feel at home in the industry. Here is a scene from inside the marble halls of the old Arsenal stadium, after a game in 1995: Arsenal's black Dutch winger Glenn Helder is introducing his black teammate Ian Wright (one of Ron Noades's ex-players) to some Dutch people. Then Helder says, "Ian, show these guys what I taught you." A look of intense concentration appears on Wright's face, and he begins jumping up and down and shouting in Dutch, "Buzz off! Dirty ape! Dirty ape!" He and Helder then collapse laughing. There was still racism in soccer, but by then blacks could mock it from the inner sanctums of the game's establishment.

The story of racism in American sports followed much the same arc. Right through the Second World War, baseball and basketball had segregated blacks into "Negro Leagues." In 1947 Branch Rickey of the Brooklyn Dodgers broke an unspoken rule among baseball owners and hired black infielder Jackie Robinson to play for his team. Robinson eventually became an American hero. However, the costar of his story was economics. The Dodgers had less money than their crosstown rivals, the New York Yankees. If Rickey wanted a winning team, he had to tap talent that the other owners overlooked. Racism provided him with an opportunity.

Of course, discrimination against black players persisted in American sports long after Robinson. Lawrence Kahn, an economist at Cornell University, surveyed the data and found little evidence that before the 1990s baseball teams were withholding jobs or pay from blacks. But he did think they were giving black players unduly short careers, and using them in only certain positions. In basketball, Kahn did find wage discrimination. When he repeated his study in 2000, he discovered, like Stefan the second time around, that discrimination was fading.

NEW SOCCER, NEW DISCRIMINATION

Trevor Phillips points a finger at his own shaven black head: "Excuse me, here I am: bull's-eye!" The son of an early Caribbean immigrant, Phillips was raised in London, and has supported Chelsea for nearly fifty years. But in the 1970s, when darts throwing was the favorite sport of Chelsea's Shed Stand, he didn't go to matches. His head felt like too obvious a target. Hardly any black people went to Chelsea then. "Now I can take my daughters," he marvels.

But as head of Britain's Commission for Equalities and Human Rights, Phillips doesn't think soccer has slain discrimination yet. Over breakfast one snowy morning, he identified an enduring type of discrimination in British soccer: "Loads of black players on the field and none in the dugout."

You might think that this form of discrimination would eventually disappear: that just as competition pushed clubs into buying black players, it will push them into hiring black managers. But in fact, the prejudice against black managers will probably be harder to shift. That is because the market in soccer managers is much less efficient than the market in soccer players.

Like discrimination against black players, discrimination against black managers first became visible in American sports. As early as 1969 Jackie Robinson, who had become quite rebellious as he grew older, refused to attend Old Timers' Day at Yankee Stadium, in protest at baseball's shunning of black coaches and managers.

The issue hit Britain only when the first generation of black players began to retire (its being an article of faith in soccer that only ex-players have what it takes to become managers). The former England international Luther Blissett, who as a player had made that ill-fated transfer to Milan, applied for twenty-two jobs as a manager in the 1990s. He did not get a single interview. Stella Orakwue, who recounts his story in her 1998 book, *Pitch Invaders*, concludes, "I feel a British black managing a Premiership team could be a very long way off." Indeed, only in 2008, ten years after she wrote this, did Blackburn give Paul Ince a chance for a few months. Even after Ince's appointment, John Barnes, who himself had struggled to get work as a manager in Britain, said, "I believe the situation for black managers is like it was for black players back in the 1970s."

True, black managers Ruud Gullit and Jean Tigana did get jobs in the Premier League. But as Orakwue points out, the crucial point is that they were foreigners. They were perceived in Britain first of all as Dutch or French, and only secondarily as black. Gullit was cast as a typical sophisticated Dutch manager, not as an untried "black" one.

You would think that given this discrimination, unprejudiced clubs could clean up by hiring the best black (or female) managers at low salaries. A small club like Tranmere Rovers, say, could probably take its pick of the world's black managers. It could get the best female manager in history. Yet it probably won't. That's because the market in soccer managers is so different from the market in players. Markets tend to work when they are transparent—when you can see who is doing what and place a value on it. That is preeminently true of soccer players, who do their work in public. When you can't see what people do, it's very hard to assign a value to their work. Efficient markets punish discrimination in plain view of everyone, and so discrimination tends to get rooted out. Inefficient markets can maintain discrimination almost indefinitely.

Black players became accepted because the market in players is transparent. It is pretty obvious who can play and who can't, who's "got bottle" and who doesn't. The market in players' salaries, as we have seen, is so efficient that it explains 92 percent of the variation in clubs' league positions.

However, the market in managers doesn't work nearly as well. Only a few managers, like Brian Clough or Bill Shankly, consistently perform better with their teams than the players' wage bill suggests that they should. It's hard to identify what it is that these men do better than others, because if it were easy, everyone would copy them. Most other managers simply do not matter very much, and do not last very long in the job. They appear to add so little value that it is tempting to think that they could be replaced by their secretaries, or their chairmen, or by stuffed teddy bears, without the club's league position changing. Even Manchester United's manager, Alex Ferguson, who has won more prizes than anyone else in the history of soccer, has probably performed only about as well as the manager of the world's richest club should. Perhaps his unique accomplishment is not winning but keeping all the interest groups in the club united behind him for so long. If you manage to stay manager of the world's richest club for nearly twenty-five years in an era when the rich are getting ever richer, you are guaranteed to stack up prizes.

It would interesting to see what would happen if a club stopped hiring managers, and allowed an online survey of registered fans to pick the team. We suspect the club would perform decently, perhaps even better than its rivals, because it would be harnessing the wisdom of crowds. And it could use the money it saved on managers to up those crucial players' wages.

None of this is good news for black managers. Because it is so hard to measure a manager's performance, it will never become painfully obvious that clubs are undervaluing black managers. That means clubs can continue to choose their managers on the basis of appearances. Any club appointing someone who is not a white male ex-player with a conservative haircut must worry about looking foolish if its choice fails. Hiring a black manager feels risky, because as Barnes says, "Black guys haven't proved themselves as managers." White guys have—or at least some of them appear to have.

At last, soccer players get more or less the jobs that they deserve. If only other professions were as fair.

6

THE ECONOMIST'S FEAR OF
THE PENALTY KICK

Are Penalties Cosmically Unfair,
or Only If You Are Nicolas Anelka?

A famous soccer manager stands up from the table. He's going to pretend he is Chelsea's captain, John Terry, about to take the crucial penalty in the Champions League final in Moscow.

The manager performs the part with Schadenfreude; he is no friend of Chelsea. He adjusts his face into a mask of tension. He tells us what Terry is thinking: "If I score, we win the Champions League." And then, terrifyingly, "But first I have to score."

The manager begins pulling at the arm of his suit jacket: he is mimicking Terry pulling at his captain's armband. Terry is telling himself (the manager explains), "I am captain, I am strong, I will score."

Still pulling rhythmically at his suit, the manager looks up. He is eyeing an imaginary, grotesquely large Edwin van der Sar who is guarding a goal a very long twelve yards away. Terry intends to hit the ball to Van der Sar's left. We now know that a Basque economist told Chelsea that the Dutch keeper tended to dive right against right-footed kickers. Terry runs up—and here the manager, cackling, falls on his backside.

Van der Sar did indeed dive right, as the Basque economist had foreseen, but Terry slipped on the wet grass, and his shot into the left-hand corner missed by inches.

"This really is soccer," the manager concludes. A player hits the post, the ball goes out, and Chelsea's coach, Avram Grant, is sacked even though he is exactly the same manager as if the ball had gone in. By one estimate, Terry's penalty cost Chelsea $170 million.

The penalty is probably the single thing in soccer that economists have most to say about. The penalty feels cosmically unfair; economists say otherwise. Penalties are often dismissed as a lottery; economists tell both kicker and goalkeeper exactly what to do. (Indeed, if only Nicolas Anelka had followed the economist's advice, Chelsea would have won the final.) And best of all, penalties may be the best way in the known world of understanding game theory.

DIABOLICAL: ARE PENALTIES REALLY UNFAIR?

At first sight, the penalty looks like the most unfair device in all of sports. First of all, it may be impossible for a referee to judge most penalty appeals correctly, given the pace of modern soccer, the tangles of legs and ball, and the levels of deception by players. When the Canadian writer Adam Gopnik watched the World Cup of 1998 on TV for the *New Yorker*, he as an outsider to soccer immediately focused on this problem. The "more customary method of getting a penalty," he wrote, " . . . is to walk into the 'area' with the ball, get breathed on hard, and then immediately collapse . . . arms and legs splayed out, while you twist in agony and beg for morphine, and your teammates smite their foreheads at the tragic waste of a young life. The referee buys this more often than you might think. Afterward the postgame did-he-fall-or-was-he-pushed argument can go on for hours." Or decades. The fan at home is often unsure whether it really should have been a penalty even after watching several replays.

And the referee's misjudgments matter, because the penalty prob-ably has more impact than any other refereeing decision in sports. Umpires in baseball and tennis often fluff calls, but there are fifty-four outs in a baseball game, and countless points in a tennis match, and so no individual decision tends to make all that much difference. Refer-ees in rugby and football blunder, too, but because these games are higher scoring than soccer, individual calls rarely change outcomes here, either. In any case, officials in all these sports can now consult instant replays.

But soccer referees cannot. And since important soccer matches usually hinge on one goal, the penalty usually decides the match. As Gopnik says, the penalty "creates an enormous disproportion between the foul and the reward."

No wonder the penalty drives managers crazy. As Arsène Wenger lamented at the end of the 2007–2008 season, "Every big game I've seen this year has been decided, offside or not offside, penalty or not penalty." Indeed, it's now a standard tactic for managers in England, after their team has lost, to devote the postmatch press conference to a penalty given or not given. It's a ritual song of lament, which goes like this: *The penalty completely changed the outcome of the game. We were clearly winning/tying but lost because of the (diabolical, unjust) penalty.*

The manager knows that most newspapers prefer covering personal-ity clashes to tactics, and so the "match" reports will be devoted to the press conference rather than his team's losing performance. Meanwhile, the winning manager, when asked about the penalty, recites: *It made no difference whatever to the outcome of the game. We were clearly winning and would inevitably have done so without the (entirely just) penalty.*

These two ritual managerial chants amount to two different hy-potheses about how penalties affect soccer matches. The first manager is claiming that randomly awarded penalties distort results. The second manager is saying penalties make no difference. On occasion, either manager might be right. But over the long term, one of them must be more right than the other. So which is it—do penalties change results, or don't they? We have the data to answer this question.

Our guru is Dr. Tunde Buraimo. One of the growing band of sports econometricians—the British equivalent of baseball's sabermetricians—Tunde works, appropriately, in the ancient heartland of professional soccer at the University of Central Lancashire in Preston. As the saying goes, the plural of "anecdote" is "data," and Tunde prefers to work with tens of thousands of pieces of evidence rather than a few random recollections. To help us with our book, he examined 1,520 Premier League games played over four years, from the 2002–2003 season until 2005–2006. For each game he knew the pattern of scoring and, crucially, which team was expected to win given the prematch betting odds.

Our test of the two rival hypotheses about penalties is simple. We asked Tunde to divide the games into two groups:

1. Games in which penalties were awarded

2. Games in which they were not

We then asked him to compare how often the home team won when there was a penalty, and how often when there wasn't. Figure 6.1 shows what he found.

FIGURE 6.1 Comparison of home team and penalties

| | Penalty awarded in match? | | |
Result	No	Yes	Total
Home win	577	142	719
	46.76%	49.65%	47.30%
Away win	336	80	416
	27.23%	27.97%	27.37%
Tie	321	64	385
	26.01%	22.38%	25.33%
Total	1,234	286	1,520
	100%	100%	100%

Look at the last column first. Taking all games in the database, 47.30 percent ended in home wins, 27.37 percent in away wins, and 25.33 percent in ties. These frequencies reflect the intrinsic advantage of home teams. Now imagine that the first manager is right: penalties change the outcome of the game. How will they do that? It might be that they always favor home teams (because referees are cowards), in which case we would expect the percentage of home wins to be greater when penalties are given. Alternatively, it might be that penalties favor away teams (perhaps enabling a team that has its back against the wall to make an escape). If so, the proportion of away wins (or ties) would rise with penalties.

But in fact, as the first two columns show, the percentages for all results barely change whether a penalty is given or not. The percentage of home wins is about three points higher when there is a penalty (up from 46.76 percent to 49.65 percent), and the percentage of ties is commensurately lower (down to 22.38 percent from 26.01 percent). The percentage of away wins remains almost identical (27.97 percent against 27.23 percent) with or without penalties. So in games with penalties, there are slightly more home wins and slightly fewer ties.

It's tempting to read significance into this: to think that the rise in home wins when there is a penalty is big enough to show that penalties favor the home team. However, statisticians warn against this kind of intuitive analysis. The absolute number of home wins when there were penalties in the game was seventy. Had the frequency of home wins been the same as in games when there was no penalty, the number of home wins would have been sixty-six. So the difference (four extra home wins) is too small be to be considered statistically significant. The rise is likely due to chance.

It would have been a different matter had the number of home wins when there was a penalty exceeded seventy-eight (or 55 percent of the games concerned). Then, the increase would have met the standard generally used by statisticians for confidence that there was a statistically reliable difference in outcomes depending on the award of a penalty. As it is, though, the data suggest that the award of a penalty does not affect either home wins, away wins, or ties.

But perhaps penalties have a different effect on match results. Perhaps they help favorites (if refs favor the big team). Or maybe they help underdogs (if penalties truly are given randomly, they should help the worse team more than the better one). Tunde tested these hypotheses, too.

FIGURE 6.2 Penalty effects on match results

	Penalty awarded in match?		
Result	No	Yes	Total
Favorite win	633	147	780
	51.30%	51.40%	51.32%
Underdog win	254	67	321
	20.58%	23.43%	21.12%
Tie	347	72	419
	28.12%	25.17%	27.57%
Total	1,234	286	1,520
	100%	100%	100%ᵃ

ᵃThe totals should add up to 100%, but there are rounding errors.

It's obvious even to the naked eye that penalties have no impact at all on whether the favorite wins: favorites win 51.3 percent of games without a penalty, and 51.4 percent with a penalty. It's true that underdogs win nearly 3 percent more often when there is a penalty than when there is not, but once again the tests demonstrate that this fact has no statistical significance. We can put the increase down to chance. Match results appear to be the same with or without penalties. Penalties do not matter.

Now, this is a statistical statement that requires a very precise interpretation. Penalties do matter in that they often change the outcome of an individual game. Clearly, a team that scores from a penalty is more likely to win, and so, whatever a manager says, a converted penalty will affect the evolution of almost any game.

However, *on average*, taken over a large sample of games, a penalty does not make it any more likely that home teams or away teams or favorites or underdogs win. If penalties were abolished tomorrow, the pattern of soccer results would be exactly the same.

This sounds counterintuitive. After all, we argued that penalties look like the most unfair device in sport. They are often wrongly awarded, they cause a lot of goals, and many of these goals decide matches. So surely penalties should make results less fair.

To explain why penalties don't change the pattern of match results, we need to consult Graham Taylor. The retired manager is now remembered as the "turnip" whose long-ball game cost England qualification for the World Cup of 1994. However, the long-ball game had previously served Taylor very well at Watford and Aston Villa. No wonder, because it rested on one crucial insight into soccer: you will score goals only if you get possession in the opposition's final third of the field.

Much the same insight applies to penalties: in practice you will get them only if you have possession (or at least a decent chance of winning possession) in the opponent's penalty area. A penalty is often wrongly given. But it is almost always a reward for deep territorial penetration. That makes it, on average, a marker of the balance of power in the game. That's why good teams get proportionately more penalties than bad teams, and why home teams get more than away teams. On average, a penalty is given with the grain of a game.

RIGHT, LEFT, OR LET VAN DER SAR DECIDE FOR YOU? GAME THEORY IN BERLIN AND MOSCOW

The next question is how to take them. Economists may have no idea when housing prices will crash, but they do know something about this one.

A surprising number of economists have thought hard about the humble penalty kick. Even Steve Levitt, author of *Freakonomics* and winner of perhaps the most important prize in economics (the Clark Medal, which some insiders think outranks the Nobel), once cowrote a little-known paper on penalties. Probably only a trio of economists would have watched videos of 459 penalties taken in the French and Italian leagues. "Testing Mixed-Strategy Equilibria When Players Are Heterogeneous: The Case of Penalty Kicks in Soccer" is one of those you might have missed, but it always won Levitt handshakes from European economists. Here's an American who *gets it*, they must have thought. Levitt, P.-A. Chiappori, and T. Groseclose explain that they wrote the paper because "testing game theory in the real world may provide unique insights." Economists revere the penalty as a real-life example of game theory.

Game theory was developed in the 1940s by the likes of John von Neumann, a brilliant mathematician who also helped create the architecture of the modern computer. It is the study of what happens when people find themselves in situations exactly like a penalty taker facing a goalkeeper: when what I should do depends on what you do, and what you should do depends on what I do.

The American government used game theory extensively during the cold war to plan its interactions with the Soviet Union and to try to predict Soviet moves. (It is said that game-theoretic advice was given during the Cuban missile crisis to consider questions like, "If we bomb Cuba, then the Russians will seize West Berlin, and then we'll have to attack Russian troops, and then they'll use nuclear bombs, and then . . .") Today economists use game theory all the time, particularly to plan government policies or analyze business strategy. Game theory even plays a big role in research on biology.

The key to game theory is the analysis of how the strategies of different actors interact. In a penalty kick, for instance, the kicker and the keeper must each choose a strategy: where to kick the ball and where to dive. But each person's strategy depends on what he thinks the other person will do.

Sometimes in game theory, what's best for the actors is if they both do the same thing—going to the same restaurant to meet for dinner, for instance. These kinds of situations are known as coordination or cooperative games. But the penalty kick is a noncooperative game: the actors succeed by achieving their objectives independently of others. In fact, the penalty is a "zero-sum game": any gain for one player is exactly offset by the loss to the other side (plus one goal for me is minus one goal for you).

The issue of game theory behind the penalty was best put in "The Longest Penalty Ever," a short story by the Argentine writer Osvaldo Soriano. A match in the Argentine provinces has to be abandoned seconds before time when a bent referee, who has just awarded a penalty, is knocked out by an irate player. The league court decides that the last twenty seconds of the game—the penalty kick, in effect—will be played the next Sunday. That gives everyone a week to prepare for the penalty.

At dinner a few nights before the penalty, "Gato Díaz," the keeper who has to stop it, muses about the kicker:

> "Constante kicks to the right."
> "Always," said the president of the club.
> "But he knows that I know."
> "Then we're fucked."
> "Yeah, but I know that he knows," said el Gato.
> "Then dive to the left and be ready," said someone at the table.
> "No. He knows that I know that he knows," said Gato Díaz, and he got up to go to bed.

Game theorists try to work out strategies for players in different types of games, and try to predict which strategy each player will pursue. Sometimes the prediction is easy. Consider the game in which each player has only two choices: either "Develop a nuclear bomb" or "Don't develop a nuclear bomb." To make a prediction, you have to know what the payoff is to each player depending on the game's outcome. Imagine the players are India and Pakistan (but it could be Israel and Iran, or any other pair of hostile nations). Initially, Pakistan does not know if India will or won't develop a bomb, so it figures:

If India has no bomb:
(a) We don't get a bomb: we can live alongside each other, but there will always be incidents.
(b) We get a bomb: India will have to treat us with respect.

If India has a bomb:
(c) We don't get a bomb: we can't resist anything India does.
(d) We get a bomb: India will have to treat us with respect.

Plainly, if you are Pakistan, you will end up developing the bomb, whether India has the bomb or not. Likewise, India will choose the same strategy, and will develop the bomb whether Pakistan does or doesn't. So the *equilibrium* of this game is for both nations to acquire a bomb. This is the gloomy logic of an arms race. The logic of a soccer match is much the same, and there are many examples of arms races in soccer, from inflation of players' wages to illegal doping.

PIECES OF PAPER IN
STUTTGART, MUNICH, BERLIN, AND MOSCOW

The problem for experienced penalty takers and goalkeepers is that over time, they build up track records. People come to spot any habits they might have—always shooting left, or always diving right, for instance. Levitt and his colleagues observed "one goalie in the sample who jumps left on all eight kicks that he faces (only two of eight kicks against him go to the left, suggesting that his proclivity for jumping left is not lost on the kickers)."

There have probably always been people in the game tracking the past behavior of kickers and keepers. Back in the 1970s, a Dutch manager named Jan Reker began to build up an archive of index cards on thousands of players. One thing he noted was where the player hit his penalties. The Dutch keeper Hans van Breukelen would often call Reker before an international match for a briefing.

Nobody paid much attention to this relationship until 1988. That May, Van Breukelen's PSV reached the European Cup final against Benfica. Before the match in Stuttgart, the keeper phoned Reker. Inevitably, the game went to a penalty shoot-out. At first Reker's index cards didn't seem to be helping much—Benfica's first five penalties all went in—but Van Breukelen saved the sixth kick from Veloso, and PSV was the European champion. A month later, so was Holland. They were leading the USSR 2–0 in the final in Munich when a silly charge by Van Breukelen conceded a penalty. But using Reker's database, he saved Igor Belanov's weak kick.

In Berlin in 2006, the World Cup quarter-final of Germany-Argentina also went to penalties. Jens Lehmann, the German keeper, stood in goal with a crib sheet tucked into his sock. On a page of hotel notepaper ("Schlosshotel, Grunewald," it said), the German keeper's

trainer, Andreas Köpke, had jotted down the proclivities of some potential Argentine penalty takers:

1. Riquelme   left
2. Crespo   long run-up/right
               short run-up/left
3. Heinze   left low
4. Ayala   2 [His shirt number, presumably given for fear that
               Lehmann would not recognize him]
               waits long time, long run-up right
5. Messi   left
6. Aimar   16, waits long time, left
7. Rodriquez   18, left

Apparently, the Germans had a database of thirteen thousand kicks.
The crib sheet might just have tipped the balance. Of the seven Argen-
tines on the list, only Ayala and Rodriquez actually took penalties.
However, Ayala stuck exactly to Lehmann's plan: he took a long run-
up, the keeper waited a long time, and when Ayala dutifully shot to
Lehmann's right, the keeper saved. Rodriquez also did his best to
oblige. He put the ball in Lehmann's left-hand corner as predicted, but
hit it so well that the keeper couldn't reach.

By the time of Argentina's fourth penalty, Germany was leading 4–2.
If Lehmann could save Esteban Cambiasso's kick, the Germans would
maintain their record of never losing a penalty shoot-out in a World
Cup. Lehmann consulted his crib sheet. Sönke Wortmann, the German
film director, who was following the German team for a fly-on-the-wall
documentary, reports what happened next: "Lehmann could find no indication on his note of how Cambiasso would shoot. And yet the piece
of paper did its job, because Lehmann stood looking at it for a long time.
Köpke had written it in pencil, the note was crumpled and the writing
almost illegible."

Wortmann says that as Cambiasso prepared to take his kick, he
must have been thinking, "What do they know?" The Germans knew

nothing. But Cambiasso was psyched out nonetheless. Lehmann saved his shot, and afterward there was a massive brawl on the field.

Both Van Breukelen's and Lehmann's stories have been told before. What is not publicly known is that Chelsea received an excellent crib sheet before the Champions League final in Moscow in 2008.

In 1995, the Basque economist Ignacio Palacios-Huerta, who was then a graduate student at the University of Chicago, began recording the way penalties were taken. His paper, "Professionals Play Minimax," was published in 2003.

One friend of Ignacio who knew about his research was a professor of economics and mathematics at an Israeli university. It so happened that this man was also a friend of Avram Grant. When Grant's Chelsea reached the final in Moscow in 2008, the professor realized that Ignacio's research might help Grant. He put the two men in touch. Ignacio then sent Grant a report that made four points about Manchester United and penalties:

1. Van der Sar tended to dive to the kicker's "natural side" more often than most keepers did. This meant that when facing a right-footed kicker, Van der Sar would usually dive to his own right, and when facing a left-footed kicker, to his own left. So Chelsea right-footed penalty takers would have a better chance if they shot to their "unnatural side," Van der Sar's left.
2. Huerta emphasized in his report that "the vast majority of the penalties that Van der Sar stops are those kicked to a mid-height (say, between 1 and 1.5 meters), and hence that penalties against him should be kicked just on the ground or high up."
3. Cristiano Ronaldo was another special case. Ignacio wrote in the report: "Ronaldo often stops in the run-up to the ball. If he stops, he is likely (85%) to kick to the right hand side of the goalkeeper." Ignacio added that Ronaldo seemed able to change his mind about where to put the ball at the very last instant. That meant it was crucial for the opposing keeper not to move early. When a keeper moved early, Ronaldo *always* scored.

4. The team that wins the toss before the shoot-out gets to choose whether to go first. But this is a no-brainer: it should always go first. Teams going first win 60 percent of the time, presumably because there is too much pressure on the team going second, which is always having to score to save the game.

Ignacio doesn't know how his research was used, but watching the shoot-out on TV, he was certain it was. Indeed, once you know the content of Ignacio's note, it's fascinating to study the shoot-out on YouTube. The Chelsea players seem to have followed his advice almost to the letter—except for poor Anelka.

United's captain, Rio Ferdinand, won the toss, and turned to the bench to ask what to do. Terry tried to influence him by offering to go first. Unsurprisingly, Ferdinand ignored him. United went first, meaning that they were now likely to win. Carlos Tevez scored from the first kick.

Michael Ballack hit Chelsea's first penalty high into the net to Van der Sar's left. Juliano Belletti scored low to Van der Sar's left. Ignacio had recommended that Chelsea's right-footed kickers choose that side. But at this early stage, he still couldn't be sure that Chelsea was being guided by his report. He told us later, "Interestingly, my wife had been quite skeptical about the whole thing as I was preparing the report for Coach Grant, not even interested in looking at it. But then the game went into extra time, and then into a penalty shoot-out. Well, still skeptical."

At this point Cristiano Ronaldo stepped up to take his kick for United. Watching on TV, Ignacio told his wife the precise advice he had given Chelsea in his report: Chelsea's keeper shouldn't move early, and if Cristiano paused in his run-up, he would most probably hit the ball to the keeper's right.

To Ignacio's delight, Chelsea's keeper, Petr Cech, stayed motionless—"not even blinking," in the Spanish football phrase. Then, exactly as Ignacio had recommended, Cech dived to his right and duly saved Ronaldo's shot. Ignacio recalled later, "After that, I started to believe that they were following the advice quite closely." As for his wife, "I think she was a bit shocked."

What's astonishing—though it seems to have passed unnoticed at the time—is what happened after that. Chelsea's next four penalty takers, Frank Lampard, Ashley Cole, John Terry, and Salomon Kalou, *all* hit the ball to Van der Sar's left, just as Ballack and Belletti had done. In other words, the first six Chelsea kicks went to the same corner.

Ashley Cole was the only one of the six who partly disregarded Ignacio's advice. Cole was left-footed, so when he hit the ball to Van der Sar's left, he was shooting to his own "natural side"—the side that Ignacio had said Van der Sar tended to choose. Indeed, the Dutchman chose correctly on Cole's kick, and very nearly saved the shot, but it was well struck, low (as Ignacio had recommended), and just wriggled out of the keeper's grip. But all Chelsea's right-footed penalty takers had obeyed Ignacio to the letter and kicked the ball to their "unnatural side," Van der Sar's left.

So far, Ignacio's advice had worked very well. Much as the economist had predicted, Van der Sar had dived to his natural side four times out of six. He hadn't saved a single penalty. Five of Chelsea's six kicks had gone in, while Terry's, as the whole world knows, flew out off the post with Van der Sar in the wrong corner.

But after six kicks, Van der Sar, or someone else at Manchester United, figured out that Chelsea was pursuing a strategy. Admittedly, the keeper didn't quite get its strategy right. Wrongly but understandably, he seems to have decided that Chelsea's strategy was to put all the kicks to his left. After all, that's where every kick he had faced up to that point had gone.

As Anelka prepared to take Chelsea's seventh penalty, the gangling keeper, standing on the goal line, extended his arms to either side of him. Then, in what must have been a chilling moment for Anelka, the Dutchman pointed with his left hand to the left corner. "That's where you're all putting it, isn't it?" he seemed to be saying. (This is where books fall short as a medium. We urge you to watch the shoot-out on YouTube.)

Now Anelka had a terrible dilemma. This was game theory in its rawest form. United had come pretty close to divining Chelsea's strategy: Ignacio had indeed advised right-footed kickers like Anelka to put the ball to Van der Sar's left side.

So Anelka knew that Van der Sar knew that Anelka knew that Van der Sar tended to dive right against right-footers. What was Anelka to do? He decided to avoid the left corner, where he had presumably planned to put the ball. Instead, he kicked to Van der Sar's right. That might have been fine, except that he hit the ball at midheight—exactly the level that Ignacio had warned against. Watching the kick on TV, Ignacio was "very upset." Perhaps Anelka was at sea because Van der Sar had pressured him to change his plans at the last moment. Van der Sar saved the shot. Alex Ferguson said afterward, "That wasn't an accident, his penalty save. We knew exactly where certain players were putting the ball." Anelka's decision to ignore Ignacio's advice probably cost Chelsea the Champions League.

RANDOMIZATION: FRANCK RIBÉRY CRACKS GAME THEORY

Crib sheets like Lehmann's might just work on penalty shoot-outs. Many of the players who take kicks in a shoot-out aren't regular penalty takers. (After Gareth Southgate missed England's crucial kick at Euro '96, his mother said that the last time he'd taken a penalty was three years before, and he'd missed that one, too.) These inferior penalty takers are not skilled or steady-headed enough to be able to vary their strategy. Quite likely, they will just aim for their favorite corner, hoping that their lack of a track record means the other side won't know their preference.

But that is not how a good penalty taker—his team's regular man—thinks.

Suppose the good kicker always chose the same corner for his penalty (game theorists call this a "pure strategy"). It would be easy to oppose: if the kicker always kicks left, then the goalkeeper knows what to do. Pure strategies don't work for penalty taking. As Levitt and Company found, "There are no kickers in our sample with at least four kicks who always kick in one direction." Take that, Jens Lehmann.

Even a more complicated pure strategy does not work. For example, suppose the kicker always shoots in the opposite corner to the one he chose last time. Then a future opponent studying this player would discover the sequence—left, right, left, right, left, right—and with a bit of thought guess what comes next. The essence of good penalty taking is unpredictability: a good penalty taker will be one whose next penalty cannot be predicted with certainty from his history of penalty taking.

This is a particular kind of unpredictability. It does not mean that the kicker should go left half of the time and right half of the time. After all, most kickers have a natural side, and favoring that side gives them a higher chance of scoring. But even if you naturally shoot to the keeper's right, as most right-footed kickers do, sometimes you have to shoot to his left, just to keep him honest. In fact, if a kicker knows his chances of scoring for either corner of the net (depending also on which way the goalkeeper dives), he can choose the proportion of kicks to his natural side that maximizes the probability of scoring. A right-footed kicker won't put 100 percent of his kicks to his natural "right" side, because that would give the goalkeeper certainty. Even a small change, like kicking right only 99 percent of the time, would raise the chances of scoring considerably by creating uncertainty in the goalkeeper's mind.

Kicking to the left half the time would leave the keeper very uncertain. However, it would also entail the kicker hitting many poor shots to his unnatural side. So the kicker does best by hitting somewhere over half his kicks to his natural right side.

Likewise, we can calculate the proportion of times a goalkeeper should dive left or right. (Note that we are assuming the goalkeeper cannot know which way the ball is going before he decides which way to dive.) Kickers and keepers who mix it up like this are pursuing what game theorists call "mixed strategies."

Mixed strategies are peculiar because they require the actor to incorporate randomness into decision making. Should I go to the pub or the cinema? A mixed strategy requires me to toss a coin, which sounds odd, since one might expect that I prefer one to the other. With a mixed strategy, you let the coin make the decision for you.

Game theorists have wondered for years whether people in the real world follow mixed strategies. They have found in tests that people tend not to use mixed strategies even when it is profitable for them to do so. In fact, our behavior seems to fall short of mixed play in a very specific way: in most cases, our sequence of choices is predictable, because people tend to do the opposite of what they have done in the past. For instance, they choose first left, then right, then left, then right, left, right, left, right, confusing *change* with *randomness*. These guinea pigs would not make good penalty takers.

Eventually, game theorists began to test mixed strategies in the natural laboratory of penalty taking. Years before Ignacio Palacios-Huerta advised Chelsea, he collected a database of 1,417 penalties taken between 1995 and 2000. First, he calculated the proportion of successful kicks based on whether the kicker went to his natural side (left or right). The success rate was 95 percent if the kicker went to his natural side and the goalkeeper went to the opposite side (the remaining 5 percent of kicks missed the goal). The success rate was 92 percent if the kicker went to his "unnatural" side and the goalkeeper went to his natural side. Obviously, the kicker's success rates were lower if the keeper chose correctly: a scoring rate of 70 percent if both keeper and kicker went to the kicker's natural side, and 58 percent if both went to the other side.

Using these figures, Ignacio calculated the optimal mixed-strategy choices for each player. To maximize his chances of scoring, an imaginary penalty taker would have to hit 61.5 percent of his kicks to his natural side, and 38.5 percent to the other side. In reality, the penalty takers Ignacio observed got pretty close to this: they hit 60 percent to their natural side, and 40 percent the other way.

A keeper's best strategy (if he insists on diving rather than standing still) is to dive to the kicker's natural side 58 percent of the time and to the other side 42 percent of the time. The actual figures, Ignacio found, were scarily close: 57.7 percent and 42.3 percent. Levitt's team, using a different database of penalties, found that keepers went to the right 57 percent of the time. So it looks as if keepers as well as penalty takers really do follow mixed strategies.

But what we most want to know are the choices of individual kickers and goalkeepers, not the overall averages. Ignacio studied twenty-two kickers and twenty goalkeepers, each of whom was involved in more than thirty penalties in his database. Again, Ignacio calculated the success rates depending on the side the kicker and goalkeeper chose, and calculated the frequencies in each direction that would maximize the chances of success for kickers and keepers.

In real life, the actual frequencies the players observed were indistinguishable from the best mixed-strategy choices in more than 95 percent of cases. We can say with a high degree of confidence that penalty takers and goalkeepers really do use mixed strategies. Levitt's paper found the same thing: except for the bizarre keeper who always dived left, almost all the other kickers and keepers played mixed strategies.

Finally, Ignacio tested the most important question of all: are soccer players capable of constructing a truly random sequence in their penalty-taking decisions, as the mixed-strategy theory requires? Careful statistical testing showed that indeed they are. In other words, it is impossible to predict which way a regular penalty taker will kick based on his history of kicks. Each time he chooses his corner without any reference to what he did the last time.

Randomization of penalties is a completely logical theory that against all odds turns out to be true in practice. As long as the penalty taker is a pro, rather than some terrified Southgateian innocent roped in for a job that he doesn't understand, lists like Lehmann's are useless.

All this shows the extraordinary amount of subconscious thought that goes into playing top-level soccer. Previous studies in game theory had shown that people could construct random sequences if the problem was first explained to them in some detail. Nobody is suggesting that soccer players have sat at home reading up on mixed-strategy equilibria. Rather, the best players intuitively grasp the truth of the theory and are able to execute it. That is what makes them good players.

Franck Ribéry is the designated penalty taker for Bayern Munich and France. Needless to say, the scar-faced little playmaker places his kicks according to a randomized mixed strategy. But more than that, one of his former managers explains, even once Ribéry has embarked on his jagged hither-and-thither run-up, *he himself* does not know which corner he will choose. When the born economist Arsène Wenger was told this, he gushed with admiration.

As good a player as Ribéry is, he might do even better as a game theorist.

7

THE SUBURBAN NEWSAGENTS
City Sizes and Soccer Prizes

The scene: the VIP room at the Athens Olympic Stadium, a couple of hours before the Champions League final of 2007 between Milan and Liverpool kicks off. Michel Platini and Franz Beckenbauer are being buttonholed every couple of yards by other middle-aged men in expensive suits. There is a crush at the buffet, and another across the room, where a familiar silver cup with "big ears" stands on a dais. You line up, assume a conquering pose beside the Champions League trophy, and grin. Nice young ladies from UEFA slip the picture into a frame for you.

An Englishman watching the scene, a soccer official, confides that he first got this close to the cup thirty years ago. Where? In Bramcote, a suburb of Nottingham. One of Brian Clough's brothers ran the local post office-cum-newsagents, and Clough himself would sometimes pop in and serve customers, or just stand behind the counter reading the papers. One Sunday morning when the future official went in with his grandfather, there was the European Cup freshly won by Forest, plunked on top of a pile of *Nottingham Evening Posts*. Behind it stood Brian Clough, holding an open newspaper in front of his face. He neither moved nor spoke, but he knew the boy would remember the scene forever. The official remembers: "I was too young and shy to speak to the man, which I regret to this day."

It's odd to think of the game's biggest club trophy ending up in a place like Bramcote (population 7,318). Yet it's not that exceptional. Provincial towns like Nottingham, Glasgow, Dortmund, Birmingham, or Rotterdam have all won European Cups, while the seven biggest metropolitan areas in Europe—Istanbul, Paris, Moscow, London, St. Petersburg, Berlin, and Athens—never have. This points to an odd connection between city size, capital cities, and soccer success. Here's why Arsenal and Chelsea haven't won the Champions League (but may soon).

GENERAL FRANCO'S TRANSISTOR RADIO: THE ERA OF TOTALITARIAN SOCCER

The best measure of success in club soccer is a simple list: the names of the clubs that have won the European Cup since the competition began in 1956. Study this list, and you'll see that the history of the European Cup breaks down into three periods.

The first, from 1956 through the late 1960s, is dominated by the capital cities of fascist regimes. Of the first eleven European Cups, eight were won either by Real Madrid (favorite club of General Franco) or Benfica (from the capital of the Portuguese dictator Salazar). Seven of the losing teams in the first sixteen finals also came from fascist capitals: Real, Benfica, and, in 1971, Panathinaikos from the Athens of the colonels' regime.

But by the start of the 1970s, the dominance of fascist capitals was eroding. Fascist governments seldom outlast their leaders, and Portugal's had entered a twilight after Salazar died in 1970. Meanwhile, everyone was waiting for Franco to go, too.

Yet even after fascism disappeared, teams from Europe's remaining dictatorial capitals continued to thrive. Steaua Bucharest, run by a son of the Romanian dictator Nicolae Ceauşescu, won the cup in 1986. Red Star Belgrade triumphed in 1991 just as Yugoslavia was breaking into pieces. The same phenomenon was at work in the communist countries as in the fascist capitals before them. Dictators send resources to the capital because that is where they and their bureaucrats and soldiers and secret policemen live. Also, it's the last place where they want a popular uprising. So the dictators do up the main buildings, boost the local economy, and help the soccer club. That's totalitarian soccer.

A communist takeover of Britain could have done wonders for a capital team like Arsenal. Just look at the triumphs of Dynamo Berlin, founded in the former East Germany with the express purpose of keeping the league title in the capital. The club president until the Berlin Wall fell was Erich Mielke, feared octogenarian chief of the East German secret police, the Stasi. Mielke loved Dynamo. He made all the best East German players play for it. He also talked to referees, and Dynamo won a lot of matches with penalties in the ninety-fifth minute. Dynamo won the East German league title every year from 1979 to 1988. This was possibly Europe's most extreme case of politicians rigging the soccer market.

Dynamo never got far in the European Cup, but General Franco's local team did. The general made a point of catching Real Madrid's games on the radio, taking a transistor along with him if he was out partridge shooting, writes Jimmy Burns in his *When Beckham Went to Spain*. It wasn't so much that Franco fixed referees or gave Real money. Rather, he helped the club indirectly, by centralizing Spain's power and resources. And he believed that Real's European Cups helped him. Fernando María Castiella, foreign minister under Franco, called Real Madrid "the best embassy we have ever had."

DOWN AND OUT, PARIS AND LONDON:
THE FAILURE OF DEMOCRATIC CAPITALS

Totalitarian capitals got off to a great start in the European Cup. But for the first forty-one years of the trophy's life, the democratic capitals of Europe never won it.

There is only one caveat: Amsterdam is nominally the Dutch capital, and Ajax of that city won the Champions cup four times. However,

Amsterdam really is only nominally the capital. The government, Queen Beatrix, and the embassies are all in The Hague, a city that often does not even have a team in the Dutch premier division. The Hague's only professional club, ADO, traditionally plays its games in front of a couple of thousand people, a large proportion of whom are nuts. Little happens on the field beyond the occasional smoke bomb or plague of rabbits. This is the curse of the democratic capital.

Instead of western capitals, provincial western European cities have dominated the competition. The rule of the provinces holds true even in the most obsessively centralized countries. Teams from five provincial British cities have won the European Cup, but never one from London. Olympique Marseille won the cup in 1993, but Paris St Germain never has. Porto has won it twice since Portugal went democratic, while the Lisbon clubs have been winless since 1962. Clubs from Milan and Turin win all the time, but never one from Rome. The cup has gone to Munich and Hamburg, but never to Bonn or Berlin. For many years, in fact, neither of those cities even had a team in the Bundesliga. Hertha Berlin, the only big club in the current capital, has not been champion of Germany since the Weimar Republic.

Capitals—especially London, Paris, and Moscow—tend to have the greatest concentrations of national resources. It's therefore striking how badly their clubs seem to underperform. We can speculate about why this is. But perhaps the main reason teams from democratic capital cities are not up to much is psychological. In capital cities, no soccer club can matter all that much. There was an instructive sight, sometime in the late 1990s, of a group of visiting fans from an English provincial town wandering down London's Baker Street yelling their club songs at passersby. In their minds, they were shaming the Londoners, invading the city for a day, making all the noise. But the Londoners they were shouting at—many of them foreigners anyway—didn't care, or even understand the point they were making.

Capitals simply have less to prove than provincial cities. They have bigger sources of pride than their soccer teams. Londoners don't go around singing songs about their city, and they don't believe that a prize for Arsenal or Chelsea would enhance London's status. Roman Abramovich and David Dein brought trophies to Chelsea and Arsenal, but neither could ever have been voted mayor of London. Soccer matters even less in Paris, where it's possible to spend a lifetime without ever knowing that soccer exists. Paris St Germain, whose ground is not even entirely within the city's Peripherique ring road, is hardly going to become the main focus of Parisian pride.

London, Paris, and Moscow don't need to win the Champions League. It is a different type of city where a soccer club can mean everything: the provincial industrial town. These are the places that have ousted the fascist capitals as rulers of European soccer.

DARK SATANIC MILLS:
WHY FACTORY TOWNS BECAME SOCCER TOWNS

In 1878 a soccer club started up just by the newish railway line in Manchester. Because the players worked at the Newton Heath carriage works of the Lancashire and Yorkshire Railway Company, their team was called Newton Heath. They played in work clogs against other work teams.

Famously, Newton Heath became Manchester United. But what matters here are the club's origins, well recounted in Jim White's *Manchester United: The Biography*. White describes the L&YR's workers, "sucked in from all over the country to service the growing need for locomotives and carriages." Life in Manchester then was neither fun nor healthy, he writes. "In the middle of the nineteenth century the average male life expectancy in Little Ireland, the notorious part of Manchester . . . was as low as seventeen." This was still the same brutal Manchester where a few decades before Karl Marx's pal Friedrich Engels had run his father's factory, the industrial city so awful it inspired communism.

Industrial Manchester had grown like no other city on earth. In 1800 it had been a tranquil little place of 84,000 inhabitants, so insignificant that as late as 1832 it did not even have a member of Parliament. It was the Industrial Revolution that changed everything. Workers poured in from English villages, from Ireland, from feeble economies everywhere. By 1900 Manchester was the sixth-biggest city in Europe, with 1.25 million inhabitants, more than Moscow at the time. Inevitably, most "Mancunians" were rootless migrants. Unmoored in their new home, many of them embraced the local soccer clubs. Soccer must have given them something of the sense of the community that they had previously known in their villages.

The same thing happened in Britain's other new industrial cities: the migrants attached themselves to soccer clubs with a fervor unknown in more established towns. When the English Football League was founded in 1888, six of the twelve founding members came from industrial Lancashire, while the other six were from the industrial Midlands. Montague Shearman wrote for the Badminton Library that year: "No words of ours can adequately describe the present popularity [of soccer] which, though great in the metropolis, is infinitely greater in the large provincial towns. . . . It is no rare thing in the north and midlands for 10,000 people to pay money to watch an ordinary club match, or for half as many again to assemble for a 'Cup Tie.'" It helped that workers in the textile industry in the Northwest began to get Saturdays off in the 1890s, a luxury that workers elsewhere in Britain did not enjoy.

By 1892, all twenty-eight English professional clubs were from the North or the Midlands. Soccer was as northern a game as rugby league. The champions in the Victorian era came from northern industrial towns like Preston, Sheffield, or Sunderland, then still among the richest spots on earth. When these places became too poor and small to support successful clubs, the league title merely migrated to larger northern cities.

The legacy of the Industrial Revolution still shapes English fandom. Today the combined population of Greater Merseyside, Greater Manchester, and Lancashire County is less than 5.5 million, or a little more than 10 percent of the English population. Nonetheless, in the 2009–2010 season 40 percent of all clubs in the Premier League were based in this region. Their advantage: more than a century of brand building. Manchester United became arguably the most popular club on earth largely because Manchester had been the first industrial city on earth. The club is only the biggest local soccer relic of that era. The forty-three professional clubs within ninety miles of Manchester probably represent the greatest soccer density on earth.

Almost all of Europe's best soccer cities have a profile like Manchester's. They were once new industrial centers that sucked in hapless villagers. The newcomers cast around for something to belong to, and settled on soccer. Supporting the club helped them make a place for themselves in the city. So clubs mattered more here, and grew bigger, than in capital cities or ancient cathedral towns with old-established hierarchies.

The market research company Sport+Markt has been studying fandom since 1994. In 2008 it asked ninety-six hundred people interested in soccer, spread over sixteen European countries, to name their "preferred" club. The top twenty are shown in figure 7.1.

FIGURE 7.1   Europe's favorite clubs

Club	Estimated number of fans (in millions)
Barcelona	44.2
Real Madrid	41.9
Manchester United	37.6
Chelsea	25.6
Zenit St Petersburg	23.9
Liverpool	23.0
Arsenal	21.3
AC Milan	21.0
Bayern Munich	19.8
Juventus	17.5
CSKA Moscow	11.1
Inter Milan	10.3
Olympique Lyon	9.4
Olympique Marseille	9.4
Galatasaray	9.0
Spartak Moscow	8.1
Fenerbahce	7.3
Wisła Kraków	6.5
Ajax Amsterdam	6.5
Dynamo Moscow	5.7

It would be wrong to treat the results as at all precise. The figures differed significantly from those in Sport+Markt's survey of the previous year. In that one year Chelsea, for instance, had supposedly gained almost 6 million fans. Enormous numbers of people change their answers to the question, "Which is your preferred team?" depending on who just won the league or where David Beckham happens to be playing. However, the survey does tell us something. Few would dispute that this top twenty includes most of Europe's best-supported clubs. And there is something remarkable about this list: the biggest clubs are not in the biggest cities. They are in the formerly industrial ones.

Of course, some teams from capitals are popular. They would be, given that London, Paris, Rome, and Moscow are by far the largest cities in their countries. Clubs in capitals have unparalleled catchment areas, even given the profusion of local teams. But in none of the seven largest European countries surveyed does the best-supported club come from a capital city. Here is the favorite team of each large country, according to Sport+Markt:

FIGURE 7.2   Favorite teams of each large country

Country	Best-supported club
England	Manchester United
France	Olympique Lyon
Germany	Bayern Munich
Italy	AC Milan
Poland	Wisła Kraków
Russia	Zenit St Petersburg
Spain	Barcelona

In six out of seven countries, the number-one team comes from a provincial town with a strong industrial history. The sole exception is France, where Lyon is a provincial town but was mostly bypassed by the Industrial Revolution. We saw how its popularity has come from nowhere since just 2002, thanks to their brilliant gaming of the transfer market under president Jean-Michel Aulas.

Taken together, the provincial industrial towns in Sport+Markt's top twenty dominate European soccer. Between them they won twenty-seven out of forty-seven European Cups from 1963 to 2009. The smaller industrial or port cities Glasgow, Nottingham, Birmingham, Porto, Dortmund, Eindhoven, and Rotterdam have won another nine between them. And all these cities have a story much like Manchester's, although their growth spurts happened later. Peasants arrived from the countryside, leaving all their roots behind. Needing something to belong to in their new cities, they chose soccer. That's why in all these places, the soccer clubs arose soon after the factories.

In most of the cities on Sport+Markt's list, the industrial migrants arrived in a whoosh in the late nineteenth century. Munich had 100,000 inhabitants in 1852, and five times as many by 1901. Barcelona's population trebled in the same period to 533,000 people. Turin, for centuries a quiet Piedmontese town, began acquiring factories in the 1870s. Milan surged with the new railways that followed Italian reunification.

Once the local merchants had grown wealthy and discovered English ways, they founded soccer clubs: Juventus in 1897, Barcelona and AC Milan two years later, Bayern in 1900. The clubs then grew with their cities. Newly industrial Milan, for instance, sucked in so many migrants that it could eventually support two of the three most popular teams in Italy.

The second stage of the soccer boom in the continent's industrial cities happened after the war. The 1950s and 1960s were the years of Italy's "economic miracle," when flocks of poor southern Italian peasants took the "train of the sun" north. Many of these people ended up in Turin, making cars for Fiat. The historian Paul Ginsborg writes, "So great and persistent was the flow from the South, that by the end of the sixties Turin had become the third largest 'southern' city in Italy, after Naples and Palermo." The migrants found jobs, but not enough schools or hospitals or apartments. Often there was so little space that roommates had to take turns sleeping. Amid such dislocation, soccer mattered all the more. Goffredo Fofi, author of a study of southern immigration to Turin in the 1960s, said that "during a Juventus-Palermo match, there were many enthusiastic immigrant Sicilian fans whose sons, by now, like every respectable FIAT worker, backed the home team."

It's one of the flukes of history that this mass migration to Turin began soon after the Superga air disaster of 1949 had decimated the city's previous most popular team, Torino. The migrants arrived soon after Juve had established itself as the local top dog, and they helped make it a global top dog. For starters, they transmitted the passion to their relatives down south.

Barcelona experienced the same sort of growth spurt at about the same time as Turin. In the 1950s and 1960s perhaps 1.5 million Spaniards moved to the Barcelona area. Entire villages in the country's interior were left almost empty. On wastelands outside Barcelona, self-built shantytowns sprang up—the sort of thing you might now see on the outskirts of Jakarta—packed with peasants who had left behind everything they knew. Many were illiterate. Hardly any spoke the local language, Catalan. A lot of them attached themselves to Barça. In Spain's new Manchester, it was the quickest way to belong.

The link between industry and soccer is almost universal across Europe. The largest average crowds in all of continental Europe in the 2008–2009 season have been at Borussia Dortmund (average: 72,400), one of many clubs in the industrial Ruhr region. In France, too, it is the industrial cities that have historically loved their clubs best. The country's few traditional hotbeds of soccer are the mining towns of Lens and Saint-Étienne, and the port of Marseille.

All these industrial cities were products of a particular era. In all of them the Industrial Revolution ended, often painfully. But besides the empty docks and factory buildings, the other legacy of industrialization was beloved soccer clubs. The quirk of a particular era gave Manchester United, Barcelona, Juventus, Bayern Munich, and the Milan clubs enough fans to dominate first their own countries, and then Europe.

If Sport+Markt had polled the popularity of soccer clubs in Turkey, it would have found the universal principle holding there, too. The country's capital of soccer is not the capital city, Ankara, but the new industrial powerhouse, Istanbul. The city is home to all three of Turkey's most popular clubs: Galatasaray, Fenerbahce, and Besiktas.

It's true that Istanbul, like St. Petersburg, was once the seat of government, but both cities lost that role more than eighty years ago, long before soccer amounted to anything in their countries. Even as late as 1950, Istanbul was a sleepy place with barely a million inhabitants. Then it became possibly the last big European city to experience an industrial revolution. Migrants were sucked in from all over Anatolia. Between 1980 and 1985 alone, Istanbul's population doubled. Today it is the largest city in Europe, with nearly 12 million inhabitants. The rootless peasants needed somehow to belong in their new home, and so they attached themselves to one of the city's great clubs. Often, these were their strongest loyalties in Istanbul.

Admittedly, almost all cities in Europe have some experience of industrialization. But very few have had as much as Manchester, Turin, Milan, Istanbul, or Barcelona. These were the European cities with the most flux, the fewest long-standing hierarchies, the weakest ties between people and place. Here, there were emotional gaps to fill. This becomes obvious when we contrast the industrial cities with old towns that have a traditional upper-class streak. In England, Oxford, Cambridge, Cheltenham, Canterbury, York, and Bath are all decent-size places, with somewhere between 100,000 and 180,000 inhabitants each. Many industrial towns of that size or even smaller—Middlesbrough, Reading, Ipswich, Blackburn, Watford, Burnley—have serious soccer traditions. Yet Oxford, Cambridge, Bath, Canterbury, York, and Cheltenham between them currently have just one team in the English Football League: Cheltenham Town, which joined it only in 1999. In towns like these, with age-old hierarchies and few newcomers, people simply didn't need soccer clubs to root themselves.

Oxford's face to the world is the university. In industrial cities it is the soccer club. Barcelona, Marseille, and (even now) Newcastle are the pride of their cities, a symbolic two fingers up at the capital. When Barcelona wins something, the president of Catalonia traditionally hoists himself up on the balcony of his palace on the Plaça Sant Jaume, and shouts at the crowds below, "Barça wins, Catalonia wins!"

These provincial clubs have armies of fans, players who will bleed for the club, and backing from local plutocrats. Bernard Tapie put money into Olympique Marseille, the Agnelli family into Juventus, and Sir John Hall into Newcastle because they wanted to be kings of their towns. Local fans and sponsors invest in these clubs partly because they feel civic pride is at stake. In the Middle Ages they would have built a cathedral instead.

Usually, provincial cities such as these only have one major club, which often becomes the only thing that many outsiders know about the place. For instance, there must be many Manchester United fans around the world who don't know that Manchester is a city in England. True, most provincial cities have two teams that compete for top-dog status: United and City in Manchester, Inter and AC Milan in Milan, Torino and Juventus in Turin, United and Wednesday in Sheffield, Celtic and Rangers in Glasgow, Forest and County in Nottingham, Everton, and Liverpool, Bayern and 1860 in Munich, Barça and Espanyol in Barcelona. Many of these rivalries have something to do with religion or politics or both. But usually one team struggles. Manchester City, Torino, and 1860 Munich have all spent long phases in the lower divisions. Everton last won the league in 1987. FC Amsterdam went bust. Midsize provincial cities are simply not big enough to sustain two big clubs for long. In the end, one club pulls ahead.

"THEY MOVED THE HIGHWAY":
THE RISE AND FALL OF SMALL TOWNS

Provincial industrial towns began to dominate the European Cup in the late 1960s. But their rule breaks down into two main periods. The first, from 1970 to 1981, is the small-town era, when clubs from some very modest places won the European Cup. Figure 7.3 shows them, with the populations not just of the cities themselves but of their entire metropolitan areas, including people in all the local suburbs.

FIGURE 7.3 European Cup winners

Club	Year(s) they won it	Metropolitan area
Feyenoord Rotterdam	1970	1 million
Ajax Amsterdam	1971–1973	1 million
Bayern Munich	1974–1976	2.9 million
Liverpool	1977–1978 and 1981	1.4 million
Nottingham Forest	1979–1980	470,000

Note that we are estimating the size of these places very generously, going way beyond the city borders. The figure for Liverpool, for instance, includes all of the local Merseyside region.

The rule of the small is even more striking when you consider some of the losing teams in European Cup finals in this era. In a remarkable four-year period from 1976 to 1979, the towns of Saint-Étienne, Mönchengladbach, Bruges, and Malmö all had teams in the final.

FIGURE 7.4 Winning towns

Club	Size of town	Size of total metropolitan area
Saint-Étienne	175,000	320,000
Mönchengladbach	260,000	260,000
Bruges	115,000	270,000
Malmö	240,000	600,000

Perhaps the emblematic small-town team of the seventies is Borussia Mönchengladbach, whose rise and fall encapsulates that of all these towns.

In the 1970s Gladbach won five German titles and reached four European finals. The Bökelberg stadium, perched on a hill among the gardens of smart houses, saw the best years of Gunter Netzer, Rainer Bonhof, and Alan Simonsen. Fans drove in from neighboring Holland and Belgium, as well as from the town's British army barracks. Decades later, a German marketing company showed that the knee-jerk response of the country's fans to the word *counterattack* was still *Gladbach*.

It was a cozy little club: Berti Vogts spent his whole career here, and when Netzer later played in Zurich he often used to drive up, sometimes to scout players for Spanish clubs, but often just to eat sausages in the canteen.

Like David Cassidy, Gladbach would have done well to combust spontaneously at the start of the eighties. In 1980 it lost its last UEFA Cup final to Eintracht Frankfurt, and the decades since have been disappointing. There was the spell in 1998, for instance, when it just couldn't stop getting thrashed. "We can only get better," announced Gladbach's coach, Friedel Rausch, just before his team lost 8–2 to Bayer Leverkusen. "I feel I can solve our problems," he said afterward. When Gladbach lost its next match 7–1 to Wolfsburg, Rausch was sacked. Gladbach has spent most of the decade since in Germany's second division.

This upsets leftist, educated fortysomethings all over Germany, who still dislike Bayern, revere the socialist Netzer, and on Monday mornings check the Gladbach result first. But there is nothing to be done. The glory days cannot come back, because what did in Gladbach was the modern era.

In the words of Norman Bates in Hitchcock's *Psycho*: "They moved the highway." In the seventies Gladbach's coach, Hennes Weisweiler, was able to build a team of boys from the local towns. The part-Dutch Bonhof came from nearby Emmerich, Vogts was an orphan from Neuss-Buttgen, and Hacki Wimmer, who did Netzer's dirty work, spent decades after his playing career running his parents' stationery shop just down the road in Aachen.

These stars stayed at Gladbach for years because there was little more money to be earned anywhere else in soccer, because most rich clubs were allowed only a couple of foreign players at most, and because their own club could generally stop them from leaving. In short, there were market restraints. That's why Gladbach, Nottingham Forest, Bruges, and Saint-Étienne could thrive in the 1970s. Even then big cities had bigger resources, but they had limited freedom, or limited desire, to use them.

The beginning of the end for small towns was the day in February 1979 when Trevor Francis became soccer's first "million-pound man."

In fact, Clough agreed to a fee of only £999,999 (then about $2 million) to bring him from Birmingham to Forest, but there were taxes on top. Three months later Francis headed the goal (against Malmö) that gave Forest the European Cup. But the swelling of the soccer economy that he embodied would eventually do in small clubs like Forest.

In the 1980s TV contracts grew, and Italy opened its borders to foreigners. Later teams around Europe began renovating their stadiums, which allowed the ones with a lot of fans to make more money. After the European court of justice's "Bosman ruling" in 1995, big clubs could easily sign the best players from any country in the European Union. Around the same time, the clubs with the most fans began earning much more from their television rights. Big clubs everywhere got bigger. Bayern Munich, previously Gladbach's main rival, mushroomed into "FC Hollywood."

After that, clubs like Gladbach could no longer keep their best players. Lothar Matthäus made his debut for "*Die Fohlen*" at the end of the golden era, but when he was only twenty-three he graduated to Bayern. The next great white hope, the local lad Sebastian Deisler, left Gladbach for Hertha at age nineteen in 1999, as soon as he distantly began to resemble Netzer. Small towns couldn't afford the new soccer.

"THAT'S NOT COCAINE, IT'S SAFFRON": THE DEMISE OF THE CATHEDRAL CITIES

Wandering around Florence, you can still imagine it as the center of the universe. It is the effect of the great cathedral, the endless Michelangelos, and all the tourists paying ten dollars for an orange juice. A Medici ruler returning from the dead, as in one of Florence's umpteen paintings of the Day of Judgment, might feel his city had won the battle of prestige among European city-states.

But he would be wrong. These days a midsize city in Europe derives its status less from its cathedral than from its soccer club. Here towns the size of Florence (600,000 people in its metropolitan area) have slipped up.

Fiorentina's last flurry came in 1999, when it beat Arsenal in a Champions League match at Wembley thanks to a goal by Gabriel Batistuta, with Giovanni Trapattoni sitting on the bench. In those days "Trap's" biggest problems were his players' insistence on busing the 150 yards from the locker room to the training ground and the Brazilian Edmondo's ritual late return from the Rio Carnaval. But those days will never return. In the Champions League, the midsize cities are now finished.

Fiorentina's demise can be dated to the day in July 2001 that the Italian police raided the home of the team's owner, the Italian film baron Vittorio Cecchi Gori. What happened was exactly what should happen when police raid a film baron's home, as if Cecchi Gori had read up on Jackie Collins beforehand.

The police broke into his apartment in the Palazzo Borghese in Rome, but then took ninety minutes to find him. This was because his bedroom door was concealed inside a mirrored wall. Only after the Filipina maid had pointed this out did they enter the bedroom to find Cecchi Gori asleep with his girlfriend, Valeria Marini, a Caprice-like figure who calls herself a singer-actress but in fact can do neither.

The police told Cecchi Gori to open his safe. Donning his silk dressing gown, he did so. When the police remarked on the stash of cocaine stored inside, Cecchi Gori replied nonchalantly, "Cocaine? That's not cocaine, it's saffron!"

Meanwhile, his business empire was untangling. It should be said that he acquired the empire only by inheritance from his father, Mario, who before dying in 1993 had warned his old business partner, Silvio Berlusconi, "Take care of Vittorio, he is so impulsive and naive."

Vittorio's problem was that he wanted to be Berlusconi. He bought commercial TV channels (a failure), pumped fortunes into his soccer team (no titles), dabbled in politics (getting no further than senator), but might have been okay had he not gotten caught in a divorce expected to be so expensive that it alone could have funded Fiorentina for years. Cecchi Gori remained admirably upbeat even after all this, leaning out of the window of his Mercedes limousine on Rome's Via Veneto to shout "*La dolce vita!*" to friends. However, he ruined Fiorentina.

It was hard to work out which bit of Cecchi Gori's empire owed what to which, but it was clear that he had borrowed tens of millions of dollars from the club. After everything went wrong, he tried the traditional Italian remedy, putting his eighty-two-year-old mother in charge, but even she could not save Fiorentina. A fax from a Colombian bank offering to pay off the club's entire debt proved, amazingly, to be a forgery.

In 2002 Fiorentina went bankrupt, slipping into Italy's fourth division, where it had to visit Tuscan village teams most of whose players were Fiorentina fans. Now it is back in Serie A, but the days of Trap, Batistuta, and "The Animal" Edmondo won't return. Florence is just too small now.

Florence is typical. Midsize European cities (between 150,000 and 1 million inhabitants) have all but dropped off the map of European soccer. They can no longer afford to compete with clubs from bigger places. In early 2004 it was the turn of Parma, whose owners, the dairy company Parmalat, turned out to have mislaid 10 billion euros. Leeds United is the great English example. In Spain Deportivo La Coruña, pride of a midsize Galician city, suddenly discovered that its debt had hit the strictly notional figure of 178 million euros. Valencia followed a few years later. These clubs fell short because they had hardly any supporters outside their own city walls. Other midsize cities—Glasgow, Amsterdam, Nottingham—have retreated with less fanfare, but they too must know they will never again produce a European champion. Even Newcastle is now beginning to emerge from denial.

The third period of the European Cup began in 1982 and hasn't ended yet: rule by sturdy provincial city. There were still a few undersize winners: Porto and Liverpool twice each, and Eindhoven, Marseille, and Dortmund. However, these towns are not exactly midgets. Four of the five are agglomerations of 1.2 million inhabitants or more. Only Eindhoven has just 210,000 people and a metropolitan area—if you draw it very generously—of only 750,000. In general, European champions are getting bigger. In modern times, the race has usually gone to the rich.

The swelling of the soccer economy—the bigger TV contracts, the new stadiums, the freer movement of players, and so on—favored the most popular clubs. For historical reasons, these tended to be the ones in big provincial cities. Their teams came to dominate the Champions League in a sort of endless loop. Every club that has won the trophy since 1998 had won it at least once before. Most had won it several times before. Are their fans growing blasé? When you have won the thing nine times, the buzz probably starts to fade.

The new dominant clubs aren't from the megacities of Moscow, London, Paris, or Istanbul but from urban areas with 2 to 4 million inhabitants: Milan, Manchester, Munich, and Madrid. These M cities are big enough to produce the required fan base yet provincial enough to generate a yearning for global recognition.

Strangely, one of these cities, Madrid, is a democratic capital. How could Real break the golden rule of the Champions League and win the trophy in 1998, 2000, and 2002? Because it had built its mammoth stadium, brand, and support in the days when Madrid was the capital of a dictatorship. Spain may have gone social democratic, but Real's players still enter the Santiago Bernabeu in those white "meringue" shirts as if it were 1955. The club's global standing is a relic of the fascist era.

GEORGE ZIPF COMES TO LONDON: THE FUTURE METROPOLITAN ERA?

George Kingsley Zipf is an almost forgotten Harvard linguist. Born in 1902, died in 1950 just as he was starting to make a name, Zipf is now known only for having formulated a law that explains almost everything. Among other things, Zipf's law tells us that London or Moscow should start winning Champions Leagues soon.

Consider the following: if you rank every American city by the size of its population, the difference in population between two consecutive cities is simply the ratio of their ranks. So if you compare cities number 1 and 2, city 2 has half (or 1/2) the population of city 1. If you compare cities number 2 and 3, city 3 has two-thirds (2/3) the population of city 2.

City 100 has 99/100ths the population of city 99 and so on down the list. Statistically speaking, the fit of this relationship is almost as perfect as it is possible to be.

This is a particularly elegant example of a more general relationship known as Zipf's law, and it applies to a lot more than city sizes. For instance, it is also true of the frequency with which words are used in English. *The* is the most commonly used word in the language, *of* is second, and so *of* is used about half (1/2) as often as *the*. All in all, Zipf's law has been called possibly "the most accurate regularity in economics."

Zipf's law also works for European cities, though not quite as neatly. City sizes in most European countries are more closely bunched, and so the second city is closer to the first city's size than in the United States, the third closer to the second, and so on.

Why might this be? Zipf's law must have something to do with migration. People will always try to migrate to where the money is. In the United States, with its open markets and very high mobility of labor, they generally do. But in Europe, political and cultural barriers have limited migration. That might explain why city sizes are more compressed there. Nonetheless, Kwok Tong Soo from the London School of Economics has shown that if you measure European metropolitan districts, Zipf's law works well in eight out of nine European countries (Denmark, France, Germany, Greece, the Netherlands, Norway, Switzerland, and Britain).

For a long time nobody could understand why Zipf's law should hold for so many different phenomena. Now, though, economists and scientists are starting to generate models of growth in which the natural outcome of a process is a distribution obeying Zipf's law. Recently, the MIT economist Xavier Gabaix came up with an explanation for why Zipf's law applies to city sizes. He said Zipf's law emerges when all cities grow at the same rate, regardless of their size and their history, but subject to random variation. This implies that common factors drive the growth of cities within a country, while the differences in growth are due to a series of random events ("shocks" in the economic jargon), like, for instance, bombing during the war, which in principle could occur anywhere. A story as simple as this is enough to explain the city sizes predicted by Zipf's law.

Two consequences of Zipf's law are crucial to soccer. First, giants—whether giant cities, giant soccer clubs, or giants of any other kind—are rare. That is because becoming a giant requires a long sequence of positive shocks, like tossing a coin fifty times and coming up "heads" every time. It can happen, but it is rare. Second, once a city becomes a giant, it is unlikely to shrink into the middle ranks unless it experiences a long series of repeated misfortunes (fifty "tails" in a row). By contrast, small cities are unlikely ever to become giants. In other words, the hierarchy of cities, which has established itself over centuries, probably won't change much in the foreseeable future.

This "law of proportionate growth" has some other consequences. What's true for cities is also true for many other social phenomena. For example, if your kid is behind at school, don't worry: he or she will almost certainly catch up, since all children tend to learn at the same rate, plus or minus a few shocks. Likewise, if you think your brilliant six-year-old soccer player is going to become another Beckham or Rooney, don't. More likely the boy had a few positive shocks in his early years, which will cancel out. Rooneys and Beckhams almost never happen. The distribution of talent is thus a bit like the distribution of city sizes: a few great talents stand out at the top, the Maradonas and Ronaldinhos, but as you go down the list, the differences become smaller and smaller.

This brings us back to European cities: there are only a few giants, chiefly Moscow, Istanbul, Paris, and London. You would expect these giant cities to produce the biggest clubs, yet none of them has ever won a Champions League.

But soon they might. Soccer is changing. It is becoming more of a free market, as fascist dictators no longer interfere and the best players are free to move between clubs almost at will. Inevitably, the best players are starting to move to the biggest markets, as happens in major league baseball. And so you would expect dominance in European soccer to move, too: after rule by dictatorial capitals, midsize provincial towns, and big provincial cities, now London and possibly Moscow and Paris should get in on the act at last.

Moscow might, because it is Europe's last large nondemocratic capital. Russia's resources are being sent to the center, and with all that oil and gas under the soil, that's a lot of resources. Paris might, because it has nearly 12 million inhabitants and only one top-division soccer club, Paris St Germain, which surely cannot be appallingly run forever.

London might do it, because even after the implosion of the City, London has the largest local economy in Europe. London already supports two of Europe's biggest teams, and could probably cope with more. This represents quite a change. In the early 1990s, London rather resembled Moscow circa 1973. Tired people in gray clothes waited on packed platforms for 1950s Tube trains. Coffee was an exotic drink that barely existed. Eating a meal outside was forbidden. The city center was almost uninhabited, and closed at 11 p.m. anyway. There was a sense of permanent decline.

Nor had London ever been even the soccer capital of Britain. Only in 1931 did a southern club—Arsenal—first win the league. Even after that, though, the title generally went north.

But in the 1990s London transformed. Cheap flights from five airports took Londoners around Europe. Trains began running to Paris and Brussels. Today it is quicker to get there than to the shrinking northern cities of Liverpool and Manchester, and less of a culture shock when you arrive. London became a European city, detached from the rest of Britain. The geographer Daniel Dorling said Britain was starting to look like a city-state. Moreover, the city was starting to grow again. Greater London's population had been falling from the Second World War until the 1980s, but boom-time London changed that.

From the late 1990s until 2008, London offered a Technicolor vista of raucous young people from all over the world dressed in weird youth-culture outfits chucking cash at each other. The Tube trains ceased to be antique curios. The place came to smell of money. All this started to give London soccer dominance.

At the same time as the city became fully international, so did the market in soccer players. The best ones could now work wherever they wanted. Many of them—like many investment bankers and actors—chose London.

Black and foreign players liked living in a city where 95 percent of the inhabitants agree with the statement, "It is a good thing that Britain is a multicultural society." When Thierry Henry was spending his best years at Arsenal, he said, "I love this open, cosmopolitan city. Whatever your race, you never feel people's gaze on you." In a virtuous cycle, foreigners attract foreigners. The Frenchman Jacques Santini, Tottenham's manager for about five minutes, wanted to come to London because his son Sebastien already lived there—a classic example of chain migration.

Equally to the point, even in the current economic crisis a soccer player can still earn a living in London. The capital's clubs have been coining it. First, their customers can still afford to pay the highest ticket prices in global soccer. Arsenal charges about seventeen hundred dollars for its cheapest season ticket, which is a lot more than Barcelona charges for its most expensive. So many Londoners were happy to fork out this kind of money that Arsenal was able to build a new stadium with sixty thousand seats and sell it out. No club in London's history has drawn such a large regular crowd. For the 2007–2008 season, the business advisory firm Deloitte ranked Arsenal and Chelsea among the world's six richest clubs.

Even now, no other European city has as many investors. When Roman Abramovich decided to buy a soccer club, it was inevitable that he would end up owning Chelsea rather than, say, Blackburn. The word is that he chose it because it was the nearest club to his house on Eaton Square. Similarly, Mohamed Al Fayed, who lives on Park Lane, bought Fulham. Even Queens Park Rangers were bought up by the Indian Lakshmi Mittal, the world's fifth richest man, who of course lives around the corner in Kensington. Yes, other rich foreigners have bought Manchester City and Aston Villa, but London is still a touch more appealing to billionaires.

The handful of biggest provincial clubs—Manchester United, Liverpool, Bayern, Barcelona, the two Milan clubs—have built up such strong brands that they will remain at the top of European soccer. However, their new challengers will probably not be other provincial clubs but teams from London, Moscow, and perhaps Paris.

At last, being in a giant capital city is becoming a strategic asset to a soccer club. When Arsenal and Chelsea finished in the top two spots in the Premier League in 2004, it was the first time in history that two London teams had achieved that feat. In 2005 they did it again. From 2006 to 2008, they figured in two out of three Champions League finals. Soon one of these clubs could become the first London team to be champion of Europe. Then the city will dominate every aspect of British life.

8

FOOTBALL VERSUS FOOTBALL

When Nelson Mandela was a teenager in the Transkei region of South Africa, he was sent to a mock British boarding school. The Clarkebury Institute taught black students, but was of course run by a white man, the Reverend C. Harris. "The school itself consisted of a cluster of two dozen or so graceful, colonial-style buildings," Mandela recalled in his autobiography, *Long Walk to Freedom.* "It was the first place I'd lived in that was western, not African, and I felt I was entering a new world whose rules were not yet clear to me."

Like the Victorian British schools that it imitated, Clarkebury aimed to turn its pupils into Christian gentlemen. A gentleman, to Victorian Britons, was someone who spoke English and played British games. As Mandela describes his school days, "I participated in sports and games as often as I could, but my performances were no more than mediocre. . . . We played lawn tennis with home-made wooden rackets and soccer with bare feet on a field of dust."

He had encountered the British Empire. The British colonial officers, merchants, and sailors who went around the world in the nineteenth century didn't merely aim to exploit the natives. They also tried to teach them British values. They succeeded spectacularly with Mandela, who at an earlier school had acquired a new first name

(Admiral Nelson was a British naval hero) and eventually became the epitome of the courtly British gentleman. However, his story is exemplary of millions of people around the world, both in Britain's official colonies and in the "informal empire," the countries where the Brits supposedly didn't rule.

From about 1917 to 1947, the British gradually stopped running the world and handed over the keys to the Americans. But the American empire was much less ambitious. It barely spread Americanism. Football, the American empire's most popular sport, still hardly exists outside the home country. In fact, when the American troops in Afghanistan wanted to woo natives, they were reduced to handing out soccer balls. (The exercise failed: Allah's name was found to be printed on a ball, a blasphemy for an object designed for kicking.)

At this point, let's agree to call the global game "soccer" and the American game "football." Many people, both in America and in Europe, imagine that *soccer* is an American term invented in the late twentieth century to distinguish the game from gridiron. Indeed, anti-American Europeans often frown on the use of the word. They consider it a ma:k of American imperialism. This is a silly position. "Soccer" was the most common name for the game in Britain from the 1890s until the 1970s. As far as one can tell, when the North American Soccer League brought soccer to the Americans in the 1970s, and Americans quite reasonably adopted the English word, the British stopped using it and reverted to the word *football*. We will compare soccer with football, and the readers will know what we mean.

What follows is a tale of two games and two empires. Soccer spread around the world whereas football did not, largely because Victorian Britons were instinctive colonialists whereas today's Americans are not. But now, for the first time, the empires are going head-to-head as if in a kid's computer game. Both the Premier League and the NFL want to rule the world. This is a struggle between two very different types of empire: the British (which contrary to popular opinion still exists), and the American (which contrary to popular opinion may not exist). Emerging from the struggle is a new breed of sports fan.

GENTLEMEN WITH LEATHER BALLS

In 1884 a nine-year-old boy named Charles Miller embarked on the S.S. *Elbe* in Brazil and set off for England. Miller's father had emigrated from Britain to Brazil, where he became an engineer for the Sao Paolo Railway Company. Now Charles was making the return journey, to enroll at an English boarding school. Like Mandela at Clarkebury, Miller at Banister Court learned games. "Just as a schoolboy, in the Garden of Childhood, listens to the teacher, so I, fascinated, saw my first game of Association Football," he later wrote.

In 1894 Miller returned to Brazil with a leather ball and a set of rules in his luggage. He set up the first Brazilian soccer league, and lived long enough to see Brazil host the World Cup of 1950 and reach the final. He also introduced rugby to Brazil, though with rather less success. He died in 1953.

Miller's story was typical of soccer pioneers in many countries. First, he was posh, or at least posh enough to go to boarding school. (Contrary to myth, it wasn't on the whole British sailors who gave the world soccer. The upper classes had considerably more soft power.) Second, Miller was typical in that he spread soccer to a country that wasn't a British colony. In the colonies, places like Australia or India, the British administrators mostly taught the natives cricket and rugby. Soccer did best in the informal empire, the noncolonies: most of Europe, Latin America, and parts of Asia. Here, it probably benefited from not being seen as a colonial ruler's game. Brits in the informal empire were supposedly just businesspeople, even if in practice their commercial clout gave the British prime minister vast influence over many unlikely countries.

From about 1850 until the First World War, Britain was the sole economic superpower. As late as in 1914, Britons still owned about 42 percent of all the world's foreign investment. The British expats who inhabited the informal empire represented the empire's economic might. The men tended to work in the railways (like Miller's father), or as businessmen (like the Charnock brothers, who set up Russia's first soccer club for their mill employees outside Moscow), or as school-teachers (like Alexander Watson Hutton, the Scottish teacher who in the early 1880s introduced soccer in Argentina).

These people had only "soft power": the wealth and prestige of the British gentleman. That was enough to spread their games. Men like Hutton taught foreigners to see sports as an upper-class and hence aspirational product. If you were a young man like Mandela who wanted to become a British gentleman, one of the things you did was play soccer. That's why the game's early adopters in the informal empire tended to be rich people who had contact with British gentlemen. Pim Mulier, for instance, who introduced a whole list of sports to the Netherlands, first encountered soccer as a five year old at a Dutch boarding school that had some British pupils. In 1879, when Mulier was fourteen, he founded the first Dutch soccer club.

Soccer conquered the world so fast largely because the British gentleman was such an attractive ideal. A century later a new British archetype, the hooligan, in his own way probably added to the game's glamour.

By the 1930s, when Mandela went to Clarkebury, the British Empire had already begun to fade. However, many of the empire's global networks outlived the loss of the colonies. The most important survivor would be the English language, even if it sustained its global reach largely thanks to the Americans. English gave people around the world an easy connection with Britain. Steven Stark, an American soccer fan, former speechwriter of Jimmy Carter, and a teacher of English rhetoric, asks, "Isn't the best thing the Premiership has going for it that it's in English? I mean, if everyone in France spoke English and everyone in England spoke French, we'd all be following the French league. In an international economy, English trumps the competition."

Many people in former British colonies grew up absorbing British football from British media outlets that had also outlived the empire. Peter Draper, when he was marketing director of Manchester United, noted that English football has been televised for decades in many Asian countries. That built loyalty. Real Madrid, Draper told us, "didn't have the platform. Spanish television is nowhere in Asia. Best team of the 1950s? Sorry, didn't see them in Asia."

Mike Abrahams is a gangster-turned-intellectual who grew up in a poor nonwhite Cape Flats township outside Cape Town. As a child he used to sit in the local library reading British boys magazines like *Shoot* and *Tiger*. He admits that classic British soccer cartoons like *Billy's Magic Boots* shaped him.

Abrahams was a leftist who identified with only one product of white capitalist imperialist Britain: soccer. He says, "People in the Cape follow English football very seriously. One of my friends, his first child's name is Shankly [after Bill Shankly, the former Liverpool manager]. And this is an activist! You can say England is a bitch on Friday night, and on Saturday afternoon you go to a sports pub to watch English soccer."

People are always complaining that American culture has conquered the world. In fact, British culture probably remains more dominant. This fading midsize island has kept a bizarre grip on the global imagination. It's not only their sports that the Brits have exported. The world's six best-selling novels of the past hundred years are all British: four Harry Potters, one Agatha Christie, and one J. R. Tolkien. The world's best-selling band ever is the Beatles. And the sports league with the biggest global impact is surely the Premier League. England has produced few great soccer players, yet on an average Saturday people in Soweto and Shanghai gather in bars for the kickoff at White Hart Lane rather than for anything from Germany.

They certainly aren't watching the NFL. In fact, the United States has rarely even aspired to vast cultural reach. The country fought wars, but mostly tried to avoid creating long-term colonies, notes John Gray, a professor at the London School of Economics. In Vietnam and Iraq, for instance, the aim was to "go in, do the job, get out." Unlike Britons, Americans generally didn't want to be in the business of empire. We know an American lawyer who spent a few months working for the British government during the occupation of Iraq. In the "Green Zone" in Baghdad he noticed a difference between the way Brits and Americans operated. When American officials wanted an Iraqi to do something, the lawyer said, they would generally call the person into the Green Zone and if necessary "bawl him out." Sometimes this strategy worked. Sometimes it didn't. But the Americans summoned Iraqis only when something needed fixing. British officials worked differently, said the lawyer. They were always inviting Iraqis in, for parties or just for chats, even when there was nothing in particular to discuss. This was exactly how the British had operated both in their colonies and in their "informal empire": they made long-term contacts. The Reverend Harris at Clarkebury school may not entirely have known it, but in effect he was a British agent charged with teaching Mandela Britishness.

By contrast, few American Harrises ever taught baseball or football to budding foreign rulers. There have been a handful of prominent American colonialists, but they are so rare as to stand out. Douglas MacArthur ruled Japan for years. Hollywood makes its blockbusters chiefly for the global market. And in sports, the NBA's commissioner, David Stern, has spent a quarter century interesting foreigners in basketball. But most American sporting moguls, like most American producers in general, have been satisfied with their giant domestic market. Baseball's last great overseas tour was in 1913–1914, after which Americans barely even tried to spread baseball or football abroad until the 1990s.

The American empire's favorite games have been no good at cultural imperialism. It's a story told in one statistic: the media agency Futures Sport & Entertainment estimates that of the 93 million people who saw the Super Bowl live in 2005, only 3 million were outside North America.

WHILE AMERICA SLEPT: HOW SOCCER INVADED THE US

After the British Victorians spread their games, sports experienced a century of relative stability. The Indians played cricket, the US resisted soccer, and the isolated town of Melbourne favored Australian Rules football, which barely existed even in other parts of Australia. But from

the 1980s, new TV channels—free, cable, and satellite—began mush-
rooming almost everywhere. They took up the burden of carrying sports
around the world. When Britain's Channel Four was created in 1982,
for instance, it began broadcasting NFL games. They were a hit.
Suddenly, there were people in Norwich or Manchester who called
themselves 49ers fans. William "the Refrigerator" Perry, the supersize
Chicago Bears lineman, became a cult hero in Britain. Alistair Kirkwood, the NFL's UK managing director, fondly recalls that for a year or
two in the 1980s, the Super Bowl had higher ratings in Britain than the
beloved soccer program *Match of the Day* on the same weekend.

It didn't last. English soccer cleaned up its stadiums, kicked out
most of its hooligans, sold its rights to Sky Television, and revived.
Eventually, Channel Four dropped the NFL. The halfhearted American invasion—albeit led by British TV—had been repelled.

Meanwhile, across the ocean, soccer was slowly infecting American
life. Even though the US already had four big team sports and seemed
to have no need of another, in the 1970s the game came from almost
nowhere to conquer American childhoods. It turned out there was a
gap in the American sports market after all. The country's most popular sport, football, was too dangerous, too male, and too expensive for
mass participation. Fitting out a kid with all the necessary equipment
for football costs around three to four hundred dollars, a significant
cost, especially if the child quickly decides that he doesn't like being
beaten up. Today, probably fewer than 1 million people in the world
play tackle football, compared to the 265 million who (according to
FIFA) play soccer.

Victorian Britons had conceived of soccer as a "man's game." But
Americans saw that it was a soft sport, safe for girls as well as boys. So
soccer in the US became an unlikely beneficiary of feminism. It did almost as well out of another post-1960s social trend, Mexican immigration. The estimated 43 million Hispanics now living in the US (up
threefold since 1980) outnumber the population of Spain.

And so more American children under twelve play soccer than
baseball, football, and ice hockey put together. The strange American

equilibrium, whereby kids play soccer and follow football, has been in place since the 1980s.

Contrary to popular opinion, soccer in America has been a success. When David Beckham joined the LA Galaxy, the cliché was that his task was to "put soccer on the map" in America. In fact, this was impossible, because soccer was already "on the map" in America. The US has a strong soccer culture. It's just different from any other country's soccer culture. In particular, it doesn't require a strong domestic men's professional league.

Major League Soccer is not American soccer. It's just a tiny piece of the mosaic. Kids' soccer, college soccer, indoor soccer, Mexican, English, and Spanish soccer, the Champions League, and the World Cup between them dwarf the MLS. To cite just one example: nearly 17 million Americans saw the World Cup final of 2006, 4 million more than watched an average game in the NBA finals and almost as many as saw the average World Series game in 2006. Moreover, soccer has penetrated most branches of the American entertainment industry, from *The Sopranos* to presidential elections in which "soccer moms" are considered pivotal figures.

American soccer people often fret over the MLS's marginality. As Dave Eggers has noted, "Newspaper coverage of the games usually is found in the nether regions of the sports section, near the car ads and the biathlon roundups." Some TV ratings for MLS games "are in the realm of—or, in some cases, actually below—tractor pulls, skate boarding competitions, and bass fishing tournaments," writes Andrei Markovits, politics professor at the University of Michigan. The lowliest MLS players earn as little as fifteen thousand dollars a year.

But to worry about this is to misunderstand why so many American suburban families like soccer. The game has thrived as a pastime for upscale kids in part precisely *because* there is no big soccer in the US. Many soccer moms are glad that soccer is not a big professional American sport like basketball or football. Like a lot of other Americans, they are wary of big-time American sports, whose stars do lousy and unethical things like shooting their limousine drivers.

By contrast, many moms see soccer as an innocent game, free of certain aspects of modern America: not violent, not drenched in money, and not very black. A large number of MLS players are white college boys. American soccer has no Charles Barkley.

ANY GIVEN SUNDAY: IS THE NFL REALLY SO EQUAL?

Clearly, though, the NFL is doing something right. Here are the average attendance rates of the most-watched leagues of all the world's ball games:

1. NFL	68,241 (regular season, 2008)
2. German soccer, Bundesliga	41,446 (2008–2009 season)
3. Australian Football League (Australian Rules football)	36,996 (2008 season)
4. English Premier League	35,341 (2008–2009 season)

The Premier League outdraws the NFL in per-capita terms, if we take into account that England has only a sixth as many inhabitants as the US. But in absolute terms no league can begin to rival the NFL. When people try to explain the NFL's popularity, they often mention its famous slogan: "On any given Sunday any team in our league can beat any other team." This is a boast the Premier League would never dare make. English soccer looks horribly unbalanced, with the "Big Four" teams dominating at the top, whereas the NFL claims to be a league of equals.

Indeed, the NFL is often called "the socialist league." Its clubs share TV income equally, and 40 percent of each game's gate receipts goes to the visiting team. This aspiration to equality is a general American sporting trait. Clubs in American baseball, basketball, and the MLS also share far more of their income than European soccer does. Take the ubiquitous New York Yankees baseball cap. Outside of New York, the Yankees receive only one-thirtieth of the profit on each cap sold, the same as every other team in baseball. By contrast, Manchester United wouldn't dream of giving Bolton or Wigan a cut of its shirts.

Many in European soccer, and particularly in England, have come to envy the NFL. English fans often complain that their sport is getting boring because the big clubs win everything. The "Big Four" of Manchester United, Chelsea, Liverpool, and Arsenal dominate not only the Premier League but the Champions League, too. In all of continental Europe, only Barcelona can match them. Even Emilio Butragueño, sporting director of plucky little Real Madrid, told the BBC, "You need uncertainty at the core of every competition. . . . We may eventually have something similar to the [salary cap] system in the US, to give a chance to all the clubs."

Andy Burnham, Britain's culture secretary, warned in 2008 that although the Premier League was "the world's most successful domestic sporting competition," it risked becoming "too predictable." He added: "I keep referring to the NFL, which has equal sharing. . . . In the US, the most free-market country in the world, they understand that equal distribution of money creates genuine competition."

Michel Platini, president of the European soccer association UEFA, seems to agree. Searching for a way to even things out in European soccer, in the spring of 2009 he put a team of UEFA officials on a plane to the US. Perhaps there was something over there that soccer could copy.

People who think like this tend to accept two truisms: The NFL is much more equal than European soccer. And sports fans like equality. Unfortunately, neither of these truisms is true. First, the NFL isn't nearly as balanced as it pretends. Second, we have data to show that overall, fans prefer unbalanced leagues.

At first glance, you could be forgiven for believing that the NFL really is much more equal than the Premier League. In the decade to 2009, seven different teams have won the Super Bowl. In the same period, only three teams have won the Premier League, with Manchester United bagging a snore-inducing six titles. On any given Sunday (or Saturday lunchtime, Tuesday night, whenever), Blackburn or Bolton can beat United, but the fact is that they usually don't.

Yet is the NFL much more equal than the Premier League? Does it have a more even distribution of wins? Measuring the level of equality in both leagues is tricky, first because there are no ties in the NFL and second because the NFL's regular season consists of just sixteen games and the Premier League's of thirty-eight. In any given season, a weak English team has many more chances to get lucky.

Happily, there is a way to allow for these differences so that we can compare the two leagues. We will do this by dreaming up another league, a totally equal one in which every team always has an equal chance of winning any given game. This equal league would be a league of coin flips. Obviously, in the coin-flip league each team would be expected to win an average of 50 percent of its games. Even so, the outcome of any sixteen- or thirty-eight-game sequence would produce some random inequalities. Hardly any team in the coin-flip league would win exactly half its games. Rather, the win percentages for the season would be randomly dispersed around 50 percent. The question then is: which looks more like the totally equal coin-flip league, the NFL or the Premier League?

To work this out, we must calculate how random the dispersion of wins is in each of our three leagues. The measure of dispersion is commonly called the standard deviation. Let's calculate standard deviation for the coin-flip league, and then for the NFL and the Premier League. (And please feel free to skip the next few paragraphs if you aren't interested in the math.)

The standard deviation of win percentages for any league is calculated by first taking the difference between each team's win percentage and 50 percent (the difference will be positive when the team has a winning season, negative for a losing season). Then we square the difference, to make sure pluses and minuses don't cancel out. Next we add up the difference for all teams in the league, and take the square root. That gives a number that is comparable to the average win percentage.

Now we are ready to find the figure we want: the standard deviation, or dispersion of win percentages. If our average win percentage is 50, a standard deviation of 1 would mean that most teams are close to the average. If the standard deviation were 20, it would mean that there is quite a lot of dispersion. In coin-tossing leagues, we know what the standard deviation should be: close to half of the reciprocal of the square root of the number of games played. This is easy to calculate. If you play sixteen games, the square root is four, the reciprocal is one-quarter, and half of that is one-eighth, or 12.5 percent.

That is what the standard deviation of win percentage in the NFL would be if on any given Sunday any team in the league really had a fifty-fifty chance of beating its opponent. Well, the NFL is not a coin-tossing league. This century, the standard deviation of win-loss records has fluctuated between 16 and 21 percent, and has averaged 20 percent. That's well above the 12.5 percent of the coin-tossing league.

The Premier League is only slightly less equal than the NFL. If the Premier League were a coin-tossing league, the expected standard deviation would be just over 8 percent. In fact, this century the Premier League's standard deviation has averaged 14 percent. So it's not a coin-tossing league, either, but the difference is not much greater than for the NFL. To put it another way, the NFL has a standard deviation about 60 percent larger than a coin-tossing league, while the EPL has one about 70 percent larger. This is a difference, but in the scale of things a fairly negligible one.

You might object that even if the NFL and Premier League are statistically almost equally balanced, the identity of the dominant teams and doormats changes each season in the NFL but not in the Premier League. After all, each season the worst NFL team gets the first draft pick, a very large human being who is in fact a device for bouncing back. As the distinguished "Chicago school" economists Sherwin Rosen and Allen Sanderson have pointed out, the Premier League punishes failure, while the NFL punishes success.

But for all the NFL's efforts, the identity of winners and losers is pretty stable in both leagues. The best teams in the NFL, the Patriots and Colts, have won more than 70 percent of their games so far this century, just as Manchester United, Chelsea, and Arsenal have won more than 70 percent of theirs. Likewise, there are as many losers in the NFL as in the Premier League. The Detroit Lions have won less than 30 percent of their games since the millennium, a feat matched in England only by Bradford City. The difference is that Bradford was relegated after its only season in the Premier League, whereas the Lions look set to sustain their peculiar brand of misery unto eternity.

So the NFL isn't much more equal than the Premier League. It just looks like it is. It does so thanks largely to randomization devices that ensure that the best team doesn't always win the Super Bowl: first, the small number of regular-season games; second, the playoffs. Both these devices ensure that no NFL team is likely to dominate for years like Manchester United has. However, this randomization comes at the expense of justice. Fans often feel that the best team in the NFL did not win the Super Bowl. In fact, the NFL looks a lot like the Champions League, where the knockout rounds add a random element that often ambushes the best team.

This disposes of our first truism: the claim that the NFL is much more equal than the Premier League. What about the second one: the notion that sports fans, like French revolutionaries, desire equality?

If fans want all teams to be equal, then they will shun games in which results are predictable. If so, more of them will watch games whose outcome is very uncertain. How to test whether fans really behave like that? Researchers have tried to gauge expected outcomes of games either by using prematch betting odds or the form of both teams over the previous half-dozen games. Studies of soccer, mostly in England, show mixed results. Some studies find that more balanced games attract more fans. Others find the reverse.

The British economists David Forrest of Salford Business School and Robert Simmons of Lancaster University have done some of the best work in this field. They found that a balanced English game could sometimes increase attendance. However, they also carried out a simulation to show that if the English leagues became more balanced, they would attract *fewer* fans. That is because a balanced league, in which all teams are equally good, would turn into an almost interminable procession of home wins. By contrast, in real existing soccer, some of the most balanced games occur when a weak team plays at home against a strong team (Stoke versus Manchester United, for instance).

Forrest and Simmons found that the people who care most about competitive balance are television viewers. The spectators at the grounds tend to be the hard core: they simply want to see their team win. However, most TV viewers are "floating voters." When the outcome of a game seems too predictable, they switch off. The two economists found that the closer a televised English soccer game was expected to be (measured by the form of both teams going into the game), the higher the viewing figures on Sky TV. Still, the size of this effect was modest. Forrest and Simmons said that even if the Premier League were perfectly balanced (in the sense that each team had an equal probability of winning each game), TV audiences would rise by only 6 percent. That would be a small effect for such a revolutionary change.

A moment's thought suggests why some unequal games might be very attractive. Most fans in the stadium are fans of the home team, and so they do not really want a balanced outcome. Often the most attractive games involve strong home teams playing weak visiting teams (Manchester United versus Stoke, again), in which case the home team typically has a lot of supporters who enjoy watching their heroes score a lot of goals, or they are games between weak home teams and strong away teams (Stoke versus Manchester United), in which local fans come to see the visiting stars, or in the hope of an upset.

Furthermore, big teams have more fans than small ones, and so if Manchester United beats Stoke, more people are happy than if Stoke wins. Also, fans are surprisingly good at losing. Psychological studies show that they are skilled at transferring blame: "We played well, but the referee was garbage." This means that fans will often stick with a team even if it always loses. It also explains why, the morning after their team gets knocked out of the World Cup, people don't sink into depression but get on with their lives.

Last, dominant teams create a special interest of their own. Millions of people support Manchester United, and millions of others despise it. In a way, both groups are following the club. United is the star of English soccer's soap opera. Everyone else dreams of beating it. Much of the meaning of supporting a smaller club like West Ham, for instance, derives from disliking Manchester United. Kevin Keegan, when he was chasing the title as manager of Newcastle in 1996, thrillingly captured that national English sentiment with his famous, "I will love it if we beat them! Love it!" monologue. (United beat him instead.) Big bad United makes the Premier League more fun.

Another way of looking at competitive balance is to view the league as a whole, rather than match by match. Do more spectators come when the title race is exciting than when one team runs away with it?

It turns out that a thrilling title race does little to improve attendance. English fans will watch their teams play in the league even when they haven't a hope of winning it (or else dozens of English clubs would not exist).

It is true that a game has to be significant to draw fans, but that significance need not have anything to do with winning the title. A study by Stephen Dobson and John Goddard showed that when a match matters more either for winning the league *or* for avoiding relegation to a lower league, then attendance tends to rise. In every soccer league in Europe, the bottom few teams are "relegated" at the end of the season to a lower tier. The worst three teams in the Premier League, for instance, drop to the Championship. It's as if the cellar teams in Major League Baseball got exiled to Triple A. Relegation is brutal, but the device has a genius to it. The annual English relegation battle boosts fans' interest to the point that teams at the bottom often outdraw teams at the top as the season comes to an end. The NFL, too, could do with a system of relegation. That would replace losers like the Lions with rising teams. This would be in the fans' interest, but not in the owners'.

Fans need a reason to care. Most matches in the Premier League are significant for something or other, even if it's only qualifying for European competition. Given that games can be significant in many different ways, it is unclear why a more balanced Premier League would create more significance.

There is a third way of looking at balance: the long term. Does the dominance of the same teams year in, year out turn fans off?

Let's compare a long period with dominance in English soccer to a long period without dominance: the fairly equal era that ran from 1949 to 1968, and the "unfair" era that began around 1989 and still continues today.

In the first, "equal," twenty-year period, eleven different teams won the English league. The most frequent champion, Manchester United, won five titles in the period. The second period was far more predictable: only six teams won the title, with United taking it ten times. Yet during the first "equal" period, total annual attendance in the top division fell from an all-time high of 18 million in 1949 to only 15 million in 1968 (and even that figure got a temporary boost from England winning the World Cup in 1966). During the second, "unequal," period, total attendance rose from 8 million to 13 million, even though tickets became much more expensive and people had many more choices of how to spend their free time.

Anyone who dismisses the Premier League as "one of the most boring leagues in the world" (in the words of Kevin Keegan), a closed shop that shuts out smaller clubs from the lower divisions, has to explain why so many people now watch all levels of English league football. In the 2006–2007 season, 29.5 million spectators paid to see professional games in England, the highest number since 1970. The Premier League pulls fans even though, as Keegan has noted, everyone knows the top four finishers in advance. But more than half of those 29.5 million spectators in 2006–2007 watched the Football League, the three divisions below the Premier League. The clubs in the Championship, the second tier of English soccer, have supposedly been doomed to irrelevance by Manchester United, and can only dream of one day clinging on at the bottom of the Premier League, yet their division in 2006–2007 had the fifth-highest-average crowd of any league in Europe.

The Premier League's inequality coexists with rising attendance, revenues, and global interest, not least from North American businessmen schooled in American major league sports: the Glazer family at United itself, Randy Lerner at Aston Villa, Tom Hicks and George

Gillett at Liverpool. These people do not seem too worried about competitive balance in English soccer.

They have reasons to feel relaxed. The Premier League's TV income is starting to catch up with the NFL's. In the 1970s the NFL generated hundreds of millions of dollars annually when soccer in Europe was generating almost nothing. By 1980 the average NFL team still had nearly as much income a year as all the clubs in the English top division put together. Today the average Premier League team earns about $60 million a year from TV, or half as much as an NFL team. That's pretty good given that England has 250 million fewer inhabitants than the US. Moreover, the gap between the two leagues has been closing, and is likely to close further as English soccer finally begins to make money out of the global market. One day, we might see English soccer chairmen buying NFL teams.

Some of English soccer's critics have not digested these figures. When we pointed out to Platini at UEFA's headquarters on Lake Geneva that English stadiums are full nowadays, he replied, "Not all. They're full at the teams that win." This argument is often made but flawed nonetheless. Whenever rows of empty seats appear at struggling teams like Blackburn or Middlesbrough, it is back-page news, and regarded as ominous for the Premier League as a whole. Yet it's natural that some fans should desert disappointing teams, while others flock to exciting ones. Sunderland, Arsenal, Manchester United, and other clubs have built bigger stadiums and filled them. Not every English team has gained spectators since 1992, but most have. All twenty clubs in the Premier League in 2008 had a higher average attendance than in 1992. If the team had been in the Premier League in 1992, the average increase was 63 percent; if it had risen from a lower division, the average increase was an even more handsome 227 percent. Of all ninety-two teams in the four highest English divisions, only seventeen had lower average crowds in 2008 than in 1992. The rising English tide had lifted almost every boat.

Admittedly, today's large crowds don't in themselves prove that dominance attracts fans. After all, many other things have changed in

England since the more equal 1949–1968 period. Crucially, the country's soccer stadiums have improved. However, the rising attendance rates do make it hard to believe that dominance in itself significantly undermines interest. Indeed, pretty much every soccer league in Europe exhibits more dominance than the American major leagues, yet fans still go.

WHY DAVID BEAT GOLIATH

Strangely, it was the British fanzine *When Saturday Comes* that best expressed the joys of an unbalanced league. *WSC* is, in large part, the journal of small clubs. It publishes moving and funny pieces by fans of minnows like Crewe or Swansea. Few of its readers have much sympathy with Manchester United (though some, inevitably, are United fans). Many of *WSC*'s writers have argued for a fairer league. Yet in September 2008 Ian Plenderleith, a contributor who lives outside Washington, D.C., argued in *WSC* that America's MLS, in which "all teams started equal, with the same squad size, and the same amount of money to spread among its players' wages," was boring. The reason: "No truly memorable teams have the space to develop." The "MLS is crying out for a couple of big, successful teams," Plenderleith admitted. "Teams you can hate. Dynasties you really, really want to beat. Right now, as LA Galaxy coach Bruce Arena once memorably said: 'It's a crapshoot.'"

In short, the MLS lacks one of the joys of an unbalanced league: the David versus Goliath match. And one reason fans enjoy those encounters is that surprisingly often, given their respective budgets, the Davids win. The economist Jack Hirshleifer called this phenomenon "the paradox of power." Imagine, he said, that there were two tribes, one large, one small. Each can devote its efforts to just two activities, farming and fighting. Each tribe produces its own food through farming, and steals the other tribe's food through fighting. Which tribe will devote a larger *share* of its efforts to fighting?

The answer is the small tribe. The best way to understand this is to imagine that the small tribe is very small indeed. It would then have to devote almost all its limited resources to either fighting or farming. If it chose farming, it would be vulnerable to attack. Everything it produced could be stolen. On the other hand, if the tribe devoted all its resources to fighting, it would have at least a chance of stealing some resources. So Hirshleifer concludes—and proves with a mathematical model— that smaller competitors will tend to devote a greater share of resources to competitive activities.

He found many real-world examples of the paradox of power. He liked citing Vietnam's defeat of the US, but one might also add the Afghan resistance to the Soviet Union in the 1980s, the Dutch resistance to the Spanish in the sixteenth century, or the American resistance to the British in the War of Independence. In these cases the little guy actually defeated the big guy. In many other cases, the little guy was eventually defeated, but at much greater cost than might have been expected based on physical resources (the Spartans at Thermopylae, the Afrikaners in the Boer War, the Texans at the Alamo).

In soccer as in war, the underdog tends to try harder. Big teams fight more big battles, and so each contest weighs a little less heavily than it does with their smaller rivals. Little teams understand that they may have few opportunities to compete at the highest level, and so they give it everything. They therefore probably win more often than you would predict based on ability alone.

NOTHING WORSE THAN NEW MONEY

Fans enjoy unbalanced modern soccer. Yet the complaints about its imbalance continue. The curious thing is that these complaints are relatively new, a product of the past fifteen or so years. Contrary to popular opinion, soccer was unbalanced in the past, too, but before the 1990s fewer people complained.

It is a fantasy that Europe was ever a very balanced soccer continent. In smaller countries, clubs from the capital have tended to rule. The Italian league was always dominated by Juventus, Milan, and Inter, and the Spanish league by Barcelona and Real Madrid. By the 1980s Bayern

Munich controlled the Bundesliga, and in the postwar era English soccer has been dominated by Manchester United, Arsenal, and Liverpool. United's ten titles in the past twenty years may sound boring, but Liverpool won ten in twenty between 1969 and 1988. Almost all other clubs are so firmly excluded from power that even giant Newcastle has not won the title since 1927. The imbalance in England as in all European leagues was reinforced by the European Cup (now the Champions League), which handed the dominant teams more money.

The old European Cup was seldom much fairer than the Champions League is now. We saw earlier in the book that only between 1970 and 1981 did clubs from modest-size towns regularly win the trophy. Usually, the cup went to the biggest provincial cities, or to Madrid. Even Platini admits, "For forty years it's been the biggest clubs that won the Champions League; when I played, too. With or without homegrown players, it was Real Madrid, Liverpool, Manchester, Juventus who won. English clubs won the cup ten times in a row, I think. No? In the 1980s."

Oh, dear. Platini is not going to win any bar quizzes anytime soon. In fact, English clubs won six straight European Cups from 1977 through 1982. But his point stands: inequality in European soccer is nothing new.

Platini smiles, thinking again of that English dominance in the 1980s: "It's funny. There were no great debates then, saying, 'We have to change everything.' Today it's the money that makes the difference."

That is precisely the point. Today's inequality in soccer bothers people not because it is unprecedented, but because it is more driven by money than it used to be. In the old days, a middling soccer team could suddenly enjoy years of dominance if it happened to hire an excellent manager who signed excellent players. That's what happened in the 1970s to Liverpool under Bill Shankly, or to Nottingham Forest under Brian Clough. Today, a middling team can suddenly enjoy years of dominance if it happens to be bought by a billionaire who hires an excellent manager who signs excellent players. That is what happened to Chelsea under Roman Abramovich, and what may happen to Manchester City under Abu Dhabian rule. So inequality in soccer, as well as not being boring, is not even new. All that's new is the money.

Many people tend to feel that inequality becomes unfair when it is bought with money. It disgusts them that Chelsea (or the New York Yankees) can sign the best players simply because it is a rich club. This is a moral argument. It's a form of idealistic egalitarianism, which says that all teams should have more or less equal resources. This stance may be morally right (we cannot judge), but it is not a practical political agenda, and it probably doesn't reflect what most soccer fans want. Spectators vote with their feet. It's certainly not the case that millions of them are abandoning the Premier League because the money offends them. Based on the evidence of what they go to watch, they want to see the best players competing against each other. Many people will say they find Manchester United evil. Not many seem to find them boring.

COUCH POTATOES AND
THE STRUGGLE FOR WORLD DOMINATION

Sometime in the early 2000s, when Paul Tagliabue was NFL commissioner, he told the team owners something like this: "You have to ask yourself, 'Do you want a potential fan base of 400 million or 4 billion in twenty or thirty years?'" His point was that if they wanted 4 billion, they'd have to find them abroad.

That was when the sporting struggle between the American and British empires finally got serious. The NBA had been trying to conquer the world since the 1980s, but at last the NFL plunged in, too. It now plays games each year in London and Toronto, and that may be just a first step.

The market in sports fans is becoming more global. This means that a century-old model of fandom—the man who supports the hometown team he inherited from his father—is collapsing. The new globalized sports fan will happily snub his local domestic league. If you live in London and you like football, you probably support an NFL team rather than some bunch of no-hopers playing on a converted rugby field a few miles from your house. Similarly, if you live in the US and like soccer, you are more likely to support Manchester United than your local MLS team, which in any case may be hundreds of miles from your house. Even in Argentina, with its great historic soccer clubs, people increasingly watch United on TV. That's all the more true in the US, China, or Japan, countries whose soccer fans mostly came of age during the second wave of sporting globalization.

These people want to see the real thing. Global fans want global leagues. For most of them, that means the NBA, the NFL, or the Premier League. It was therefore wrong to imagine that Beckham could save American soccer by playing for the Galaxy. American soccer is alive and well and lying on the sofa watching Manchester United on the Fox Soccer Channel.

The Premier League is going to spread ever further, and the NFL will try to. This struggle won't be fought to the death. There is room for them both. "I personally don't know anybody who follows only one sport and nothing else," Kirkwood, the NFL's UK managing director, told us. "I don't think it's as competitive as it looks. We don't have a vision of being a top-three sport in Britain. If you go into a big-enough market, you can carve a niche. So you can be an Arsenal fan and a New York Giants fan."

Some Arsenal fans are going to become Giants fans, but probably a lot more Giants fans are going to become Arsenal fans. Long after the sun set on the British Empire, it is achieving a posthumous victory in sports.

PART II
The Fans

Loyalty, Suicides, Happiness, and
the Country with the Best Supporters

9

THE COUNTRY THAT
LOVES SOCCER MOST

Which country loves soccer most?

This might sound like a matter of the heart that is hard to measure, but in fact the data exist. Loving soccer expresses itself in three main ways: playing the game, going to the stadium, and watching soccer on television. We have international figures for all three.

First, a caveat: not all the numbers are reliable. There are lies, damned lies, and statistics, and statistics from outside the Western world tend to be even worse. We will therefore limit our quest to Europe. Using a bit of judgment, by the end of the chapter we will be able to say with some confidence which European country cares most about the game.

PLAYERS: OH, TO BE A TINY ISLAND

In 2006 FIFA tried to count how many people in the world played soccer. The "Big Count" came up with 265 million soccer players, more than 90 percent of them males. Some were registered with proper clubs. The overwhelming majority, though, were "unregistered occasional players" who kicked around with friends on playgrounds and beaches and five-a-side courts. The only way to find out whether these people played soccer was by asking them—or at least a tiny representative sample of them.

None of these obstacles put off FIFA. The organization is a bit vague about exactly how it got ahold of the figures, saying it used "the standard practice of a questionnaire as well as an online tool." It also threw in its Big Count 2000, plus a UEFA survey and other "internal analyses," to "supplement missing data from associations and for plausibility purposes." Reading between the lines of the survey, it seems that more than a fifth of national FAs didn't even bother to take part. The whole endeavor was "scientifically observed by Lamprecht & Stamm SFB AG, a social research company based [handily] in Zurich."

Anyway, the most ambitious survey of soccer participation in history came up with a list of the most enthusiastic soccer-playing countries. China and the United States were found to have the most players (26 million and 24 million, respectively), but of course the key question is which countries had the largest proportion of their inhabitants playing. Figure 9.1 shows FIFA's list.

It's striking how many of the most enthusiastic soccer players live on little islands where there presumably isn't much else to do but play soccer and watch the waves roll in. The Faeroe Islands, Aruba, Barbados, Vanuatu, Anguilla, Bermuda, Iceland, and the Cook Islands (combined population about 1 million) all make the top twenty.

FIFA's list is interesting if true. Let's take the case of Mali, tenth on the list. This is a vast country with poor or nonexistent roads. It stretches much of the way across the Sahara. The average inhabitant has a daily income of about three dollars. Who worked out that 11 percent of the 12 million Malians play soccer?

Even the European figures are dubious. When the Mulier Instituut in the Netherlands set out to collate data on sports participation in the EU, it began its report with a series of caveats. Different countries use different methods to establish how many people play sports, it said. "Even within a single year, research conducted in one and the same

FIGURE 9.1 Most enthusiastic soccer-playing countries

Country	Percentage of population that plays soccer
Costa Rica	27
Germany	20
Faeroe Islands	17
Guatemala	16
Chile	16
Paraguay	16
Aruba	15
Barbados	13
Vanuatu	13
Mali	12
Anguilla	12
Austria	12
Norway	12
Slovakia	11
Sweden	11
Bermuda	11
Iceland	11
Netherlands	11
Ireland	10
Cook Islands	10

country can result in significant differences in the recorded figures for sport participation for up to 40 per cent."

Still, when it comes to European countries at least, FIFA's list probably has some value. That's because Europe is an organized sort of continent where a high proportion of the people who play soccer are actually registered with a club. We have a good idea of how many registered soccer players there are, because every one of them belongs to the country's soccer federation. So the number of registered players in a European country is a fair indicator of the total of all its soccer players. By way of reality check, let's see whether the European countries on FIFA's overall list of most enthusiastic players have a lot of *registered* soccer players, too.

It turns out that Germany, Holland, Austria, and Sweden—all in the top twenty of most enthusiastic soccer countries per capita—also figure in FIFA's top-twenty countries with the most registered players. Furthermore, Slovakia is in the top-twenty countries with the most registered *male* players, even though it has only 5.4 million inhabitants. In the Faeroes, Norway, and Ireland, also on FIFA's list of enthusiastic countries, a mammoth 10 percent or so of the population are registered players. Of the most enthusiastic European countries identified by FIFA, only Iceland lags a bit in registration: just 7 percent of Icelanders were registered players.

So it seems that the European countries in FIFA's top twenty per capita might really play a lot of soccer. Without treating the Big Count as gospel, let's give those nine Europeans countries on FIFA's list a little star each, and continue our quest to find the most enthusiastic of them all.

SPECTATORS: GREAT HORDES OF PEOPLE NOT GOING TO SOCCER MATCHES

Playing is one way of expressing a love of soccer. Going to watch matches is another.

When you think of packed soccer stadiums, you think of England. Visually, soccer crowds are one of the things that the English do best. And everyone knows that the Premier League has the biggest crowds in the world.

Well, the second-biggest crowds, anyway. The average attendance in the Premier League in the 2007–2008 season was 36,076. That was 3,000 fewer than went to see the average Bundesliga game that same year.

This fact comes from a weirdly addictive statistics Web site. The best thing about www.european-football-statistics.co.uk (run by the Dutchman Paul in 't Hout) is its collection of average attendance rates for almost every soccer league in Europe, though, sadly, not Albania. These stats give surprising insights into fandom, and help reveal which European country is maddest about the game.

The first thing you notice on the Web site is how much attendance figures fluctuate over time. The data on the site go back decades. Back in the 1980s, when Italian stadiums were as safe as family restaurants

and Serie A was the world's best league, Italians watched far more soccer than the English. In the 1984–1985 season the average crowd in
Serie A was 38,872. Napoli, for crying out loud, drew more than
77,000. Meanwhile, in the English first division in that year of Bradford and Heysel, only 21,080 braved the average league match.

How times change. By the 2007–2008 season, according to the
stats obtained by In 't Hout, Serie A and the Premier League had
pretty much changed places: the average Italian game drew only
23,180 people, a good 13,000 fewer than the Premier League. Juventus, the Old Lady herself, averaged just 20,930. Here are a few teams
in Europe that outdrew her that season: Genk in Belgium, Heeren-
veen in Holland, 1860 Munich (averaging more than 35,000 in Germany's second division), nine clubs in the English Championship
including both Sheffield sides, and Leeds United in League One, the
third tier of English soccer.

Many other European leagues also have sharp trends in attendance
over time, further evidence that fans behave much more like consumers
than like addicts. French, German, and Dutch attendance rates have
soared since the 1990s. In eastern Europe, by contrast, we see what
Brian Clough once called the great hordes of people not going to soccer matches. These empty stadiums are a postcommunist phenomenon.
Back in 1989, Nicolae Ceauşescu's last year in power, the average crowd
at a Romanian first-division match was officially 17,000, nearly as many
as in England at the time. Now it is just 5,800.

The least-popular league in Europe is Estonia's, with an average attendance in the country's top division of 184 (presumably not so hard to
count). And even given that Russian men are dying at such a startling
rate, it's disappointing that only 13,334 on average bother to turn up to
Premier League matches there. The English Championship (average:
17,483) is more popular, and in fact outdraws every league in Europe
east of Germany. The English and Germans are the only Europeans
who go to watch mediocre soccer in numbers.

However, as a friend of ours in Moscow once advised, "Never believe any Russian statistic." In 't Hout admits to doubting the stats for

certain eastern European countries. He gets particularly suspicious when the official attendance for a game is reported as a round number—3,000, for instance—as opposed to a precise one, like 3,142. He e-mails us, "In some leagues I found figures for one game of for example 2,000 and 5,000."

The western European data tend to be more reliable. Even there, though, there are doubts. In England, is the attendance the number of people who actually went to the game or the number who held tickets for it? After all, many season-ticket holders skip some matches. At a small club at the end of a disappointing season, they might have trouble passing on their tickets. In countries such as Italy, ticket sellers have been known to wave through hundreds of scary-looking away fans without anyone paying. Some turnstile attendants might slip the odd bribe into their pockets and click somebody through, or let in friends for free. Clubs in some countries might report a lower attendance number than the real figure, to reduce the tax they pay on their ticket income. Anyway, there's often nobody assiduously counting butts in seats.

Still, the figures on In 't Hout's Web site do tell us something. Most of them are not made up. Especially in western Europe, they probably correlate to a large degree with the number of people who actually went to games. And we can accept the general finding that eastern European crowds are low. A glance at the pictures on TV tells us that. Admittedly, we can't make a precise ranking of average crowds in all European countries, but we can identify a few countries where attendance at soccer seems to be particularly high as a share of their populations.

The way to identify these hot spots is first to count the combined average crowds for the main professional divisions in each country. Let's start with the largest European countries, which typically have three serious divisions each. England has four, but so as to compare it to France, Germany, Italy, and Spain, we will analyze only its top three divisions.

The sixty-eight English league clubs in those three divisions averaged about 1.3 million spectators between them in 2007–2008. (The clubs in League Two had another 104,000 in total, too few to make much difference to the national total.) That is, over two normal match days, in which every club played at home at least once, you would expect 1.3 million people to show up in England's top three divisions. That is by no means a precise figure, but it is probably a decent indication.

We then divided that spectator average by the country's population. England has 51 million inhabitants; 1.3 divided by 51 = 0.025. That means that the total combined spectator average of English clubs equals 2.5 percent of the English population.

It turns out the English are the most enthusiastic stadium-goers of all the large European countries. Figure 9.2 shows the (very rough) stats for the top three divisions of each big country.

FIGURE 9.2 Total spectator average as percentage of population, part 1

Country	Total spectator average as percentage of population
England	2.5
Spain	1.9
Germany	1.5
Italy	1.2
France	0.9

Spain's average included only the top two divisions—all that In 't Hout's Web site had. However, in the other large countries the crowds for the third division added only between 0.1 and 0.2 percent to the national total.

So far the English have lived up to their reputation as great consumers (if not players) of soccer. But when we compare them to the smaller western European nations, their spectating becomes less spectacular. The Scots, for one, are much more eager watchers of soccer. The average Scottish Premier League match drew a crowd of 15,580 in 2007–2008, which is not bad for a country of 5.1 million people. If the English went in equal proportions, taking into account the fact that the English Premier League has eight more teams than Scotland's, the average top-flight English match would draw a crowd of about 90,000.

You might even say that the English are somewhat lackluster fans, given that they have the best teams on earth playing on their local fields. On the other hand, they also have to pay the highest ticket prices on earth.

The Scots are among the European spectating elite, if not at the very top. Figure 9.3 shows the European countries whose inhabitants, according to www.european-football-statistics.co.uk, are most inclined to watch professional soccer.

FIGURE 9.3 Total spectator average as percentage of population, part 2

Country	Total spectator average as percentage of population
Cyprus	4.8
Iceland	4.4
Scotland	3.9
Norway	3.7

For Scotland and Norway, we counted attendance figures in the top two divisions; for even smaller Cyprus and Iceland, only the top one. All the clubs in the Icelandic top division put together had a total average attendance of just 13,284, about the same as Bradford City all by itself. However, that was pretty good for a country of just over 300,000 people who were also busy buying up the world's subprime mortgages and running West Ham at the time.

It would be silly to treat these figures as exact to the decimal point. On the other hand, these are countries that tend to produce fairly reliable statistics. Norway is wealthy and hyperorganized. Iceland was wealthy until it discovered subprimes, and it remains hyperorganized. Scottish soccer has modern stadiums and voracious marketing officials, who keep elaborate electronic databases of their supporters. They have a pretty good idea of how many come to matches. Paul in 't Hout says he considers the Norwegian, Icelandic, and Scottish attendance data quite reliable, because they are reported as exact figures—3,921 or 5,812 spectators. He is more suspicious of Cyprus, where the figures are reported as round numbers like 2,000 or 9,000. Also, he admits, "I only have one source in Cyprus and so I cannot verify the figures."

Still, we can say with some confidence that these top four nations love going to watch soccer. Their position at the top of these rankings is not a one-shot deal. When we did this exercise in 2001, Cyprus was also in first place, and Scotland's lead over England was as large as it was in 2008. People in these countries watch in astonishing numbers, given how poor their leagues are. To quote Nick Hornby, marveling at the thousands of people who watch even the most pathetic English clubs, "Why, really, should anyone have gone at all?"

Each of the top four gets a star in our quest to find Europe's most enthusiastic soccer nation. Two of the top four—Norway and Iceland—also appeared in our very cautious list of the countries that played the most soccer. They now lead the pack with two stars each. The other eager playing nations had unspectacular average crowds, with the Netherlands the best of the lot at 2.5 percent of the country's population. As for the Faeroes, even In 't Hout doesn't have the attendance figures.

NATIONS OF COUCH POTATOES:
THE MOST POPULAR TV PROGRAMS IN HISTORY

In our quest to establish which country cares most about soccer, one statistic towers over all the others: TV viewing figures. After all, relatively few people actually play soccer—seldom more than 10 percent of a country's inhabitants—and even fewer watch it in stadiums. In any case, we have seen the flaws in the data for playing and spectating. But we do have good figures for the most popular way to consume soccer: watching World Cups and European championships on TV. Viewing figures are the final piece of evidence to assess before we can name the most soccer-mad country in Europe.

TV ratings have plunged over the past thirty years. Once upon a time only the BBC broadcast in Britain, and so every program the BBC aired had a market share of 100 percent of viewers. Then television expanded: first came other free channels like ITV and Channel Four, and later satellite and broadband cable. Audiences in all rich countries splintered among the different channels. The share that any one show could command slumped. In the US, for instance, thirty-six of the top forty-five shows ever aired were shown before 1990. But here's the thing: all the top nine American programs after 1990 were sports events. Seven were Super Bowls, and the other two were ladies' figure skating events from the 1994 Winter Olympics, which people watched because they knew that one American skater had paid someone to hobble her rival on the national team. Only sports could still unite Americans on the sofa.

It is the same in Germany, where seven out of the eight highest-rated programs of all time involve the German soccer team playing in a major tournament. In Britain only the 1966 World Cup final and the 1970 FA Cup final replay between Leeds and Chelsea make the top eight. Still, here too big soccer tournaments provide some of the communal glue once supplied by trade unions, churches, and royal weddings. Possibly the best chance English people get to bond with each other nowadays, unless they are weeping over the passing of a reality-TV star, is during a World Cup.

Big soccer matches have that sort of unifying role in most European countries. Their appeal goes beyond men. Forty percent of the global audience for Euro 2004 was female. In fact, it is the long-term rise in female viewers that has made televised soccer more popular than ever before.

Before we can work out which country watches most soccer on TV, we need to separate the reliable viewing data from the false ones. Organizations like FIFA and the International Olympic Committee report the highest numbers they can. The more TV viewers an event attracts, the more advertising that will flow to the event, and the more that broadcasters will pay to screen it. Hence the improbable tallies that organizers sometimes cite for their games. According to FIFA, a cool 715 million people watched the World Cup final in 2006. Even this claim looks modest compared to the 1.5 billion who supposedly saw the opening ceremony of the Commonwealth Games in Melbourne. What to believe?

This is where Kevin Alavy comes in. Alavy is head of analytics at Futures Sport & Entertainment. His job is to sit in London working out how many people really watch different sporting events, though in fact he is far more charming than that description implies. This is how he defines his work: "Very simply, are these sports events worth the massive investment that they typically cost, and how can my clients get even more value from their association with sport?"

Alavy can both explain how the inflated numbers were invented and give advertisers (and some of the rights holders) the more reliable estimates they need. He also extracts trends from the mountains of broadcasting data that exist nowadays. For this book, he gave us some insight into the data he has been gathering on World Cups and European championships since 1998. Using it, we can identify the most fanatical soccer nation in Europe.

Around the world, TV data are extrapolated from the viewing habits of a sample of the population—in the US, about 10,000 people. Individuals used to get paid a small fee to keep a diary of their TV consumption. Then came the "people meter": a little electronic box attached to a TV set that allows each person in a household to indicate when they are watching. Invented in Britain, the people meter is now used in most wealthy countries to measure viewing. Alavy calls it "the gold standard of global media research."

To see how "people meter" data differ from the inflated data, consider the Super Bowl. It is indisputably the most watched event in the US. The last ten Super Bowls have been the ten most watched American TV programs of the last decade. But exactly how watched were they? Figures of 750 million to 1 billion global viewers per game get cited. Instead, using the "people meter" data, Alavy puts a typical Super Bowl's average live audience at about 100 million viewers, or about one-third of all Americans excluding the under-five set. (That is a mammoth figure, except when compared to the viewing figures for big soccer games. For instance, six matches at Euro 2004 drew a larger live global audience than that year's Super Bowl.) The inflated figure of "750 million to 1 billion" is not an outright lie. Rather, it is a reasonable guess as to the number of people in the world who could have watched the Super Bowl on TV because they subscribe to the right channels.

Using the "people meter," Alavy has collected verifiable viewing figures for sports in fifty-four countries. Thirty-one of the countries on his
list are in Europe, twelve in Asia, ten in the Americas, and only one
(South Africa) in Africa, a continent where there is almost no serious
measurement of viewing habits. Many poorer countries still use diaries
rather than people meters. Sadly, there are no reliable viewing figures
either for Cyprus, Iceland, or Scotland, three of the four European
countries with the highest relative attendance rates in stadiums. Cyprus
and Iceland are too small for Futures Sport & Entertainment to have
bothered to measure their viewing habits, and the Scottish figures are
lumped together with Britain as a whole. Even so, for thirty-three of
Alavy's fifty-four countries, we have figures for at least four of the six
major soccer tournaments covered since the World Cup of 1998.

The viewing figure Alavy uses for any given game or event is the
"average program audience." That is the average number of viewers
during the entire event, rather than the peak figure, which would typically be one and a half times higher, or the "reach," which includes anyone who caught at least three minutes.

Alavy reports the viewing figure for any game as a percentage of all
the people in each country who live in households with TV sets. In
most European nations almost every household has owned a set since
the 1970s. However, that is not true in less developed nations. Only
about a quarter of India's population of 1.1 billion, for instance, lives in
households with TVs.

Alavy's collection is a treasure chest: thousands of TV ratings covering hundreds of games between national teams screened in fifty-four
countries since 1998. However, there is an obvious problem: Germans
probably watch a lot of games involving Germany, and Germany has a
pretty good record; how to compare the viewing figures of the successful Germans with the not-quite-so-successful English? Indeed, how to
compare German viewing of Euro 2008, where their team made the
final, to viewing by the English, whose team didn't even qualify? Or to
cite another complication: a casual fan who watches only his own national team is surely not to be compared to the fanatic who glues herself

to the sofa for every match of the tournament. Going one step further, viewers in Malaysia or Colombia who follow the Euro must surely be considered to have reached the acme of perfection in fandom.

There are other problems. The World Cup in Japan and Korea had disastrous TV ratings in Europe, because most games were played in the European late morning or at lunchtime. That is why FIFA was so keen to keep the World Cup of 2010 in South Africa despite all the problems there: Johannesburg is usually just one hour ahead of central European time, making it ideal for European viewers. It's less convenient for Americans. In all the agonizing over the refusal of Americans to watch soccer on TV (as opposed to playing it, which American children do in great numbers), an obvious but overlooked explanation is that most of the best games are played in Europe at times when most Americans are working.

We also need to control for the significance of each match. Obviously, the final will draw more viewers than a group match, but how many more?

In short, no two of our thousands of ratings are strictly comparable. Happily, there is a way to control for the differences, and so to strip down to the essence of TV fandom. We can expect viewing levels in every country to rise for the final of a tournament. We can also expect an uplift when the country's own national team plays, or when a game is shown in prime time. Once again, we need to wheel out the technique of multiple regression. A reminder: multiple regression is the mathematical formula for finding the closest statistical fit between one thing (in this case TV viewing figures) and any other collection of things (here time of match, who is playing, and so forth). When you have many observations—like the thousands we have here—the regression technique is extremely powerful. Not only does it give you a precise figure for the influence of one factor on another, but it can also tell you how reliable that statistical estimate is. For example, the regression can show that playing a game in prime time will add, say, 4 percent to the size of the audience, and it can also say that the probability that this estimate is mistaken is less than 1 percent.

Running a regression will allow us to isolate each contributory factor—such as kickoff time—and measure its impact on attendance. Not only will this tell us a great deal about what attracts viewers to televized soccer, but the final figure that we are left with after these regressions consists of two parts. One part is what is called a "random error": that which we cannot explain because we know too little about what happened on the day. The other part, though, is a "fixed effect": an estimate of the viewing share that a soccer match will achieve in a given country, stripped of all other characteristics like kickoff time, identity of teams, stage in the tournament, and so on. The "fixed effect" is what we are after. The size of the fixed effect in each country will tell us how eager that country is to watch international soccer on TV.

The method works like this: Our data show that the "fixed effect" for the UK is 6.98. This means that just under 7 percent of all British households with TV sets will watch a World Cup or European championship game, regardless of its characteristics. Seven percent is the proportion of Brits that we can expect to have watched, say, Tunisia versus Saudi Arabia at the World Cup of 2006. However, if the game is played in the middle of prime time (meaning a kickoff between 7 p.m. and 8:45 p.m.), the total of British viewers rises by about 4.3 percent. If the game is a semifinal, viewing goes up another 5.6 percent.

So our regressions would lead us to estimate the British audience for each World Cup semifinal in 2006 at 16.9 percent: the core audience of 7 percent would have risen by 4.3 percent because each game kicked off in prime time, and by another 5.6 percent because it was a semifinal. The actual viewing figures for each game were within 2 percentage points of our estimates.

By no means perfect, but over the hundreds of games seen in fifty-four countries, the errors are relatively small. The average rating figure for each game taken across all fifty-four countries is 8.6 percent. Again: that is the proportion of households with TV sets that watched the game. For more than three-quarters of our estimates, the error was smaller than half this number. So while we cannot place too much weight on any single estimate for a particular match seen in a specific country, overall the regression summarizes the data pretty well. The regression captures just over two-thirds of the variation in viewing figures. The remaining third of the variation is due to unexplained random factors.

Before we ask which countries are the biggest soccer couch potatoes, let's pick apart the other regression effects for what they tell us about fandom. We found that only two time-of-day effects mattered: games played during "sleep time" (midnight to 5:40 a.m.) reduced the average audience by 3.6 percentage points, while prime time added about 4 percentage points depending on the exact time.

The significance of a match was crucial. In the group stages, if one or both teams playing in the third match were already knocked out, the TV rating fell. If both teams were out, the game lost 4.7 percentage points of its rating—a giant loss, since a rating of 4.7 percent is usually enough to keep a series on TV in the first place.

Yet when one or both teams in a third group game had nothing much to play for because they had already qualified for the next round, viewing figures barely fell. Soccer is soap opera. We watch it because of the story that unfolds after the game, not just because of the game itself. As long as a team is still in the tournament, its story continues.

Viewing figures rise steadily for each round of a tournament. The World Cup's round of sixteen adds 1.4 percent to the audience, while quarter-finals add 2.5 percent, semifinals 5.6 percent, and the final itself 10.1 percent. Even the match for third place, often mocked as meaningless, raises audiences by 4.9 percent—only slightly less than the semifinal effect. The UEFA dropped the third place play-off from the European championship in 1984 because the game was thought to be boring. Perhaps the UEFA should reconsider.

Besides time and significance of the match, a third effect sometimes matters: who is playing. Brazil is everybody's "second team." Despite getting duller since 1970, it still commands a viewing premium of 2.2 percent whenever it plays. Weirdly, only one other team consistently enhanced viewing figures across all fifty-four nations in Alavy's database: not Italy or Holland or Argentina but, yes, England. Its games boost global TV ratings by 1.4 percent.

To sum up, imagine a World Cup final played in mid–prime time between England and Brazil. This would add 10.1 (the final effect) + 4 (prime time effect) + 1.4 (England effect) + 2.2 (Brazil effect) = 17.7 percent to average viewership expected in any country.

There is one last factor to consider: nationalism. Its effect is enormous. For any game, for any country, broadcasting the national team added an average of 17.9 percent to the audience. It appears that for the average person on earth, simply watching his own national team in a humdrum group match is more attractive than watching England versus Brazil in the World Cup final. People who love soccer are vastly outnumbered by nationalists who tune in only for "our boys."

If England did play Brazil in a World Cup final in prime time, how many Britons would watch? Our model would predict 7 percent (the core audience) + 17.9 (the nationalist effect) + 16.3 (the prime time, final, and "Brazil" effects) = 41.2 percent. That would equal about 25 million viewers. In fact, this is almost certainly an underestimate, partly because it wouldn't count the people watching in pubs and other public places. Predictions about events that are both extremely rare and important are inevitably subject to wide margins of error. The same problem afflicts forecasting in financial markets: no statistical model can accurately predict a crash in the stock market. We have a good idea of how regular "small" factors like the time of day will affect viewing figures. We are much less precise about the effect of big one-shot deals like the country's own national team playing a final.

Now we can finally open the last door: after correcting for all incidental factors, which country has the highest TV ratings for World Cups and European championships?

And the winner is: Croatia! Alavy notes that Croat passion goes beyond soccer. "They also have very high ratings in other major sporting events," he says. For instance, when Croatia and Spain met in the world handball final in 2005, average ratings in Croatia were nearly four times higher than in Spain. This enthusiasm may stem from having recently fought for independence in a nationalist war, or it may just be because Croatia has excellent sports teams.

FIGURE 9.4 The biggest soccer couch potatoes

Team	Core TV viewing rating for soccer as percentage of households with TV sets
Croatia	12.4
Norway	11.9
Netherlands	11.5
Uruguay	10.7
Denmark	9.1
Serbia	9.0
Ecuador	9.0
Brazil	8.8
Korea	8.7
Sweden	8.6
Germany	8.6
Hungary	7.9
Italy	7.8
Argentina	7.4
Indonesia	7.3
Singapore	7.1
Romania	7.1
UK	7.0
Lebanon	7.0

The other European countries that watch most international soccer—the Norwegians, Dutch, Danes, and Serbs—also have relatively small populations and relatively big soccer reputations. Quite likely, small nations score high in our rankings because they tend to be more interested in what is going on outside their borders than big nations like France or Mexico. Alavy notes, "To have high average ratings, it's all about having a high tendency to watch when your local heroes are *not* playing."

Britain, for all its claims of soccer obsession, is stuck in what Alavy calls "a kind of midtable mediocrity," sandwiched in eighteenth place between Romania and Lebanon. Germany has the most eager couch potatoes among Europe's big countries. Eleventh in the table, they would be even higher but for their new custom of "Public Viewing," as they call it in their impenetrable language. Since 2006, Germans have taken to watching games in huge crowds on big screens outside. About 12 million Germans are estimated to have chosen this method to watch their team lose to Italy in that year's World Cup semifinal. The figure was particularly impressive given that the 30 million other Germans who watched at home were by themselves the country's largest-ever TV audience. At Euro 2008, the "Fan Mile" by the Brandenburg Gate in Berlin had to be closed nearly three hours before the final because it was already packed with nearly half a million singing and dancing "Public Viewers." Yet these people do not show up in Germany's "people meter" data.

Generally, European countries dominate at the top of Alavy's table. Partly this is because most World Cup games are played at times designed to suit them. There is a vicious (or virtuous) cycle here: because Europe has high viewing figures for soccer, World Cups are often held in Europe, and so European teams do well, and so European viewing figures are high. Only as Asians become richer and more enthusiastic about soccer might this change. Chinese prime time could be a very lucrative market one day.

The Asian figures in our table need a pinch of salt. The Korean figures are for 2002 to 2008, so they benefited from the "halo effect" created by South Korea's run to the semifinal in 2002. Moreover, in Korea and Indonesia the World Cup is hard to escape because it is often shown "wall-to-wall" on several channels simultaneously. By contrast, Singapore scores high partly because only the best World Cup matches are shown there—and partly because Singaporeans love betting on soccer the way other people love soccer.

Figure 9.5 shows Alavy's least-enthusiastic nations.

The Taiwanese must really not like soccer. Of course, even they cannot achieve a negative rating in practice, but our data combine the actual viewing figures with the specific characteristics of each game (time of day, group match, and so forth) to produce a final figure. In real life the Taiwanese numbers do not come out far from zero. Nor do the ratings for the US and India. An oddity of the US is that it is the only country where the nominal national team does not draw the highest ratings. At

FIGURE 9.5 Least-enthusiastic nations

Team	Core TV viewing rating for soccer as percentage of households with TV sets
Australia	2.7
New Zealand	2.5
Ukraine	2.1
Mexico	2.0
Lithuania	1.8
Canada	1.7
Latvia	1.6
India	1.2
US	0.6
Taiwan	-0.8

the World Cup of 2006, viewers there preferred watching Brazil, Italy, and Mexico. For many people living in the US, of course, these are their true "home" teams.

Americans, Indians, and Taiwanese at least have an excuse for not watching soccer: they prefer other sports. The nations that stand out among Alavy's least enthusiastic are Mexico and Ukraine, which both have respectable traditions in soccer. Indeed, several other countries that don't care much—Spain, Portugal, and France—have some of the best soccer teams on earth. Alavy notes that Spanish audiences for international sports tend to be relatively low, perhaps because of the country's regional divides. Basques, say, might not want to follow a Spanish "national" team. That may now be changing: Spanish viewing figures shot up during Euro 2008 even before they reached the final.

THE KING AS SPURS FAN:
THE COUNTRY IN LOVE WITH SOCCER

Heia, Norge. Norway is officially Europe's kookiest nation about soccer. "Why soccer in Norway?" ruminates Matti Goksøyr, the well-known Norwegian sports historian, when we break the happy news to him. He admits to being baffled: "Norway, a winter nation. Impossible to play soccer in wintertime. It's really a mystery."

Just to recap: here is how Norway won our award. In our first category, playing soccer, Germany and the Faeroes scored highest in Europe, at least according to FIFA. Austria, Norway, Slovakia, Sweden, Iceland, Holland, and Ireland followed at some distance.

Of these enthusiastic playing countries, the only ones that were also unusually enthusiastic on spectating were Norway and Iceland. Cypriots and Scots were avid spectators, too.

So our third category, TV viewing, had to provide the decider between the front runners, Norway and Iceland. It may be that the entire Icelandic population watches every game of every World Cup, even the goalless tie between Bolivia and South Korea in 1994, but if so we will have to wait a couple of years to find out, because the country introduced people meters only in 2007. However, Norway did register among the continent's leading couch potatoes as compiled by Kevin Alavy, alongside Denmark, Croatia, and Holland. (The Dutch and Icelanders deserve special mentions for scoring high in two of our three categories.)

Admittedly, Norway got a boost from the peculiarity of its TV market. Crucially, commercial TV took a long time to get going in the country. This means that Norwegians for a long time had fewer channels than most Europeans, which in turn means that programs on their few channels could get a larger share of the market than elsewhere. On the other hand, the Norwegian enthusiasm for watching soccer is remarkable because it isn't even their favorite TV sport. In surveys people claim to prefer biathlon and langlauf, says Knut Helland, a Bergen university professor. So Norway wins our award.

Why Norway, indeed? Early signs of dangerous obsession emerged in the late 1940s, when soccer pools were introduced into the country. Nowadays, the whole world gambles on soccer, but the Norwegian oddity was that even back then, all the games on the betting form were from English soccer. Goksøyr adds: "And that was self-evident. It had to be like that."

Had there been an award for most Anglophile country in Europe, Norway would probably have won that, too (with Scotland and Serbia finishing joint last). When the Germans invaded in 1940, it seemed natural that King Haakon and his Oxford-educated son Olav should flee to London, along with the Norwegian government. Later, after Olav became king he always tried to make an autumn pilgrimage to England, where as well as dropping in on his cousin Queen Elizabeth he did his best to catch a soccer match. Olav supported Arsenal, which must have made for awkward dinnertime conversation with his son Harald, the current king, who is a Spurs fan.

Obsession with English soccer is now almost a human universal—South African cabinet meetings sometimes get interrupted by quarrels over the previous night's English games—but Norway got there first. On Saturday, November 29, 1969, decades before the Premier League formulated its secret plans for world domination, Norwegian TV broadcast its first-ever live English soccer match: Wolves 1, Sunderland 0. Naturally, the nation was hooked. The Saturday game from England fast became an institution. "The most important thing in Norway when it comes to affection for soccer is the Saturday TV games," says Andreas Selliaas, special adviser to the Norwegian Olympic and Paralympic Committee and Confederation of Sports. "My father supports Leyton Orient. Why?"

Orient isn't even the worst of it. Tiny British neighborhood teams like Barnet and Rushden and Diamonds have Norwegian fan clubs. According to the *Aftenposten* newspaper, fifty thousand Norwegians belonged to supporters' clubs of British teams in 2003. King Harald was an honorary member of the Spurs fan club. That's not to mention the planeloads of Norwegians who commute to Old Trafford. And while doing all this, the Norwegians still find time to lead the world at winter sports.

When they turn to soccer, in summer, the local peculiarity is that Norwegian women play it almost as enthusiastically as men. The country's FA started hunting for women way back in the 1970s. Today about one in twenty-three Norwegian females is a registered soccer player, the highest proportion of any country on earth. In fact, Norway has more registered female players than England despite having less than a tenth of its population. Even the Norwegian FA's general secretary is a woman. It's surely no coincidence that the world's most developed country (according to the United Nations' rankings) is also the one that gives the largest share of its inhabitants the opportunity to play and watch soccer.

Norwegians have always played the game, and obsessed over English teams, but for decades they barely bothered to develop an elite game of their own. Their domestic league was amateur, and the national team's matches weren't shown live on the country's sole TV channel but were squeezed into a couple of minutes on the evening news. Then, in 1992, Norwegian TV finally embraced Norwegian soccer. The league took off, gaining status from returning Norwegian players who had actually clumped around the holy sanctum that is English soccer. Many fans adopted a local team to supplement their British one.

Now one in twenty-seven of Norway's inhabitants is a regular spectator in their domestic league, a mania untempered by the dreadfulness of the teams. Other Scandinavians, reflecting on Norway's love for almost any kind of soccer, like to say, "Norwegians are not used to much."

Norway's national team has seldom been up to much either, even if it is the only team in the world with a winning record against Brazil (played four, won two, tied two). The number of Norwegians that glue themselves to a World Cup is especially outrageous given that they usually don't have a dog anywhere in the race. Though Norway didn't qualify for Euro 2004, for instance, Norwegians watched more of the tournament than most nations that were there. If they ever get a decent team, they might really start to like soccer.

10

ARE SOCCER FANS POLYGAMISTS?

A Critique of the Nick Hornby
Model of Fandom

Just this one afternoon started the whole thing off—there was no
prolonged courtship. . . . In a desperate and percipient attempt to
stop the inevitable, Dad quickly took me to Spurs to see Jimmy
Greaves score four against Sunderland in a 5–1 win, but the damage had been done, and the six goals and all the great players left
me cold: I'd already fallen for the team that beat Stoke 1–0 from a
penalty rebound.

—Nick Hornby in *Fever Pitch* (1992),
on the origin of his lifelong love of Arsenal

Fever Pitch is a wonderful memoir, the most influential soccer book ever
written, and an important source for our image of the soccer fan. The
"Fan," as most Britons have come to think of him, is a creature tied for
life to the club he first "fell for" as a child. Hornby says his love of Arsenal has lasted "longer than any relationship I have made of my own

free will." But is Hornby's "Fan" found much in real life? Or are most British soccer supporters much less loyal than the world imagines them to be?

Let's start with Hornby's version, because it is the accepted story of the British Fan. As far as life allows, the Hornbyesque Fan sees all his club's home games. (It's accepted even in the rhetoric of fandom that traveling to away games is best left to unmarried men under the age of twenty-five.) No matter how bad his team gets, the Fan cannot abandon it. When Hornby watched the Arsenal of the late 1960s with his dad, the team's incompetence shamed him but he could not leave: "I was chained to Arsenal and my dad was chained to me, and there was no way out for any of us."

"Chained" is a very Hornbyesque word for a Fan's feelings for his club. Often, the Fan uses metaphors from drugs ("hooked") or romantic love ("relationship," "fell for"). Indeed, some adult Englishmen who would hardly dare tell their wives that they love them will happily appear in public singing of their love for a club, or for a player who would snub them in a nightclub if they ever managed to sneak past his entourage.

No wonder the Fan's loyalty to his club is sometimes described as a bond stronger than marriage. Rick Parry, as chief executive of the Premier League in the 1990s, recited the then dominant cliché about fandom: "You can change your job, you can change your wife, but you can't change your soccer team. . . . You can move from one end of the country to another, but you never, ever lose your allegiance to your first team. That's what English soccer is all about. It's about fierce loyalty, about dedication." (The Argentine variant: "You can change your wife—but your club and your mother, never.") Recently, in more metrosexual times, soccer officials trying to emphasize the strength of club brands have extended the cliché by one more attachment: you can even change your gender, the officials say, but not your club.

Ideally, the Hornbyesque Fan supports his local team (even if Hornby did not). This gives the Fan roots, a sense of belonging. In a wonderful essay on fandom in the highbrow journal *Prospect*, Gideon Rachman quotes an archetypal declaration of faith from a Carlisle Fan called Charles Burgess, who wrote in *The Guardian*: "There never was any choice. My dad . . . took me down to Brunton Park to watch the derby match against Workington Town just after Christmas 41 years ago—I was hooked and have been ever since. . . . My support has been about who we are and where we are from."

In real life Rachman is a commentator on international politics in the *Financial Times*, but his essay in *Prospect* is a key text in the British debate about fandom. It is the anti–*Fever Pitch*. In it, Rachman outs himself as a "fair-weather fan, an allegiance-switcher," who at different times in his life has supported Chelsea, QPR, and Spurs. So casual are his allegiances that he registered with FIFA for the World Cup of 2006 as an Ivory Coast supporter, figuring that he wouldn't face as much competition for tickets. He got into every round including the final. For the World Cup in South Africa, Rachman is a registered Paraguay fan.

He treats the passions of Hornbyesque Fans as slightly bizarre. After all, in England a Fan's choice of team is largely random. Few clubs have particular religious or class affiliations, and few English people have an attachment dating back generations to any particular location. Some children become fans of their local team, however terrible it might be, but if you live in Cornwall or Somerset or Oxfordshire you will have no local team, while if you live in London or around Manchester you have many. As Rachman asks, "Why devote a huge amount of emotion to favouring one part of west London over another?"

Nonetheless, the Hornbyesque Fan is a widely admired figure in Britain, at least among men. Whereas *fanatic* is usually a pejorative word, a *Fan* is someone who has roots somewhere. As we will argue later, this respect is connected to the quirks of British history: in that country, roots of any kind are in short supply.

However, our first question is: how true is the Hornby model of fandom? Does it really describe the way most British fans feel about their clubs?

THE CHINESE SERIAL FAN

Very little is known about sports fans who are not hooligans. The academics D. L. Wann and M. A. Hamlet estimated in 1995 that only 4 percent of research on sports concentrated on the spectator.

So we start our quest into the nature of fandom with only one or two fairly safe premises. One is that foreign fans of English clubs, at least, are not all monogamous in their devotion. Rowan Simons explains in *Bamboo Goalposts*, his book about Chinese soccer, that many Chinese fans support "a number of rival teams at the same time," and are always changing their favorite club. Simons adds, "So dominant is the serial supporter in China that it is quite rare to find a fan with a real unflinching loyalty to one team."

Stephanus Tekle, senior consultant at the market researchers Sport+Markt, has polling data to back up Simons's claim. Tekle says that since the late 1990s hordes of new fans around the world—particularly women—have come to soccer without long-standing loyalties. Many of these people appear to be "serial supporters" who probably support Manchester United and Liverpool, or Real Madrid and Barcelona, simultaneously. No wonder that clubs like United or Real keep changing their guesses as to how many fans they have worldwide. Figure 10.1 presents a few of United's estimates of the past few years.

FIGURE 10.1 **Fan estimates**

Year	Estimated Fans	Source
2003	75 million	Mori
2007	About 90 million	Manchester United
2008	333 million (including 139 million "core fans")	TNS Sport

None of these estimates is necessarily wrong. There may well be 333 million people on earth who have feelings for Manchester United. However, few of these "fans" are likely to be lifelong Hornbyesque devotees. Jose Angel Sanchez, now chief executive of Real Madrid, a club with its own share of foreign serial supporters, thought many of these serial fans might eventually evolve into Hornbys. He told us in 2003, "We used to say that the chances of changing your team are less than changing your partner or even your sex. But the way that people enter soccer in Asia is different: they enter through the stars. But this will not stay this way, in my opinion." Well, perhaps.

Still, surely British fans are a lot more loyal than those fickle Chinese, right? Unfortunately, polling suggests otherwise. In 2008 Sport+Markt found that Chelsea had 2.4 million "fans" in Britain. Again according to Sport+Markt, that represented a rise of 523 percent in the five years since Roman Abramovich had bought the club. Yet even that figure of 2.4 million represented a swift decline: in 2006, when, no doubt coincidentally, Chelsea had just won the league twice running, Sport+Markt credited the club with a mammoth 3.8 million British fans.

Again, we are not saying that Sport+Markt's figures were wrong. Rather, its premise was. To serial supporters, the question "Which is your preferred soccer club?" does not make sense. It presumes that everyone who likes soccer is a one-club Hornbyesque Fan. Instead, researchers should be asking, "Which *are* your preferred soccer *clubs*?" After all, a very large proportion of people who like soccer are polygamous consumers. One of the authors of this book, Stefan, as a Saturday-morning coach of grade school children, has seen the color of the shirts switch from red to blue and back again depending on who last won the league. Newly rising clubs like Chelsea are particularly prone to attracting short-term fans, says Tekle of Sport+Markt. Clubs like Liverpool or Manchester United with stronger brands tend to have more loyal long-term supporters, he adds. In fact, the likes of Manchester United are likely to have both far more Hornbys *and* far more casual fans than other clubs. But detractors of United tend to seize upon the hordes of casual fans and don't mention the Hornbys.

Hornby himself recognized the prevalence of casual fans in soccer. Many of the people who pop up briefly in the pages of *Fever Pitch* enjoy the game but are not wedded to a particular club. Hornby calls this type the "sod-that-for-a-lark floating punter," and speaks of it with admiration:

"I would like to be one of those people who treat their local team like their local restaurant, and thus withdraw their patronage if they are being served up noxious rubbish."

SPECTATORS: THE HARD CORE

We know there are, broadly speaking, two types of soccer fan: the Hornbys and the sod-that-for-a-lark floating punters. We know that the sod-that-for-a-lark people are heavily represented among foreign fans of clubs like United, and even seem to be pretty common in Britain. By 2006, if we can believe Sport+Markt's figures, about 90 percent of Chelsea's fans were people who had not supported them in 2003. No doubt a club like Hartlepool has a higher percentage of devoted Hornbys among its fans, but then clubs like Hartlepool don't have many fans anyway.

One might carp that the sod-that-for-a-lark lot are mostly just armchair fans, and that "real" fans tend to be Hornbys. However, it would be wrong to dismiss armchair fans as irrelevant. The overwhelming majority of soccer fans in Britain are armchair fans, in the sense that they hardly ever go to games. In a Mori poll in 2003, 45 percent of British adults expressed an interest in soccer. But we've seen that the total average weekly attendance figures of all professional clubs in England and Scotland equal only about 3 percent of the population. In other words, most of the country's soccer fans rarely or never enter soccer stadiums.

Fletcher Research, in one of the first serious market analyses of English soccer, in 1997 found that only about 5 percent of supporters of Premier League clubs attend even one match in an average season. If only a small minority of soccer fans get to the stadium at all, even fewer see every single home game for years on end, as Hornby did.

Most soccer fans are armchair supporters. If we want to unearth the Hornbys, we need to concentrate on the elite of fans who actually go to games: the spectators.

We know that in the Premier League at least, most spectators now watch every home game their club plays. Often they have to: at the most successful clubs, only season-ticket holders can get seats. Many of these regular spectators may be sod-that-for-a-lark punters at heart, who have been enticed by ticketing policies to show up every week. However, it's among this group of week-in and week-out spectators that we must look for the small hard core of lifelong Hornbys in English soccer. At moments of high emotion, the TV cameras like to zoom in on spectators in the stands—heads in hands, or hugging their friends—as if these people incarnated the feelings of the club's millions of supporters. They don't. Rather, they are the exceptions, the fanatical few who bother to go to games. Some of these spectators presumably support their club "through thick and thin," watching them unto eternity like Hornby does.

At least, that is the theory. But we studied attendance numbers in English soccer over the past sixty years, and found that even among the actual spectators, a startlingly high proportion appeared to be sod-this-for-a-lark types.

| |

Nobody seems to have tried before to calculate how many British fans are Hornbys. Yet the figures required to make some sort of estimate do exist. Paul In 't Hout's marvelous Web site, www.european-football-statistics.co.uk, has statistics on attendance rates and league performance for all clubs in the top four divisions of English soccer from 1947 through 2008. Using these data, we can find out (a) the annual mortality rate of soccer spectators; that is, how many of the people who watched last season don't come back the next? and (b) the sensitivity of new spectators to the success of teams. Do most newcomers flock to Chelsea when Chelsea wins the league?

Our model itself reveals some of the logic of soccer fandom. Generally speaking, teams cannot both have very loyal Hornbyesque Fans (that is, a low mortality rate) and at the same time be capable of attracting large numbers of new spectators when they are successful. If most of the crowd consisted of Hornbys who never gave up their seats, then when a team did well, there would be no room in the stadium for all the new fans who wanted to watch them. So floating supporters can get tickets only if the mortality rate of the existing spectators is high enough.

Previous studies have shown that a club's attendance tends to rise and fall with its league position. (The rare exceptions include Newcastle, Sunderland, and the Manchester City of the late 1990s.) In our data for the sixty-one-year period, there were 4,454 changes in clubs' league position. In 64 percent of the cases where the club rose in the league, its home crowd increased, too. In 74 percent of the "down" years, home attendance fell. This means that 69 percent of all cases confirmed the simple hypothesis that fans respond to performance. Simply put: there is a market in soccer spectators. The few academics who study fandom—most of them in the US—explain the fans' motives through the psychological phenomenon of "BIRGing," or "basking in reflected glory."

To account for the ebb and flow of English soccer fans, we have constructed a very simple model. It consists of two elements. First, there are the "new fans" coming into the game. New fans are estimated as the difference between the total attendance for the season and the number of loyal fans left over from the previous season. We divide new fans into two groups: the BIRGers, who come to watch the team depending on its success, and those who come for reasons we can't explain. We will treat these reasons as random factors, although each person probably had a good reason to come to the game at the time—a friend invited him, a girlfriend left him, or some such.

The second element of our model is the "loyal fans": those who came back from the previous season. Loyal fans are estimated as the difference between the total attendance for the season and the new fans entering the game. Of course, the difference between the loyal fans plus the new fans and last season's attendance is the "lost fans." We can think of these lost fans as falling into two groups as well: the BIRGers who were lost to the club because its performance declined, and those who were lost for other reasons that we cannot measure (got back together with girlfriend, took up DIY, or whatever).

Now, we are not claiming that we can identify new fans, loyal fans, and lost fans *individually*. However, we can identify these categories *in a statistical sense*, as groups. We know how many people are in each group, even if we do not know their names.

Our model produces two results. First, it gives us an estimate of the BIRGers: the fraction of new fans that a team can expect to attract as a result of the position it achieves in the league. Looking at the annual changes in attendance figures, we found that spectators are only mildly sensitive to a team's performance. Our estimates implied that the club that won the Premier League would attract 2.5 percent of all new spectators entering the league the next season. However, a team that finished at the bottom of the Premier League, or at the top of the Championship (English soccer's second tier), does almost as well: it attracts 2 percent of all the league's new spectators. Teams in the middle of the four divisions (that is, those ranked around forty-sixth in England) would attract 1 percent of all new spectators, while teams at the very bottom of the fourth tier would attract almost nobody. In short, while new spectators do like success, the vast majority of them are not simple BIRGers, glory hunters. Judging by the ebb and flow of crowds over the sixty-one years, most people seem to go to a plausible club playing near their home.

That is the profile of the newcomers. But how many of last year's crowd do they replace? What is the mortality rate of the existing spectators?

We know how many spectators each club lost or gained, season by season for sixty-one years. We also know how many spectators the league as a whole lost or gained. That means that for every club we can calculate the average percentage of last season's fans who did not come back for the new season. And the percentage that fits the data best: 50. Yes: on average in the postwar era, half of all spectators in English soccer did not take their seats again the next season.

Here's an example of how the model works (for the sake of simplicity, we have rounded up all numbers):

Bristol City finished the 2006–2007 season in second place in League One. The team's total attendance that season was 295,000. The total attendance for all four divisions was 29.5 million.

The next season,

(a) The total attendance for all four divisions rose by 400,000, to 29.9 million
(b) Bristol City came in fourth in the Championship—a rise of twenty-two places

So to calculate Bristol City's expected attendance in 2007–2008, we estimate their numbers of loyal "returning" fans and of new fans:

(c) Loyal fans are 50 percent of the previous season's total: 148,000
(d) New fans are calculated by estimating Bristol City's share (based on league performance) of new fans of the entire league:
(e) We predict 15.1 million new spectators for English soccer as a whole. That equals this year's total attendance (29.9 million) minus loyal fans from last year (50 percent of 29.5 million = 14.8 million) = 15.1 million
(f) Given that Bristol City finished twenty-fourth out of ninety-two clubs, we estimate its share of all new fans in the country at 1.7 percent. Its number of new fans should therefore equal .017 x 15.1 million = 257,000
(g) So Bristol City's loyal + new spectators = 148,000 + 257,000 = 405,000
(h) Bristol City's actual number for 2007–2008 was 374,000, so our model overestimated their support by 31,000, or 8 percent

Obviously, the model does not work perfectly for every club. However, taking all ninety-two clubs together, the estimate that fits the data best is that 50 percent of last season's fans do not return. To quote one analysis of the English game: "One Third Division club in the London area, for example, has an estimated 'hard core' support of about 10,000; this rises to 20,000 according to the team's success and the standing of the visiting team." These words were written in 1951 in an economic study of soccer published by the London-based Political and Economic

Planning think tank. They remain a good summary of English fandom as a whole since the war.

The discovery that half of all spectators—supposedly the hardest of hard-core Fans—do not bother to return the next season conflicts with the Hornby version of loyal one-club fandom. Yet it has to be true, to explain the churn we see in attendance numbers. Even a club like Leeds, noted for its devoted fans—while stuck in League One it draws significantly larger crowds than Juventus—has seen attendance fall from a peak of 755,000 in the 2001–2002 season to only 479,000 in 2006–2007.

Nor is this high mortality rate a new phenomenon. The sixty-one years of attendance data suggest that habits of English spectators have changed little over the years. While there has always been a hard core of Hornbys, it seems it has also always been the case that the majority of people who go to English soccer matches go only once in a while, and are often quite fluid about whom they choose to watch. And given that spectators are the fans who commit most time and money to the game, their devotion is in most cases really rather limited. The long-term devoted spectator of the kind that Hornby described in *Fever Pitch*, far from being typical, is a rare species. Committed one-club lifelong fandom is a beautiful theory—or as Gandhi supposedly said of Western civilization, "It would be a good idea." The reality is that in English soccer, the loyal Hornbys are a small shoal in an ocean of casual Rachmans. England may be a nation of fans, but it's scarcely a nation of Hornbys.

CALL YOURSELVES "LOYAL SUPPORTERS"

In 1996 Alan Tapp, a professor of marketing at Bristol Business School, started to develop a relationship with a struggling club in the Premier League. Over the next four years he met the club's executives, got to see the data they had on their supporters, and assembled a team of researchers who conducted hundreds of interviews with the club's fans. Tapp eventually published two papers about his work in academic marketing journals. Together they add up to a rare, marvelous study of how the spectators of one club actually behave. Tapp titled his second paper, published in 2004, "The Loyalty of Soccer Fans—We'll Support You Evermore?" with a very pregnant question mark. What he found was that fans talk loyal, but don't always act it.

The club Tapp and his colleague Jeff Clowes studied—based in a Midlands town that is quite easy to identify—was not very good. It wasn't the sort of outfit to attract many BIRGing glory hunters. Most of the club's spectators lived locally. In a survey in 1998, a massive 87 percent of them agreed slightly or strongly with the phrase, "I would describe myself as a loyal supporter."

Well, they would say that, wouldn't they? Tapp cautions that many of those 87 percent might have been engaging in "socially desirable responding." After all, almost nobody in English soccer calls himself a "sod-that-for-a-lark floating punter." That would be socially taboo. Most fans told Tapp and Clowes that they regarded sod-that-for-a-lark types as "pariahs." As Rick Parry said, English fans pride themselves on their loyalty.

Yet when Tapp studied how these spectators behaved, he found a peculiar lack of loyalty. To start with the most basic fact: the club's average crowd during the four-year period of study slipped from about 24,000 to just 16,000.

The average across the period was about 21,000, which broke down as follows:

- About 8,000 season-ticket holders
- Another 8,000 places typically filled from a group of 15,000 or so regular attendees
- 5,000 spectators who came from "a 'revolving door' of perhaps 20,000 'casual fans'"

Tapp came up with three labels for the different groups: "fanatics," "committed casuals," and "carefree casuals."

The "fanatics," or Hornbys, were mostly season-ticket holders. Tapp said some of these people were veritable "'soccer extremists' who had commitment to the sport and the club that is arguably unparalleled in other business or leisure sectors." There was the man who, when asked by Tapp's team what he would save if there were a fire in his house, replied, "Oh my [match] programs and tapes. No question. And my wife and kids of course." Many of the fanatics came from the local area, and had supported the club since childhood.

But even some of the fanatics were less fanatical than they claimed to be. Tapp found that each season, on average, 1,000 of the 8,000 season-ticket holders did not renew their seats and were replaced by new people. "Even at the fanatic end, the loyalty bucket had significant leaks," he remarked.

The team was playing badly. In one season, a mere 2 percent of fans proclaimed themselves "very satisfied" with performances. However, it was not the bad soccer that was driving them away. When Tapp's team asked people why they were letting their season tickets lapse, the lapsers usually talked about their lives away from the stadium. Fans were much more likely to give up their season tickets if they had children aged under five, or if they described their lives as "complicated."

So it wasn't that the lapsers felt less loyal to the team than the people who kept going year in, year out. They were simply at different stages in life. Some regular fans admitted that at one point in life "they had simply lost interest, often in their late teens and early 20s." Others had been "triggered" by a son or daughter to return to the stadium. Older people, whose lives were presumably more stable, were the most likely to renew their season tickets. Tapp surmises that they "have simply settled into some form of auto-repurchase." In other words, showing up to the stadium year in, year out is not a good marker of loyalty. Rather, it is a good marker of age.

At the far end of the scale from the "fanatics" were the "carefree casuals." Few of the carefree casuals claimed to be "loyal supporters." They were "soccer fans" rather than "club fans," they preferred to see a good game than a victory for their team, and they treated soccer as just one of several possible activities on a Saturday. Tapp noted, "Being club supporters is not part of their self-image."

Many of the "carefree casuals" sometimes went to watch other teams. Tapp reckons that it is probable that some regulars at Derby County, for instance, also occasionally show up at Nottingham Forest, even if this flies in the face of everything we are always told about English soccer fans.

Tapp adds that these people are mostly not "brand switchers," who switch from supporting one club to supporting another. Very few people love Derby one year, Forest the next, and Carlisle the year after. Rather, these adulterous spectators are engaging in what marketing experts call "repertoire buying": they purchase different brands at different times. In normal consumer markets in almost every country, "repertoire buyers" are thought to outnumber both "brand-loyal" and "price buyers." In soccer, too, repertoire buyers seem to be fairly common. Tapp says, "Repertoire fans took a lot of pleasure from a multiplicity of aspects of the game itself, while single club fanatics were less interested in soccer, more devoted to the club as an entity."

Tapp's middle group of spectators at the Midlands club was made up of "committed casuals." These people didn't go to every match, but they did tend to describe themselves as "loyal supporters." They rarely watched other clubs, and were more interested than the "carefree casuals" in seeing their team win. However, they too treated soccer as just one option for their Saturday. Tapp said they "perhaps have their soccer support in perspective with the rest of their lives."

In short, through close-up study very rare in English soccer, he has gotten past the cliché of "We'll support you evermore." Instead, he found the same thing that we did: there are some Hornbys in British soccer, but even among the self-proclaimed "loyal supporters" of an inglorious club they are outnumbered by casual fans who can take it or leave it. Tapp ends by cautioning sports marketers that for all the rhetoric of undying love pervading English soccer, fans' "loyalty cannot be relied upon." He urges marketers to "look under the surface of supporter loyalty," where they will find "loyalty patterns quite similar to, say, supermarket goods sectors."

HORNBYS, CLIENTS, SPECTATORS, AND OTHERS

It turns out that few British soccer fans are either Hornbys or BIRGing glory hunters. Rather, most have a shifting relationship with the club or clubs that they support. Of the 50 percent of spectators who do not show up at their club the next season, the largest group may well continue to be monogamous fans of that club. They just can't afford to go anymore, or are busy raising children, or have moved to another part of the country, or simply care less than they used to. The object of their love might not have changed, but the intensity has. Many of them may once have been Hornbys who fell for a team as an eight year old when their father took them to their first game. However, by the time they are twenty-eight or eighty-eight they are no longer the same fan. For many people, fandom is not a static condition but a process.

Other lapsed fans will have lost interest altogether. Others still might be shifting their allegiances to another club or clubs, because they have either moved to a new town, started to follow the team their kids support, or simply fallen for better soccer elsewhere. Rachman, for example, explains in his *Prospect* essay that he stopped supporting Chelsea "because they were a terrible team, followed by violent cretins."

Instead, he made a two-and-a-half-mile journey within West London and became a QPR fan. In the rhetoric of English soccer, the choice facing the supporter is often presented as stark: either he sticks with his local team, or he becomes a BIRGing glory hunter. However, reality is more nuanced. England is so densely stuffed with professional soccer clubs—forty-three within ninety miles of Manchester, as we saw—that many people can find a new local side without going to the trouble of moving.

Then there is a dirty secret of English soccer: many fans support more than one team. If you live in Plymouth, say, you might support Plymouth Argyle, Chelsea, and Barcelona, and have a fondness for a half-dozen other clubs, even though if Plymouth ever makes the FA Cup final, you will travel to Wembley decked out as a "lifelong Plymouth fan." Hornby himself, in *Fever Pitch*, supports Cambridge United as well as Arsenal. In fact, whereas the usual analogy for soccer fandom is idealized monogamous marriage, a better one might be music fandom. People are fans of the Beatles, or the Cure, or the Pixies, but they generally like more than one band at the same time, and are capable of moving on when their heroes fade.

As usual, it was Arsène Wenger who put this best. In January 2009 he gave Arsenal's Web site an untraditional account of how he thought fandom worked. "Soccer has different types of people coming to the game," he said. "You have the client, who is the guy who pays one time to go to a big game and wants to be entertained. Then you have the spectator, who is the guy who comes to watch soccer. These two categories are between 40 and 60 [years old]. Then you have two other categories. The first is the supporter of the club. He supports his club and goes to as many games as he can. Then you have the fan. The fan is a guy between 15 and 25 years old who gives all his money to his club."

Obviously, Wenger's four categories are not exact. Here and there they even conflict with those of Tapp and Clowes, who found that many fans *lose* interest between fifteen and twenty-five. But Wenger agrees with them that there are several different categories of spectator, of varying emotional intensity, and that people move between these categories depending largely on their time in life.

Ties in soccer fandom are much looser than the rhetoric of "We'll support you evermore" suggests. In that regard, they resemble ties of real existing marriage in Britain today. People still get married promising "till death do us part," but in 2000 there were 141,000 divorces in England and Wales, six times as many as in 1960. About half of all adults in England and Wales are not presently married. A lifelong monogamous marriage has become almost as rare as a lifelong monogamous love of a soccer club.

THE INAUTHENTIC NATION

Against all evidence, the stereotype persists that the typical British soccer fan is a full-on Hornby. No wonder it does, because the tiny percentage of fans who are Hornbys dominate the national conversation about fandom. Of course they do: they are the people who are most motivated to join the conversation. For them, following soccer is not just a hobby but an identity. Also, they make up a disproportionately large share of the soccer economy—"the most valuable customers," Tapp calls them—and so clubs and media listen to them more than to the sod-this-for-a-lark punters. And the Hornbys have a compelling story to tell. Most of the best stories are about love, and these are people who proclaim their love in public every week.

Yet there is a deeper reason the Hornby account of fandom has been so easily accepted in Britain. That is because it tells a story of roots, of belonging—a lifelong love of the club your father or grandfather supported before you—in a country that is unusually rootless. In transient Britain, the story of the rooted Fan is especially seductive.

Britain was the first country on earth where peasants left their native villages to go and work in rootless industrial cities. It was among the first countries where the churches began to empty; a tie that helps root people all over the world has long been extraordinarily weak among native Britons.

Even after the Industrial Revolution, the British never settled down much. The average Briton now changes his residence about once every seven years, more often than all other Europeans except the Nordics and the Dutch, according to a Eurobarometer survey for the European Commission in 2005. Many Britons emigrate. About 6 million of them now live outside Britain, as do another 50 million–odd people with British ancestry. Probably only India and China have produced diasporas that are as large and as widely spread, says the British government.

It is hard for people this transitory to build up deep ties of any kind, even to soccer clubs. Admittedly, Tapp and Clowes found that many of the "fanatical" supporters of the club they studied had spent their lives in the local town. But it was the club's "casual" fans, who "had often moved to the area as adults," who were more typical of British migratory patterns. For instance, Tapp and Clowes identified one group whom they called "professional wanderers": "people (mainly managers/professionals) who have held jobs in a number of different places who tended to strike up (weakly held) allegiances with local teams, which they retain when they next move." Like most Britons, the professional wanderers were too rootless to become Hornbyesque Fans. *None* of the casual fans interviewed by Tapp and Clowes "felt a close part of the local community, in contrast to the fanatics."

And Britons have suffered yet another uprooting: as well as leaving their place of birth, many of them have left their class of birth, too. This upheaval began on a large scale in the 1960s. As the economy grew, and more Britons stayed on at school and went to university, a mostly working-class nation turned into a mostly middle-class one. For many people this was a traumatic change. Their fathers had been factory workers, and now they were managers/professionals, with the different set of experiences and attitudes that entails. They lost touch with their roots. Naturally, many of them began to worry about their authenticity deficits.

In the 1990s, British soccer went upscale. The price of tickets jumped. In the food stands outside the stadiums, the proverbial middle-class quiches replaced the proverbial working-class pies. All these changes prompted endless laments for a lost cloth-capped proletarian culture from people who themselves somewhere along the way had ceased to be cloth-capped proletarians. They yearned to be authentic.

All this makes the true Fan a particularly appealing character to Britons. He is the British version of a blood-and-soil myth. The Fan has roots. Generations may pass, and blue collars turn to white, but he still supports his "local" team in what is supposed to be the "working-man's game." Many Britons who aren't Hornbyesque Fans would like to be. The Fan is more than just a compelling character. He is a British national fantasy.

11

A FAN'S SUICIDE NOTES

Do People Jump Off Buildings
When Their Teams Lose?

It is one of the eternal stories that are told about soccer: when Brazil gets
knocked out of a World Cup, Brazilians jump off blocks of apartments.
It can even happen when Brazil wins. One writer at the World Cup in
Sweden in 1958 claims to have seen a Brazilian fan kill himself out of
"sheer joy" after his team's victory in the final. Janet Lever tells that story
in *Soccer Madness*, her eye-opening study of Brazilian soccer culture published way back in 1983, when nobody (and certainly not female American social scientists) wrote books about soccer. Lever continues:

> Of course, Brazilians are not the only fans to kill themselves for
> their teams. In the 1966 World Cup a West German fatally shot
> himself when his television set broke down during the final game
> between his country and England. Nor have Americans escaped
> some bizarre ends. An often cited case is the Denver man who wrote
> a suicide note—"I have been a Broncos fan since the Broncos were
> first organized and I can't stand their fumbling anymore"—then
> shot himself.

Even worse was the suicide of Amelia Bolaños. In June 1969 she was an eighteen-year-old El Salvadorean watching the Honduras–El Salvador game at home on TV. When Honduras scored the winner in the last minute, wrote the great Polish reporter Ryszard Kapuściński, Bolaños "got up and ran to the desk which contained her father's pistol in a drawer. She then shot herself in the heart." Her funeral was televised. El Salvador's president, ministers, and the country's soccer team walked behind the flag-draped coffin. Within a month, Bolaños's death would help prompt the "Soccer War" between El Salvador and Honduras.

Then there was the Bangladeshi woman who reportedly hanged herself after Cameroon lost to England in the World Cup of 1990. "The elimination of Cameroon also means the end of my life," said her suicide note. In fact, if *The Hindu* newspaper in India is right, Bangladeshis have a terrible proclivity for soccer suicides. After Diego Maradona was thrown out of the World Cup of 1994 for using ephedrine, "about a hundred fans in Bangladesh committed suicide," said an article in the newspaper in 2006. (It would be fascinating to know *The Hindu*'s source.)

By now the notion that soccer prompts suicide has become a truism. It is often cited to show the grip of the game over its devotees, and as one reason (along with heart attacks on sofas during televised matches) the average World Cup causes more deaths than goals.

We found that there is indeed an intimate connection between suicide and soccer. However, the connection is the opposite of what is commonly believed. It's not the case that fans jump off buildings when their teams lose. Working with a crack team of Greek epidemiologists, we have found evidence that rather than prompting suicide, soccer stops thousands of people from killing themselves. The game seems to be a lifesaver.

| |

Each year about a million people worldwide commit suicide, estimates the World Health Organization. That is nearly twice the number that die of breast cancer, and five times as many as died in war in 2002. To use Germany as an example: in 2005, 10,260 Germans officially died by suicide, more than died in traffic accidents, illegal drugs, HIV, and murder and other violence put together. For Germans aged under forty, suicide was the second-most-common cause of death. And the reported figures for suicides are understatements, says the University Hamburg-Eppendorf, which runs a therapy center for people at risk of suicide: "There may be a significant share of unrecognized suicides among the death types labeled 'traffic accidents,' 'drugs' and 'causes of death unknown.'"

The suicide risk varies depending on who in the world you are. If you are an elderly, alcoholic, clinically depressed, divorced Lithuanian man, be very afraid, but suicide rates are relatively low in Latin America, leaving aside for the moment the issue of World Cups. Globally, women attempt suicide more often than men do, but most "successful" suicides are males. In the US, for instance, 80 percent of the 30,000 people who manage to kill themselves each year are male. For reasons that nobody quite understands, suicide peaks in spring when daylight hours are longest. In the Northern Hemisphere, that means May and June.

The question of why people commit suicide has preoccupied sociologists since sociology began. In 1897 Émile Durkheim, descendant of a long line of French rabbis, published his study *Suicide*. It wasn't just the first serious sociological study of suicide. It was one of the first serious sociological studies of almost anything. Drawing on copious statistics, Durkheim showed that when people lost their connection to wider society because of a sudden change—divorce, the death of a partner, a financial crisis—they sometimes killed themselves. He concluded that this particular form of suicide "results from man's activities lacking regulation and his consequent sufferings."

A few decades later, sociologists began to wonder whether man's sufferings might possibly include the results of sports matches. The numbers of suicides this caused might be significant: after all, most suicides are men, and sports give meaning to many men's lives. Frank Trovato, a sociology professor at the University of Alberta in Canada, was among the first to investigate the suicide-sports nexus. He found that when the Montreal Canadiens ice hockey team—once described as the national team of French Canada—got knocked out of the playoffs early between

1951 and 1992, Quebecois males aged fifteen to thirty-four became more likely to kill themselves. Robert Fernquist, a sociologist at Central Missouri State University, went further. He studied thirty American metropolitan areas with professional sports teams from 1971 to 1990, and showed that fewer suicides occurred in cities whose teams made the playoffs more often. Routinely reaching the playoffs could reduce suicides by about twenty each year in a metropolitan area the size of Boston or Atlanta, said Fernquist. These saved lives were the converse of the mythical Brazilians throwing themselves off apartment blocks.

Later, Fernquist investigated another link between sport and suicide: he looked at the suicide rate in American cities after a local sports team moved to another town. It turned out that some of the fans abandoned by their team killed themselves. This happened in New York in 1957 when the Brooklyn Dodgers and New York Giants baseball teams left, in Cleveland in 1995–1996 when the Browns football team moved to Baltimore, and in Houston in 1997–1998 when the Oilers football team departed. In each case the suicide rate was 10 to 14 percent higher in the two months around the team's departure than in the same months of the previous year. Each move probably helped prompt a handful of suicides. Fernquist wrote, "The sudden change brought about due to the geographic relocations of pro sports teams does appear to, at least for a short time, make highly identified fans drastically change the way they view the normative order in society." Clearly, none of these people killed themselves just because they lost their team. Rather, they were very troubled individuals for whom this sporting disappointment was too much to bear.

Perhaps the most famous recent case of a man who found he could not live without sports was the Gonzo author Hunter S. Thompson. He shot himself in February 2005, four days after writing a note in black marker with the title, "Football Season Is Over":

No More Games. No More Bombs. No More Walking. No More Fun. No More Swimming. 67. That is 17 years past 50. 17 more than I needed or wanted. Boring . . .

Thompson, an occasional sportswriter, loved football. One night during the presidential campaign of 1968, he took a limousine journey through New Hampshire with his least-favorite person, the Republican candidate Richard Nixon, and they talked football nonstop in the backseat. "It was a very weird trip," Thompson wrote later, "probably one of the weirdest things I've ever done, and especially weird because both Nixon and I enjoyed it." The reminiscence, in *Fear and Loathing on the Campaign Trail '72*, segues into an ominous musing on suicide, as a Nixon aide snatches away the cigarette Thompson is smoking over the fuel tank of the candidate's plane. Thompson tells the aide, "You people are lucky I'm a sane, responsible journalist; otherwise I might have hurled my flaming Zippo into the fuel tank."

"Not you," the aide replies. "Egomaniacs don't do that kind of thing. You wouldn't do anything you couldn't live to write about, would you?"

"You're probably right," says Thompson. As it later turned out, he was wrong. His ashes were fired from a cannon in Aspen, Colorado.

So much for suicides and North American sports. We know much less about the connection between suicides and European soccer. In one of the very few European studies done so far, Mark Steels, a psychiatrist at the University Hospital in Nottingham, asked whether Nottingham Forest's worst defeats prompted local suicides. He looked at admissions for deliberate self-poisoning to his hospital's accident and emergency department on two bad days for Forest: after the team's defeats in the FA Cup final of 1991 and the FA Cup quarter-final of 1992. He found that both games were followed by an increase in self-poisonings. After the cup final, the rise was statistically significant, meaning that it was unlikely to have happened by chance. Steels concluded that "a sudden disappointment experienced through an entire community may prove one stress too many for some vulnerable members of this community."

| |

All this is fascinating but inconclusive. For starters, the sample sizes of all these studies are pretty small. How many people are admitted to a Nottingham hospital for self-poisoning after a soccer match? (Answer:

ten in the twelve hours after the 1991 cup final, nine after the 1992 quarter-final.) How many people kill themselves in Cleveland in any given month? The other problem is that almost all these researchers pursued what you might call the Brazilian apartment-building hypothesis: that when people suffer a sporting disappointment, they kill themselves. Mostly, these are studies of the dogs that barked: people who did commit suicide.

But what if the relationship between suicide and sports is deeper than that? If sports give meaning to fans' lives, if sports make them feel part of a larger family of fans of their team, if fans really do eat and sleep soccer like in a Coca-Cola ad, then perhaps sports might stop some of these fans from killing themselves. We wanted to find out if there were dogs that didn't bark: people who didn't commit suicide because sports kept them going.

It so happens that we have a case study. Frederick Exley was a fan of the New York Giants football team, whose life alternated between incarcerations in mental hospitals and equally unhappy periods spent in the bosom of his family. In 1968 Exley published what he called "a fictional memoir," *A Fan's Notes*, one of the best books ever written about sports. Nick Hornby gave *Fever Pitch* the subtitle "A Fan's Life" in part as a tribute to Exley.

The Exley depicted in *A Fan's Notes* is a classic suicide risk. He is an alcoholic loner separated from his wife. He has disastrous relationships with women, alienates his friends, and spends months at a time lying in bed or on a sofa at his mother's or aunt's house. For a while his only friend is his dog, Christie III, whom he dresses in a mini blue sweatshirt like his own and teaches to stand up like a man. "Like most Americans," Exley writes, "I had led a numbingly chaste and uncommitted existence in which one forms neither sympathies nor antipathies of any enduring consequence."

Only one thing in life provides him with any community: the New York Giants. While living in New York City he stands on the terrace every home game with a group of Brooklyn men: "an Italian breadtruck driver, an Irish patrolman, a fat garage mechanic, two or three burly longshoremen, and some others whose occupations I forget . . . And they liked me."

When the Giants are not playing, Exley spends much of his time drinking alone. But when a game is on, he watches—depending on the stage of his life—with his Brooklyn group, or with other people in bars, or with his stepfather at home. Exley is the stepfather's eternal houseguest from hell, but "things were never better between us than on autumn Sunday afternoons": "After a time, hardly noticeable at first, he caught something of my enthusiasm for the beauty and permanent character of staying with someone through victory and defeat and came round to the Giants." Fittingly, the stepfather dies just before a Giants game: "Seated on the edge of the davenport watching the starting lineups being introduced, he closed his eyes, slid silently to the floor, and died painlessly of a coronary occlusion."

Inevitably, at one point in the memoir, Exley contemplates suicide. He has convinced himself he has lung cancer. Determined to avoid the suffering his father went through, he decides to kill himself instead. Drinking with strangers in bars, he gets into the habit of working "the conversation round to suicide," and soliciting their views on how best to do it. The strangers are happy to oblige: "Such was the clinical and speculative enthusiasm for the subject—'Now, if I was gonna knock myself off . . . '—that I came to see suicide occupying a greater piece of the American consciousness than I had theretofore imagined."

Only one thing keeps Exley going. The Giants are "a life-giving, an exalting force." He is "unable to conceive what [his] life would have been without football to cushion the knocks." The real-life Frederick Exley lived to the age of sixty-three, dying in 1992 after suffering a stroke alone in his apartment. He might never have gotten that old without the Giants.

There may be a great many Exleys around. The viewing figures we saw earlier in the book suggest that sport is the most important communal activity in many people's lives. Nearly a third of Americans watch the Super Bowl. However, European soccer is even more popular. In the

Netherlands, possibly the European country that follows its national team most eagerly, three-quarters of the population watch Holland's biggest soccer games. In many European countries, World Cups may now be the greatest shared events of any kind. To cap it all, World Cups mostly take place in June, the peak month for suicides in the Northern Hemisphere. How many Exleys have been saved from jumping off apartment buildings by international soccer tournaments, the world's biggest sporting events?

This is not just a rhetorical question. A study of soccer tournaments and suicide would bring together both an incomparably compelling communal event and a sample the size of several countries. So we set about finding the data.

We needed suicide statistics per month over several years for as many European countries as possible. These figures do not seem to be published anywhere. Luckily, we found out that the Greek epidemiologists Eleni Petridou and Fotis Papadapoulos had laboriously gotten hold of these data years earlier by writing to the statistical offices of several countries. A statistician who works with Petridou and Papadapoulos, Nick Dessypris, went through the numbers for us. He found that in almost every country for which he had numbers, fewer people kill themselves while the national team is playing in a World Cup or a European championship. Dessypris said the declines were "statistically significant"—unlikely to be due to chance.

Let's take Germany, the biggest country in our study and one that always qualifies for big tournaments. Petridou and Papadapoulos had obtained monthly suicide data for Germany from 1991 through 1997. A horrifying total of 90,000 people in Germany officially killed themselves in this period. The peak months for suicides were March through June.

But when Germany was playing in a soccer tournament—as it did in the Junes of 1992, 1994, and 1996—fewer people died. In the average June with soccer, there were 787 male and 329 female suicides in Germany. A lot more people killed themselves in the Junes of 1991, 1993,

1995, and 1997 when Germany was not playing soccer. In those soccer-free Junes, there was an average of 817 male and 343 female suicides, or 30 more dead men and 14 more dead women than in the average June with a big tournament. For both German men and women, the June with the fewest suicides in our seven-year sample was 1996, the month that Germany won Euro '96.

We found the same trend for ten of the twelve countries we studied. In Junes when the country was playing in a soccer tournament, there were fewer suicides. These declines are particularly remarkable given how much alcohol is consumed during soccer tournaments, because drinking would normally be expected to help prompt suicides. Only in the Netherlands and Switzerland did soccer tournaments not seem to save lives; these two countries saw very slight increases in the suicide rate during tournaments. In the other countries, the lifesaving effect of soccer was sometimes spectacular. Our data for Norway, for instance, run from 1988 through 1995. The most soccer-mad country in Europe played in only one tournament in that period, the World Cup of 1994. The average for the seven Junes when Norway was not playing soccer was 55 suicides. But in June 1994 there were only 36 Norwegian suicides, by far the lowest figure for all eight Junes in our data set. Or take Denmark, for which we have suicide tallies from 1973 through 1996, the longest period for any country. In June 1992 the Danes won the European championship. That month there were 54 male suicides, the fewest for any June since 1978, and 28 female suicides, the joint lowest (with 1991) since the data set began.

We have tried to make some very rough estimates of how many lives these tournaments saved in each country. "Lives saved" represents the decline in deaths during the average June when a country's national team is playing in a World Cup or European championship compared to the average June when the team isn't playing. Figure 11.1 shows the tally. The figures are negative for the Netherlands and Switzerland because more people killed themselves when their teams were playing than when there was no soccer.

FIGURE 11.1 Deaths during World Cup compared to average June

	Male lives saved	Female lives saved
Austria	9	−3
Czech Republic	14	6
Denmark	4	4
France	59	8
Germany	30	14
Greece	0	5
Ireland	2	1
Netherlands	−5	0
Norway[a]	[19 lives saved spread across both genders]	
Spain	4	1
Sweden	4	15
Switzerland	−1	−2

[a]The data for Norway were not broken down by gender.

The next question is what happens after a team is knocked out. Do all the people who had been saved from suicide by soccer then fall into a void and jump off apartment buildings? If so, you would expect a rise in suicides in the period after the tournament.

However, we found that in ten of our twelve countries, suicides *declined* for the entire year when the national team played in a big tournament. Only in the Netherlands did suicides rise in the year when the team played; in Spain the difference was negligible. But in the other ten countries, even after the team got knocked out and the euphoria ended, there was no compensating rise in suicide. To the contrary: it seems that the uniting effect of the tournament lasted for a while afterward, continuing to depress the suicide rate. For each of these ten countries, more lives were saved on average over the entire year than in June alone. Figure 11.2 contains our very rough estimates for lives saved over the entire year when the national team plays in a tournament ("lives saved" represents the decline in deaths during a "soccer" year compared to the average year). Very roughly, soccer tournaments in these periods appear to have helped save several hundred Europeans from suicide.

FIGURE 11.2 Lives saved by gender in "soccer" years

	Male lives saved	*Female lives saved*
Austria	46	15
Czech Republic	55	12
Denmark	37	47
France	95	82
Germany	61	39
Greece	9	13
Ireland	19	–10
Netherlands	–10	–1
Norway	[92 lives saved spread across both genders]	
Spain	2	–3
Sweden	44	16
Switzerland	20	2

We couldn't find any monthly suicide data for any of the British nations. However, the only two previous studies on this topic that we know of in Britain suggest that the lifesaving effect works there, too.

"Parasuicide" is a suicidal gesture in which the aim is not death but rather self-harm, or a cry for help. One example of parasuicide is taking an insufficient overdose. George Masterton, a psychiatrist in Edinburgh, and his coauthor J. A. Strachan studied Scottish parasuicides during and immediately after the World Cups of 1974, 1978, 1982, and 1986. Each time, Scotland had qualified for the tournament. Each time, Masterton and Strachan found a fall in parasuicide for both genders during the tournament that "has been sustained for at least eight weeks after the last game." The Scottish case is a pretty strong piece of evidence against the apartment-building theory of soccer suicides, because if there was ever an excuse for soccer fans to try to kill themselves, it was Scotland's performance at the World Cup of 1978. (Their fantasist manager, Ally McLeod, had boasted beforehand that they would leave with a "medal of some sort.")

Later Masterton and Anthony J. Mander studied the numbers of people who came to the Royal Edinburgh Hospital with psychiatric emergencies during and after the World Cups of 1978, 1982, and 1986. The researchers found "reductions in all illness categories during and afterwards (with the exception of alcoholism during)." The decline in emergencies applied to both genders, and was more marked after each World Cup than during it. For instance, there was a 56 percent fall in admissions of male neurotics in the weeks after a tournament.

The authors then tried to explain what was going on here:

> There are few outlets which permit a wide and acceptable expression of Scottish nationhood—sport is perhaps the most powerful, and [soccer] is the national game. . . . We would speculate that such a common interest and endeavour, fused with a surge of nationalism, might enhance social cohesion in the manner proposed by Durkheim to explain the decreased suicide rates that accompany times of war.

Social cohesion is the key phrase here. This is the benefit that almost all fans—potential suicides and the rest of us—get from fandom. Winning or losing is not the point. It is not the case that losing matches makes significant numbers of people so unhappy they jump off apartment buildings. In the US, fans of longtime losers like the Chicago Cubs and the Boston Red Sox baseball teams have not killed themselves more than other people, says Thomas Joiner, author of *Why People Die by Suicide*, whose own father died by suicide.

Joiner's article "On Buckeyes, Gators, Super Bowl Sunday, and the Miracle on Ice" makes a strong case that it's not the winning that counts but the taking part—the shared experience. It is true that he found fewer suicides in Columbus, Ohio, and Gainesville, Florida, in the years when the local college football teams did well. But Joiner argues that this is because fans of winning teams "pull together" more: they wear the team shirt more often, watch games together in bars, talk about the team, and so on, much as happens in a European country while the national team is playing in a World Cup. The "pulling together" saves people from suicide, not the winning. Proof of this is that Joiner found fewer suicides in the US on Super Bowl Sundays than on other Sundays at that time of year, even though few of the Americans who watch the Super Bowl are passionate supporters of either team. What they get from the day's parties is a sense of belonging.

That is the lifesaver. In Europe today, there may be nothing that brings a society together like a World Cup with your team in it. For once, almost everyone in the country is watching the same TV programs and talking about them at work the next day, just as people used to do thirty years ago before cable TV arrived. Part of the point of watching a World Cup is that almost everyone else is watching, too. Isolated people—the types at most risk of suicide—are suddenly welcomed into the national conversation. They are given social cohesion. All this helps explain why big soccer tournaments seem to save so many female lives in Europe, even though relatively few women either commit suicide or (before about 2000 at least) watch soccer. The "pulling together" during a big soccer tournament is so universal that it drags many women along in a way that club soccer does not. It may also be that during tournaments, some troubled women benefit from a brief vacation from male partners who are distracted by soccer.

Other than sports, only war and catastrophe can create this sort of national unity. Most strikingly, in the week after John F. Kennedy's murder in 1963—a time of American sadness but also of "pulling together"—*not one* suicide was reported in twenty-nine cities studied. Likewise, in the US in the days after the September 11 attacks, another phase of national "pulling together," the number of calls to the 1-800-SUICIDE hotline halved to about three hundred a day, "an all-time low," writes Joiner. And in Britain in 1997, suicides declined after Princess Diana died.

Joiner speculates that "pulling together" through sports may particularly suit "individuals who have poor interpersonal skills (often characteristic of severely depressed or suicidal persons)." You don't have to be charming to be a fan among fans.

In 1956 Frederick Exley was drunk, unemployed, and loveless in Chicago. He writes, "Though I had completely disregarded football my first year in that happy city, during the autumn of 1956, after losing my job, I once again found that it was the only thing that gave me comfort." At some point or other in life, we have all known how that feels.

12

HAPPINESS

Why Hosting a World Cup
Is Good for You

In the 1920s, the belief arose in the poor black Transkei region of South Africa that black Americans were going to arrive in airplanes to destroy the white men and save the chosen. This was supposed to happen in 1927.

Today in South Africa you can find a similar belief: that in 2010 the rich people of the world will arrive in airplanes and save the whole nation. On the day in May 2004 that South Africa was awarded the World Cup, locals celebrating in Soweto shouted, "The money is coming!"

Half the people you meet in Johannesburg have a scheme for 2010: buying apartments just to rent them out during the tournament, selling sausage and maize pudding outside stadiums, corralling peasant women to weave bead flags in the colors of all the participating teams. Much of South African conversation now is about such schemes, and in newspaper profiles, when a celebrity describes what he is working on, he generally adds, "The key thing is to be ready for 2010." The year has become a magic number, like the Year of the Beast, or 1927.

South Africans may sound as if they are on a collective space trip organized by the government and scheduled to end with a bump on July 12, 2010, the day after the final. However, they are merely expressing in extreme form a conventional belief: that hosting a big sports event can make a place rich. Whenever a country bids to host a World Cup or an Olympics, its politicians prophesy an "economic bonanza." They invoke hordes of shopaholic visitors, the free advertising of host cities to the world's TV viewers, the long-term benefits of all the roads and stadiums that will get built. No wonder that nowadays almost every country seems to want to host these events. The bidding to stage the World Cup of 2018 is the most competitive ever.

In fact, staging sports tournaments doesn't make you rich at all. The reason countries are so eager to host is an altogether different one: hosting makes you happy. Strangely, though, the wannabe hosts don't seem to understand their own motives.

| |

The 1989 movie *Field of Dreams* is a sentimental redemption story starring Kevin Costner as an Iowa farmer. Growing up the son of a baseball nut, the farmer had dreamed of being a baseball star. As an adult, he hears a voice telling him to build a baseball diamond on his cornfield. "If you build it, he will come" is the film's catchphrase. The moral: building stadiums where they do not currently exist is uplifting and good for you. This originally American idea has since spread to soccer in Europe.

There is in the US a small industry of "consultants" who exist to provide an economic rationale for "If you build it, he will come." In almost any city in the US at almost any time, someone is scheming to build a spanking new sports stadium. The big prize for most American cities is to host a major league team, ideally an NFL franchise, but if that can't be had, then baseball, basketball, or, if nothing else is going, ice hockey or at worst soccer. Hosting an American sports "franchise" has a lot in common with hosting a World Cup. Both the franchise and the World Cup are mobile beasts. Their owners are generally willing to move to whichever city or country offers them the best deal. In the US, owners of sports teams usually demand that the host city's taxpayers pony up for a stadium, with lucrative parking lots thrown in. All this is then handed over to the franchise owner, who also gets to keep the money he makes from selling tickets. About seventy new major league stadiums and arenas have been built in the US in the past twenty years. The total cost: $20 billion, about half of which came from the public. In New Orleans, for instance, the taxpayer paid for the Superdome but not for better levees.

In one typical case in 1989, seventy investors, including the son of the then American president, George H. W. Bush, paid $83 million for the Texas Rangers baseball club. The Bush group wanted a bigger stadium. Strangely for a phalanx of right-wing millionaires, it decided that local taxpayers should finance it. If that didn't happen, the new owners threatened to move the Rangers elsewhere. The people of the local town of Arlington duly voted to increase the local sales tax by half a percent, raising the $191 million needed for the ballpark.

The president's son George W. became the Rangers' managing director. Mostly, this just meant being the official face of the club. He would sit in the stands during games handing out baseball cards with pictures of himself. When he ran for governor of Texas in 1994, he constantly cited his experience in baseball. There wasn't much else on his CV at the time. He was duly elected, and decorated his Austin office with 250 signed baseballs.

In 1998 the Bush group sold the Rangers to Tom Hicks for $250 million. Most of the value was in the stadium that the taxpayers had built. Bush personally netted $14.9 million. He admitted, "When it is all said and done, I will have made more money than I ever dreamed I would make." Meanwhile, he was already beginning to parlay his governorship into a bigger political prize.

So the trick for American club owners is to persuade the taxpayer to cough up for stadiums. This is where economists come in handy. Economists like to say that people respond to incentives. Well, economists certainly respond to incentives. Anyone hoping to persuade taxpayers to pay for a stadium in the US commissioned an economist to write an "economic impact" study. By a strange coincidence, these studies always showed that the stadium would make taxpayers rich. (One book describing this racket is aptly called *Field of Schemes*.)

The argument typically went as follows: building the stadium would create jobs first for construction workers, and later for people who worked in it. Fans would flock in from all around ("If you build it, he will come"), and they would spend money. New businesses would spring up to serve them. As the area around the stadium became populated, more people would want to live there, and even more businesses (and jobs) would spring up. "The building of publicly funded stadiums has become a substitute for anything resembling an urban policy," notes Dave Zirin in his *People's History of Sports in the United States*.

The "economic impact" study then typically clothes this model with some big numbers. If you put your mind to it, you can think up a total in benefits that runs into the billions, whatever currency you happen to be working in. Best of all, no one will ever be able to prove that number wrong. Suppose you promise that a stadium will bring a city economic benefits of $2 billion over ten years. If the city's income (hard to measure in the first place) rises by only $1 billion over the decade, then, of course, it was something completely different (the world economy, say) that restricted the income. You could prove the original estimates wrong only if you could estimate how much economic growth there would have been had the stadium never been built—but this "counterfactual" figure is unknowable, precisely because it is a counterfactual. The same economists soon branched out into writing studies that justified ever more extravagant spending on the Olympics.

It would have seemed rude to derail this industry with anything so inconvenient as the truth. But then along came Rob Baade. The quiet, courteous academic seemed an unlikely figure to be taking on the stadium lobby. After all, he is a former top-class athlete himself: at college, Baade captained the Wisconsin basketball team. When the white coach seemed antagonistic to the majority of black players, Baade found himself championing players against coach in what he describes as one of the most difficult years of his life.

Afterward he wanted to do graduate work in public finance, a branch of economics that usually involves many equations and few words. But he also wanted to coach basketball and to apply something of what he had learned while on the Wisconsin team. A colleague told him about a job at Lake Forest College, an idyllic little place just outside Chicago. To the dismay of some of his purist professors, he went to Lake Forest on a temporary appointment and ended up coaching there for eighteen years, while also rising to full professor of economics. He was a good coach, too: the year before he arrived the team had not won a single game, but within four years they were winning 85 percent of their games.

When you start out as an academic you try to write papers that will grab your colleagues' attention. Baade used his own background to enter the economics of sports, then still almost virgin terrain. At a seminar in New York he presented a paper titled "The Sports Tax." Journalists from the *New York Times* and the *Wall Street Journal* happened to be in the audience, and they zeroed in on what had been almost a throwaway line in his talk: public investment in stadiums does not provide a good return for taxpayers. As a coach himself, Baade might have been expected to join the stadium boosters. Had he done so, he could have earned himself good money in "consulting." Instead, he went into opposition.

The Heartland Institute, a conservative think tank, asked him to write up his thoughts. There are few issues in American political life where the Right joins with an intellectual liberal like Baade, but the paper he published in 1987 laid out the problem clearly: "Contrary to the claims of city officials, this study has found that sports and stadiums frequently had no significant positive impact on a city's economy and, in a regional context, may actually contribute to a reduction in a sports-minded city's share of regional income."

Baade had asked the awkward questions that stadium boosters always ignored. For instance, where would all the construction workers for the new stadium come from? Wouldn't they have jobs already, and therefore wouldn't a shortage arise somewhere else? Worse still, as competition for their skills intensified, wouldn't costs rise?

Once you start thinking of people as having alternatives rather than just standing around waiting for the stadium to arrive, the economics begin to look less appealing. For every dollar going in, there is probably a dollar going out somewhere else. In particular, if a city has to balance its budget, then spending more on stadiums must mean spending less on parks and schools. These lost jobs have to be counted against the stadium's benefits. And if the city doesn't balance its budget, isn't it storing up future burdens for taxpayers, who will have to forgo something, someday?

That is bad enough, but what if the stadium doesn't produce the promised benefits? After all, most stadiums are used for only a few hours a week, and barely at all in the off-season. Even allowing for the occasional rock concert (and there is a limit to how many times Elton John can play in your town), most of the time the neighborhood around the stadium will be deserted. Nobody wants to live in a place like that. The neighborhoods around Yankee Stadium or Shea Stadium hardly became desirable, for instance.

Nor did Baade believe that a stadium would draw in much spending from outside the city. Most out-of-town fans would buy a hot dog and beer, watch the game, and leave—hardly an economic bonanza. A mall, or a Cineplex, or even a hospital would generate more local spending.

Around the end of the 1980s other economists, too, began asking these awkward questions. However, Baade went one better. In order to show that the boosters' numbers didn't add up, he generated some numbers of his own. Perhaps he couldn't measure the counterfactual, but he could get close by comparing economic growth in cities that had major league teams with those that didn't. After all, he reasoned, if the boosters were right, then over time cities with stadiums must do better than cities without stadiums.

Baade examined data such as income per head and the numbers of new businesses and jobs created in various cities. The more he looked, the less difference he found between the economic profiles of cities with and without stadiums. All this spending was evidently producing no benefit.

Gradually, people took notice. Other economists started to replicate Baade's findings, and to find new ways to test the proposition that stadiums create wealth. "Antistadium movements" began in many American cities.

In the mid-1990s Baade was asked to testify before Congress. On the day of his testimony, Congress was also holding hearings on the Clinton Whitewater affair and on military intervention in Bosnia, but when the stadium hearings started, the other chambers emptied. One of the people in the room was Paul Tagliabue, commissioner of the NFL and someone all the congressmen wanted to be seen with. Powerful people like Tagliabue were getting quite irritated by Baade's awkward facts.

Academic freedom is a cherished value of American universities, but, as Baade was starting to realize, so is making money. He recalls an old guy coming up to him after one meeting and saying: "You might be right, professor, but if I were you I would watch my back. You're getting in the way of a whole lotta commercial projects." A university seldom likes seeing its employees upset local politicians and businesspeople. Lake Forest College always supported Baade, but at times it would have been convenient had he thought differently.

He kept on telling the truth regardless. Among economists, often not the sportiest of types, he developed a special credibility as a former athlete. This sometimes came in handy, like when a questioner in a public debate asked, "No disrespect, professor, but what does an economist like you know about athletics?"

Eventually, Baade descended on soccer. He and Victor Matheson conducted a study of the impact of hosting the World Cup of 1994 in the US. They looked for evidence of faster economic growth in the host cities, and as usual they found nothing. Yet by now, the old bogus American arguments for hosting sports had spread to other countries.

The raising and dashing of hopes of an "economic bonanza" have since become as integral a part of a modern soccer tournament as the raising and dashing of hopes that England will win it. A few months after England hosted Euro '96, for instance, a report by a body called Tourism Research & Marketing said that fewer than 100,000 overseas fans had visited England for the tournament, against a forecast—admittedly plucked out of thin air by the FA—of 250,000. Nor had the visitors spent much. Euro '96 generated about $155 million in direct income for Britain. This was peanuts compared to the $20 billion spent by all overseas visitors to the country in 1996. Meanwhile, a study by Liverpool University and the city council found that the 30,000 visitors to Liverpool during Euro '96 spent only $1.56 million among them. How many jobs did that create? Thirty, all of them temporary.

A few years later Japanese and Korean government officials were predicting that the World Cup of 2002 could boost their economies by a staggering $26 billion and $9 billion, respectively. Of course, after the event there was little sign of any such boost, and indeed some evidence that tourists had stayed away for fear of soccer hooligans.

Finally, the weight of this research was starting to stack up. It was becoming obvious that even if you build it, he doesn't necessarily come. The boosters' claims of economic benefits were growing muted. The estimates produced for the World Cup in Germany in 2006 were altogether more sober. Even a study sponsored by the German soccer federation suggested a mere $2 billion in new benefits. (Similarly in London now, estimates of the likely economic benefits from the 2012 Olympics are kept studiously vague.)

Perhaps the best estimate we have of how much visitors to soccer tournaments actually spend was done at the German World Cup. This was the biggest media event in history, a monthlong party (except for the boring soccer), yet even here the hosts didn't make much money.

A team of economists, led by Holger Preuss from the University of Mainz, decided to work out how much "new" money visitors to the World Cup actually spent. In the old days, when boosters estimated economic bonanzas, they simply multiplied the number of seats in stadiums by some imaginary spending number (counting meals, hotels, and transportation as well as tickets) to produce an enormous hypothetical sum.

The problem with this method, as serious economists pointed out, is that not every visitor to an event really injects extra spending into the economy. Preuss's team surveyed a large sample of visitors to the World Cup and found that only about one-fifth were foreigners who had traveled to Germany specifically for the soccer. More than half the "visitors" were in fact Germans. For the most part these Germans would have been in Germany anyway, and had there been no World Cup they would presumably have spent their money on other forms of entertainment (such as going to movies or restaurants). If they spent money at the World Cup, they spent less elsewhere in the German economy, which largely offset any economic benefit from the soccer. Of course, some Germans who might otherwise have been spending their money in Spanish bars stayed home for the soccer. However, their spending was probably offset by other Germans who went abroad precisely in order to avoid the madness of the World Cup.

The remaining foreign visitors to the World Cup—about a quarter of all visitors—were either "time switchers," who would have come to Germany anyway at some point and simply timed their visit to coincide with the World Cup, or foreigners who would have been in Germany during the World Cup anyway and just decided to go along and see what all the fuss was about. Preuss's team called this last category "casuals."

"Time switchers" and "casuals" would have added little to spending, because even without the World Cup they would have spent their money in Germany. Preuss's team asked their respondents detailed questions about their spending plans. They concluded that the World Cup generated spending by visitors of €2.8 billion. That was negligible beside the Paris Hiltonesque €1,000 billion–plus spent annually by consumers in Germany. It was also much less than the German state spent preparing for the tournament. Remarkably, more than a third of that visitor income came from people who never got inside a stadium but merely watched the games on big screens in public places. In short, even the World Cup was barely a hiccup in the German economy.

Almost all research shows the same thing: hosting sports tournaments doesn't increase the number of tourists, or of full-time jobs, or total economic growth. The next World Cup will not be an airplane dropping dollars on South Africa. When the country's finance ministry flew three eminent sports economists to Pretoria for a workshop, the trio argued that the best South Africa could hope for was that the World Cup would *not reduce* economic growth. Even the 500,000 or so expected foreign visitors would not be a bonanza. In 2007, South Africa attracted an average of more than 750,000 foreign visitors a month.

Added to all this are the host's costs. If the economic benefits of putting on these tournaments are muted, the expenses seldom are. Economists Brad Humphreys and Szymon Prokopowicz made some rough estimates of the costs to Poland of hosting just half of Euro 2012. Poland will need to lay on a lot more than just new stadiums, airports, and hotels for fans. UEFA requires, for its own officials and guests, the use of one entire five-star hotel within a forty-five-minute drive of every stadium. The teams need another sixteen hotels, most of them five-star. The referees have to be in five-star hotels near the stadiums. The doctors who perform the doping controls need five-stars "in the countryside." Much of the cost of these hotels will come courtesy of the Polish government. It will also have to put up surveillance cameras all over its stadiums and towns.

In all, Humphreys and Prokopowicz estimated that Poland would have to spend about $10 billion on Euro 2012. True, some of the infrastructure the country is buying will have its uses after the tournament. However, much of it won't, because the things you need for a soccer tournament are never quite the same as the things you need for daily life, which is why the Japanese stadiums for the World Cup of 2002 are now mostly empty. All those Polish cameras, roads to stadiums, and luxury hotels in provincial towns may never quite pay for themselves.

Ah, say the boosters, but the biggest economic benefits are intangible. Michael Katz is a millionaire Johannesburg lawyer who sits on the organizing committee for the South African World Cup. In his air-conditioned office in the business district of Sandton, he says the World Cup will show that "foreigners can invest here, trade here with confidence." The tournament will boost South Africa's brand.

However, that is true only if things go well. What if three days into the tournament an English fan is carjacked and later an American sponsor who has come to Johannesburg to watch games and schmooze is raped? The news will be repeated nonstop on CNN for days on end. Statistically, this is quite likely to happen. The armed robbers of Johannesburg have undoubtedly already canceled all leave for June and July 2010.

Katz responds, "On that basis you must never host a World Cup, you must never do anything in business, because something may go wrong." But we know that hosting a sports tournament can seriously damage your brand. It happened to the Olympic hosts Munich in 1972, Montreal in 1976, and Atlanta in 1996. The 2010 World Cup might persuade people that South Africa is not a poor, corrupt, diseased, crime-ridden country; alternatively, it might persuade them that South Africa is precisely that.

Most economists now agree with Rob Baade: hosting a sports tournament doesn't make a place rich. The question then is why countries still bother. Why do the US, Russia, Australia, England, Indonesia, Mexico, Japan, Spain and Portugal, Holland and Belgium all want to stage the World Cup of 2018? The answer has nothing to do with money. Rather, it reveals something about the new politics of happiness now emerging in the rich world.

In recent years, social scientists have learned a lot about happiness. Their best source in Europe is the Eurobarometer research program, which is funded by the European Commission. Each year it asks about a thousand citizens from each European country how happy they are. To quote the exact question: "On the whole, are you very satisfied, fairly satisfied, not very satisfied, or not at all satisfied with the life you lead?"

The survey has been conducted for about forty years. By now, some insights have accumulated. Perhaps the most interesting is that having money in itself doesn't make you happy. "There is a paradox at the heart of our lives" is how Richard Layard opens his book *Happiness: Lessons from a New Science*, one of a flood of recent works on the subject. "Most people want more income and strive for it. Yet as Western societies have got richer, their people have become no happier." Layard (sometimes described as the British government's "happiness czar") says that in the US, Britain, and Japan, people have gotten no happier in the past fifty years even as average incomes have more than doubled.

It seems that we humans adapt quickly to our environment. The things we once thought of as luxuries soon become necessities (although, by the same token, our sense of well-being would quickly adapt to losing half our income). What we care about is not our absolute wealth but our rung on the ladder. Ruut Veenhoven, a leading expert on happiness, says, "When we have overtaken the Joneses, our reference drifts upward to the Smiths, and we feel unhappy again."

Only in countries where income per capita is below about fifteen thousand dollars—countries such as Mexico, the Philippines, or India—has increased wealth brought some happiness. Layard writes, "The reason is clear—extra income is really valuable when it lifts people away from sheer physical poverty." But that very rarely happens in Europe anymore.

Some other truths emerge from the European data. Scandinavians are very happy; eastern Europeans are not. The Irish both north and south of the border are surprisingly happy. Age, sex, and social status matter, too. In western Europe at least, the average person's happiness tends to decline with age until he is twenty-six years old, and then starts to rise again. Women seem to be happier than men, which might help account for their much lower rates of suicide. The more educated people are, the happier they tend to be. Married people are generally happier than unmarried ones. What happens around you in society also matters: when unemployment or inflation rises, people tend to grow unhappier. Spending time with friends and family makes people happy.

And, we discovered, so does hosting soccer tournaments. Staging a World Cup won't make you rich, but it does tend to cheer you up.

The day before the World Cup final of 2006, one of the authors, Simon, visited the street where he used to live in Berlin. Fifteen years before, the Hohenfriedbergstrasse had been a dull-brown place with toilets on the stairwells and potentially fatal coal ovens in every apartment. Nobody ever spoke to anyone else. This time, he had to check the street sign to make sure it was the same place. Flags were flying from every house—German flags made in China, but also flags of many other nations—and children were playing everywhere even though they had supposedly gone extinct in Germany. The World Cup seemed to have made a usually gloomy nation happy.

This is typical. Georgios Kavetsos and Stefan Szymanski (with a lot of help from Robert McCulloch, guru of happiness research) took the European Commission's happiness data for twelve western European countries from 1974 to 2004 and checked whether it correlated at all with sports tournaments. The obvious first question was whether people became happier when their national team did well. It turned out that they didn't: there was no visible correlation. Then Kavetsos and Stefan looked at hosting and happiness, and here they found a link. After a country hosts a soccer tournament, its inhabitants report increased happiness.

What Kavetsos and Stefan did was to replicate existing studies of happiness using all the measures researchers usually consider (income, age, marital status, and so on), and then see whether living in a host country made a difference as well. Their data on happiness covered eight separate hosts of tournaments: Italy and France for the World Cups of 1990 and 1998, and for the European championships Italy (1980), France (1984), West Germany (1988), England (1996), and Belgium and the Netherlands (2000). In all but one of these eight host countries, there was a significant uptick in self-reported happiness just after the tournament. The only exception was the UK, where happiness fell slightly just after Euro '96, but then we all know that the UK is not England.

This evidence is persuasive. However, given that so many other factors influence happiness, we wanted to test whether this effect could be measured even after allowing for the other factors. To do this, several large databases had to be welded together, and in the process the data from some years were lost. For instance, it turns out that the income of respondents was not surveyed in every single year. That left us with data for five hosts: Italia '90, and the Euros of 1984, 1988, and 2000, the last of which had two hosts. Admittedly, this is a small sample, but in all five host countries, happiness rose after the tournament, even allowing for all the other effects that influence happiness. The inhabitants reported a higher level of happiness the year after the tournament than they had the year before, and they reported more happiness in the autumn surveys (that is, after the tournament) than in the spring surveys (held before the tournament).

The jump in happiness was quite large. Citizens of wealthy countries like the Netherlands or France would need to make hundreds of dollars more a month to experience a similar leap. One way to express this is that the average person gains twice as much happiness from hosting a soccer tournament as from having higher education. The effect can also be likened to an unexpected increase in income that takes someone from the bottom half of the income distribution to the middle of the top half. It's not quite winning the lottery, but very satisfying nonetheless. If you calculate this for an entire nation, then the leap in happiness from hosting can easily be worth a few billion dollars.

In general in the host countries, older men gained the most extra happiness, presumably because many of them were sitting in front of their television sets with little else to do. Lesser-educated people gained more happiness than better-educated ones. Of all the subgroups we studied, only one (a significant one) did not get any happier: women.

The gain in happiness lasts at least a couple of months, given that the tournaments are played in midsummer and the survey is carried out in the autumn. For World Cups, the gain was quite persistent: even two and four years after the tournament, every subgroup we looked at was still happier than before the tournament. European championships, though, lifted happiness only briefly. We found no impact on happiness in the host country a year after the Euro.

But if people gain a lot of happiness after hosting a tournament, they lose a little happiness before it. The ritual fuss over whether the stadiums will be ready, whether English thugs will invade their country, whether their team will be made to look ridiculous appears to cause stress. Six years and four years before hosting a tournament, many of the subgroups we studied showed a decline in happiness.

| |

It turns out that hosting doesn't make you rich, but it does make you happy. This begs a question. If countries want to host soccer tournaments (and American cities want to host major league teams) as part of their pursuit of happiness, why don't they just say so? Why bother clothing their arguments in bogus economics?

The answer is that it took politicians a long time to discover the language of happiness. Until very recently, European politicians talked mostly about money. Anything that served only to make people happy was derided with the contemptuous phrase "feel-good factor," as if politics should be above such trivialities. Most politicians simply assumed that the real business of government was to make people richer. For one thing, measuring income was easier than measuring happiness. And so, when politicians argued for hosting tournaments, they typically used the language of money. It was almost the only vocabulary they had.

But it gradually became clear that in rich countries, more money didn't make people happier. Robert Kennedy was one of the first to see this, remarking in March 1968, three months before he was murdered, that the gross domestic product "measures everything . . . except that which makes life worthwhile."

Only in the past few years have many European politicians begun talking less about money and more about happiness. In Britain, the change is obvious: Gordon Brown is an old-fashioned "money" politician, whereas David Cameron is more of a newfangled "happiness" one. In a speech in 2006, Cameron tried to introduce the acronym "GWB"—"general well-being"—to counter the decades-old "GDP" for "gross domestic product." He said, "Improving our society's sense of well-being is, I believe, the central political challenge of our times. . . . Politics in Britain has too often sounded as though it was just about economic growth." Instead, Cameron wanted politics "to recognize the value of relationships with family, friends and the world around us."

It seems that soccer tournaments create those relationships: people gathered together in pubs and living rooms, a whole country suddenly caring about the same event. A World Cup is the sort of common project that otherwise barely exists in modern societies. We've seen that the mere fact of following a team in the World Cup deters some very isolated people from committing suicide. If playing in a tournament creates social cohesion, hosting one creates even more. The inhabitants of the host country—and certainly the men—come to feel more connected to everyone else around them. Moreover, hosting can boost the nation's self-esteem, and so makes people feel better about themselves.

Even politicians are made happy by hosting. Most of their work is frustrating. You try to get money to build, say, roads, but other politicians stop you. Even when you get the money, it's hard to build the roads because people pop up to object. It's the same with housing or foreign policy or recycling: being a politician is an endless tedious struggle with your enemies.

But it isn't when you want to host a sports tournament. Suddenly, everyone gets on board. While London was bidding for the Olympics, the rower Steve Redgrave pulled an Olympic gold medal out of his pocket during a meeting at the House of Commons, and MPs of all parties began drooling over him. Even going to war doesn't create that sort of unanimous sentiment anymore.

The end of ideology—the disappearance of nationalism, socialism, religion, communism, and fascism from western Europe—has left many politicians with little better to do than to plug sports events using specious arguments. Ken Livingstone wrote when he was mayor of London, "Crucially, the Olympics will also bring much-needed new facilities: an Olympic-size swimming pool in a city that has just two Olympic pools to Berlin's 19, and a warm-up track that would be turned over to community use."

Plainly, arguments like these are just excuses. If you want to regenerate a poor neighborhood, regenerate it. Build nice houses and a train line. If you want an Olympic pool and a warm-up track, build them. You could build pools and tracks all across London, and it would still be cheaper than hosting the Olympics. The only good reason to host an Olympics is that it makes people happy. The politicians behind London's bid did not say so, because when the city was bidding in the early 2000s they hadn't yet discovered the politics of happiness. But they did sense that the voters would reward them for winning the Games.

The London Games may pay for themselves in terms of happiness. After all, in 2008 the monthly income of the third quartile of British earners was £1,033 (then about $1,800), while the top quartile earned £2,608 (about $4,500). Based on past data, the increase in happiness from hosting could be as much as $2,750 per employee, or a staggering national total of $54 billion worth of happiness. The eight million Londoners, in particular, have the highest incomes in the European Union, and so would need to receive a fortune in tax rebates to buy the happiness that the Games could bring them.

Puritans might rightly argue that even a rich country like Britain has better things on which to spend money. However, the likely gain in happiness from the Olympics does mean the politicians are canny to give the people bread and circuses. In postmaterialist countries like Britain, the math of hosting and happiness probably stacks up.

But it's much less likely that South Africa will get its money's worth in happiness from hosting the World Cup. This is still very much a sub-$15,000 country, where putting more money in people's pockets would make them happier. About a third of all South Africans live on less than $2 a day. These people need houses, electricity, vacations, doctors.

We already know that the World Cup won't make Sowetans richer. It's also questionable whether it's an efficient way to make them happier. At last count, the ever-rising bill for the stadiums alone for the World Cup stood at 13 billion rand, or about $1.6 billion (up from an initial estimate of 2 billion rand). For $1.6 billion you could buy hundreds of thousands of houses for poor people, or a lot more than the South African government builds each year. The World Cup will keep a lot of South Africans in shacks.

Driving out of Soweto, you see the pain in the advertisements painted on the roadside billboards: "Motaung Funeral Directors—We Salute the Spirit of Ubuntu!" There are also the "21st Century Funeral Brokers," or you can buy a "Rasta funeral." Just outside town, you pass a flower bed beside the road where the flowers form the shape of a number: "2010." It's the year the Americans will land in airplanes and save everybody.

PART III
Countries

Rich and Poor, Tom Thumb,
Guus Ghiddink, Saddam, and
the Champions of the Future

13

THE CURSE OF POVERTY
Why Poor Countries Are Poor at Sports

When Didier Drogba was five, his parents put him on a plane in the Ivory Coast and sent him to live with an uncle in France. The six-hour flight, alone with his favorite toy, passed in a blur of tears and tissues.

About a decade later Drogba's father lost his job at a bank in Ivory Coast, and the family moved to a suburb of Paris, where they were reunited with their exiled son. Eight Drogbas ended up living in an apartment of about 110 square feet. "A very large wardrobe, really," Drogba recalled in his autobiography. "Hard. Very hard. Even enough to drive you crazy." The apartment was cold, and his little brothers were so noisy he couldn't concentrate on his schoolwork. "Luckily, my father had allowed me to start playing soccer again."

There is a myth that poor people are somehow best equipped to make it as sportsmen. A cliché often used about them is that sport is their "only escape route from poverty." The poor are supposedly figuratively "hungrier" than the rich. If they are black, like Drogba, they are sometimes thought to have greater genetic gifts than white people. And the evidence that poor people excel at sports seems to be in front of our eyes. England is not the only national soccer team dominated by players from lowly backgrounds. France since the 1990s has generally fielded a majority of nonwhite players, and few Brazilian internationals are sons of corporate lawyers, either. Most of the world's best soccer players started life poor: South Americans like Diego Maradona, who as a toddler almost drowned in a local cesspit, Africans like Samuel Eto'o who appear to support hundreds of people back home, or European immigrants like Zlatan Ibrahimovic or Zinedine Zidane, who grew up in some of the toughest neighborhoods on the Continent. Drogba's childhood was only slightly more Dickensian than most. The origins of American basketball players and football players are mostly lowly, too. The best preparation for sporting greatness seems to be a poor childhood.

Yet it is not. The facts show that the world's poor people and poor countries are worse at sports than rich ones. It is true that poorer immigrants in rich countries often excel at sports, but the reasons for that have nothing to do with skin color or "hunger."

Let's look at poor countries first. The vast majority of countries on earth are even more firmly excluded from sporting success than England is, simply because they are poor. This becomes apparent in a simple exercise to discover which country is the world's best at sports and which country is best for its size.

To find the best countries, we combined the historical results from many major international sporting events: the Summer and Winter Olympics, World Cups in several sports, and the most popular individual sports. For some sports the data go back more than a century, for others, only a couple of decades. For all sports, we took 2006 as the end point.

Our methodology is not perfect. We started with the men's world cups in biggish sports that have seldom or never featured at the Olympics. We ranked the top five countries in these sports, based first on the number of world titles they have won, and in case of ties, on finishes in the final four. We gave the best country in each sport five points, the second four, the third three, the fourth two, and the fifth one. There is no need to read the rankings for every sport, but following are the detailed points tallies for those who are interested:

Rugby Union

Australia	5
New Zealand	4
England	3
South Africa	2
France	1

Karate (counting only team events)

Japan	5
France	4
England	3
Spain	2
Italy and Turkey	1 each

Cricket

Australia	5
West Indies	4
India	3
Pakistan	2
Sri Lanka	1

Baseball was trickier. Historically the US dominates the sport. However, it traditionally sends amateurs or minor leaguers to the world cup. The US ranks only third all-time in the tournament. But we used our judgment to rank it as the world's best country in baseball, producing this ranking:

US	5
Cuba	4
Venezuela	3

Colombia	2
South Korea	1

Basketball is an Olympic event. However, as the world's second-most-popular team game it deserves additional input in this quest. We therefore added the results of the basketball world cup. Again the US rarely fields its best players, and historically ranks second behind Yugoslavia. But using common sense we placed the US first here, too, producing this ranking:

US	5
Yugoslavia	4
USSR/Russia	3
Brazil	2
Argentina	1

Favoring the US in baseball and basketball did not affect the outcome of our quest.

The only women's world cup we counted was soccer. Women's soccer is an Olympic event, too, but far more popular than most other women's team games, and therefore it seemed to merit more input. The rankings for women's soccer:

US	5
Norway and Germany	4 each
Sweden	2
China	1

We also assessed popular individual sports that are seldom or never represented in the Olympics. We rewarded countries for triumphs by their citizens. In tennis we counted men's and women's Grand Slam tournaments—tennis being a rare sport in that it is played widely by women. We used only results from the "Open era" starting in 1968, when tennis became very competitive.

Men's Tennis

US	5
Sweden	4
Australia	3
Czechoslovakia	2
Spain and Switzerland	1 each

Women's Tennis

US	5
Germany	4
Australia	3
Yugoslavia	2
France	1

In golf we used the results of the men's majors:

US	5
Britain (including all four home countries)	4
South Africa	3
Australia	2
Spain	1

In chess we ranked countries by the number of years that they provided the world champion:

USSR/Russia	5
Germany	4
France	3
US	2
Cuba	1

In cycling we counted victories by citizens of each country in the Tour de France, a more prestigious event than the world championship:

France	5
Belgium	4
US	3
Italy	2
Spain	1

In auto racing we chose the most prestigious competition, Formula I, thus discriminating against the US, which prefers its own races. Again, we counted world championships by citizenship. The rankings:

Britain	5
Brazil	4
Germany	3
Argentina	2
France, Australia, and Austria	1 each

We did not include the world cups of popular sports like volleyball and ice hockey, because these are Olympic sports, and so we will assess them through their role in the Olympics' all-time medals table. Boxing was too hard to assess, as there are various rival "world championships." We also excluded the athletics world cup. Athletics is copiously represented at the Olympics, and for most of the history of its world cup, the entrants have been entire continents rather than single countries.

Clearly, the Summer and Winter Games deserve to carry more weight in our quest than any single world cup. In the Summer Olympics of 2004, medals were awarded in twenty-eight sports. Many of these, such as archery or kayaking, are played by very few people. Still, because of the event's profusion of sports and its prestige, we gave the Summer Games ten times the weighting of world cups in single sports. So we gave the top country in the all-time medals table 50 points rather than 5 points for a single world cup. Because the whole planet competes in the Olympics—unlike, say, in baseball or cricket—we rewarded the top ten rather than five countries in the all-time medals table. The ranking:

US	50 points
USSR/Russia	40
Britain	30
France	20
Italy	10
Hungary	8
East Germany (GDR)	6
Germany	4
Sweden	2
Australia	1

We gave the Winter Olympics three times the weighting of a world cup. Because few countries play winter sports, we rewarded only the top five in the all-time medals table:

Norway	15 points
US	12
USSR/Russia	9
Germany	6
Austria	3

Finally, the soccer world cup. Soccer is an Olympic sport, but it is also the planet's most popular game. We gave its world cup six times the weighting of world cups in other sports, and rewarded the top ten countries in the all-time points table. The ranking:

Brazil	30 points
Germany	24
Italy	18
Argentina	12
England	6
France	5
Spain	4
Sweden	3

Netherlands	2
USSR/Russia	1

We then totaled up all the points. Here are our top twenty-one best sporting countries on earth:

US	97
USSR/Russia	58
Britain	51
Germany	49
France	40
Brazil	36
Italy	31
Australia	20
Norway	19
Argentina	15
Sweden	11
Spain	9
Hungary	8
East Germany and Yugoslavia	6
South Africa, Japan, and Cuba	5
New Zealand, Austria, and Belgium	4

The winner, the US, deserves particular praise given that we omitted two of its favorite sports, football and NASCAR, because nobody else plays them. The USSR/Russia in second place can be slightly less pleased with itself, because it won most of its points when it was still a multinational empire. Third place for Britain/England shows that the country has punched above its weight, though more so in the distant past than recently. Germany, in fourth place, is a dangerous sleeper. If we credit the united country with East Germany's Olympic medals (and forget all the male growth hormones that went into winning them), then Germany jumps to second place overall with 75 points.

Australia in eighth place did brilliantly given that we ignored its prowess at its very own version of football, "Aussie Rules." Brazil was the best developing country, and would have been even if it didn't play soccer, thanks to its successful diversification into basketball and Formula I auto racing. India (1.1 billion inhabitants, 3 points for cricket) and China (1.3 billion, 1 point for women's soccer) were the biggest flops per capita.

But which country is world champion per capita? To find out, we worked out how many points each country scored per million inhabitants. That produced this top ten of overperformers:

Norway	4
Sweden	1.22
Australia	0.98
New Zealand	0.97
United Germany*	0.91
Britain/England	0.85
Hungary	0.8
West Indies**	0.77
France	0.67
Italy	0.54

* Including the GDR's Olympic medals

**Or the nations that together supply almost all West Indian cricketers, namely, Jamaica, Trinidad and Tobago, Guyana, Barbados, and Antigua

Heia Norge, again. The country that we had already crowned as the most soccer mad in Europe now turns out to be the best per capita at sport. Norway's lead is so large that it would most probably have won our sporting Tom Thumb trophy even with a different scoring system, even, say, if we had valued the Winter Olympics only as much as a cricket or baseball world cup. This is a country where at a state kindergarten in suburban Oslo in midafternoon, among the throng of mothers picking up their toddlers, someone pointed out to us an anonymous mom who happened to be an Olympic gold medalist in cross-country skiing. Norway won more points in our competition than all of Africa and Asia (excluding Oceania) put together. We could even have omitted the Winter Olympics—almost a Norwegian fiefdom—and the country would still have made the top five of our efficiency table, thanks to its prowess at women's soccer.

But the main thing the top of our rankings demonstrates is the importance of wealth. Our efficiency table for sports bears a curious resemblance to another global ranking: the United Nations' human development index. This measures life expectancy, literacy, education, and living standards to rank the countries of the world according to their well-being. We found that a nation's well-being is highly correlated with its success in sports. Which country is top of the UN's human development index for 2008 (based on data for 2006)? *Heia Norge*, again.

Tied for first in the index with Norway was Iceland, though the country that turned itself into a hedge fund and then blew itself up may have slipped a little since. Iceland, with only 300,000 inhabitants, was never going to win any of our sporting points. But Sweden was second in the world for sports and seventh for human development. And the fourth country in the UN's human development index, Australia, was our sporting number three. In all, eight of the countries in our sporting top ten were also among the UN's twenty-three most developed countries on earth. The only poorer nations that sneaked into our sporting top ten were Hungary (with its vast Olympic program under communism) and the West Indian nations. However, even these poor cousins were all classified by the UN as "highly developed" countries except for Jamaica and Guyana, whose development was "medium." Generally, the most developed countries also tend to be best at sports.

The case of Norway shows why. It's Norwegian government policy that every farmer, every fisherman, no matter where he lives in the country, has the right to play sports. Norway will spend what it takes to achieve that. Just as supermarkets have sprouted all over Britain, there are all-weather sports grounds everywhere in Norway. Even in the unlikeliest corners of the country there's generally one around the corner from your house. Usually the locker rooms are warm, and the coaches have acquired some sort of diploma. A kid can play and train on a proper team for well under $150 a year, really not much for most Norwegians. Almost everyone in the country plays something. Knut Helland, a professor at Bergen University who has written a book on Norwegian sports and media, notes that Norway has the biggest ski race in the world with about 13,000 participants. "I'm taking part in it myself," he adds. When the European Commission studied time use in European countries in 2004, it found that the Norwegians spent the most time playing sports: on average, a whopping thirteen minutes a day. People all over the world might want to play sports, but to make that possible requires money and organization that poor countries don't have.

In short, poor countries are generally poorer at sport. It's no coincidence that China won nothing at sports before its economy took off and that it topped the medals table at the Beijing Olympics afterward. Most African countries barely even try to compete in any sports other than soccer and a few track events. And the best place to find out why the world's poor do worse than the world's rich is South Africa, where some very poor and very rich neighborhoods are almost side by side, separated only by a highway or a golf course.

South Africa is the one African country to score any points at all in our sporting table. Yet it owes almost all those points to an ethnic group that makes up less than 10 percent of the country's inhabitants: white people.

Only about 4.3 million of the 48 million South Africans are white. Nonetheless, whites accounted for 14 of the 15 players in the Springbok rugby team that won the world cup in 1995, 13 of the 15 that won it in 2007, as well as all five South African golfers who have won majors, and nearly all the country's best cricketers. If we treated white South Africa as a separate country, then their five sporting points would have put it in third place in the world in our sporting efficiency table. That is entirely predictable. South African whites were nurtured under apartheid on almost all the resources of the country.

The national teams of South African whites now dominate their respective sports. At the time of this writing, the country's mostly white cricket team is ranked second in the world, while the mostly white Springbok rugby team is world champion. Nonwhite South Africa's national team does less well. As we write, the "Bafana Bafana" soccer team, sometimes known at home as the "Banana Banana," is seventy-second in FIFA's rankings, a few spots behind Panama and Gambia.

Here are five vignettes to explain why black South Africa and other poor nations fail at sport:

YOU ARE WHAT YOU EAT: JOHANNESBURG

Steven Pienaar, Everton's South African midfielder, has the frame of a prepubescent boy. There's hardly a European soccer player as reedy as he is. But in South African soccer his body type is common. Frank Eulberg, a German who very briefly was assistant coach of the Kaizer Chiefs, South Africa's best team, says that when he arrived at the club, sixteen of the players were shorter than five foot nine. "I sometimes thought, 'Frank, you're in the land of the dwarves.'"

Most likely, Pienaar is reedy because he grew up malnourished and without much access to doctors. He was born in a poor Coloured township in 1982, the height of apartheid, when almost all money and health care went to whites. Growing tall is not just a matter of what you eat. When children become ill, their growth is interrupted, and because poor children tend to get ill more often than rich ones, they usually end up shorter.

Most of the players who will represent South Africa in 2010 were born in nonwhite townships in the 1980s. And so the ghost of apartheid will bug the Bafana at the World Cup. One reason South Africans are so bad at soccer is that most of them didn't get enough good food.

Apartheid, based on the bogus ideology that races are different, ended up creating white, black, "Coloured," and Indian South Africans who really were like separate peoples. The whites on average tower over the blacks. No wonder the cricket and rugby teams are so much better than the Bafana. "Well, they have their moments," laughs Demitri Constantinou.

This descendant of Greek immigrants, an exercise scientist at Wits University in Johannesburg, directs FIFA's first medical center of excellence in Africa. When we met, he was running a project with the South African Football Association to help develop young soccer players. Constantinou's team tested the health of all the players selected for SAFA's program. In a Woolworths tearoom in one of Johannesburg's posh northern suburbs, among white ladies having afternoon tea, he says, "The biggest issue was nutrition." Is malnutrition one reason African teams perform poorly at World Cups? "I think yes. And I think it has been overlooked as a possible cause."

Hardly any players in the latter stages of the World Cup of 2006 were shorter than about five foot eight, Constantinou notes. "There is a minimum height." If a large proportion of your male population was below that height, you were picking your team from a reduced pool. Conversely, though he didn't say it, one reason that Norway and Sweden (two of the three tallest countries in the world) excel at sport is that almost all their male inhabitants are tall enough. They are picking their teams from a full pool.

A BEAST INTO A TOOTHPICK: CAPE TOWN

George Dearnaley is a big, ruddy white man who looks like a rugby player, but in fact he was once the Bafanas' promising young center forward. Dearnaley never got beyond promising, because when he was in his early twenties his knee went. He didn't mind much. He spoke a bit of Zulu, and had studied literature and journalism at college in Toledo, Ohio, and so he joined the soccer magazine *Kick Off*. Now he is its publisher as well as the author of an excellent column.

Over an English breakfast in a Cape Town greasy spoon near the *Kick Off* offices, Dearnaley reflected on the Amazulu team in Durban where his career peaked. Seven of his teammates from the Amazulu side of 1992 were now dead, out of a squad of about twenty-four. Dearnaley said, "One guy died when his house exploded, so that was probably a taxi war or something. But the rest must have been AIDS. One player, a Durban newspaper said he was bewitched. A six-foot-four beast of a man, who was suddenly whittled down to a toothpick."

Constantinou says it's quite possible that a fifth of the Bafanas' potential pool of players for 2010 carries the HIV virus. How many South Africans who could have played in 2010 will be dead instead?

THE DARK SIDE OF THE MOON:
SANDTON, JUST OUTSIDE JOHANNESBURG

It is quite a step for Danny Jordaan to be organizing a World Cup, because until he was thirty-eight he had never even seen one. The chief executive officer of the World Cup 2010 grew up a million miles from the world's best soccer. Being in South Africa under apartheid was not quite like being on the moon, or being in North Korea, but it was almost as isolated. South Africa was the last industrialized country to get television, in 1976, because the white government was afraid of the device. Even after that hardly any blacks had TV sets, and FIFA did not allow its World Cup to be broadcast in the apartheid state. So the first time Jordaan saw a World Cup on television was in 1990.

The country's isolation continued even after that. As far as most South Africans were concerned, international soccer might still as well have been happening on Mars. Jordaan says, "South Africans played on their own. We thought we were so smart. That's why when we played our first competitive match against Zimbabwe [in 1992], every South African knew we were going to hammer Zimbabwe. But Zimbabwe had this little player called Peter Ndlovu. Nobody knew Peter Ndlovu. By halftime it was 3–0 for them. That was the first entry into international soccer. That really shook this country."

As late as 1998, when South Africa entered its first World Cup, large swaths of the population assumed that the Bafana would win it. After all, everyone knew that their native style of "piano and shoeshine"—

essentially, doing tricks on the ball while standing around—was just like Brazilian soccer but better. The Bafana did not win the World Cup.

Black South Africa was isolated twice over: first by sanctions, then by poverty. However, isolation—a distance from the networks of the world's best soccer—is the fate of most poor countries. Their citizens can't easily travel to Italy or Germany and see how soccer is played there, let alone talk to the best coaches. Some can't even see foreign soccer on television, because they don't have a television. And only a handful of the very best players in these countries ever make it to the best leagues in the world.

One reason poor countries do badly in sports—and one reason they are poor—is that they tend to be less "networked," less connected to other countries, than rich ones. It is hard for them just to find out the latest best practice on how to play a sport.

Playing for national teams in Africa hardly lifts the isolation much. Most poor, isolated African countries compete only against other poor, isolated African countries. At best, they might encounter the world's best once every four years at a World Cup. No wonder they have little idea of what top-class soccer is like.

"THE ORGANIZERS. IT'S THE BIGGEST PROBLEM": LONDON

For mysterious reasons, someone decided that the Bafana should play their annual charity match, the Nelson Mandela Challenge, not in the magnificent 78,000-seat FNB Stadium just outside Johannesburg, but more than five thousand miles away at Brentford's Griffin Park in West London.

On a gray November London afternoon the day before the game in 2006, the South Africans were in their gray-colored three-star hotel on the outskirts of Heathrow Airport. In the lobby were flight crews, traveling salesmen, and cheery men in green-and-yellow tracksuits hanging with their entourage: the Bafana Bafana. Their opponents, the Egyptians, who were also staying in the hotel, had congregated in the bar. Apparently, Egypt was furious. It had been promised a five-star hotel, and a match fee that had yet to materialize.

Pitso Mosimane, the Bafanas' caretaker manager—a big, bald, bullet-headed man—was also hanging around the lobby. Mosimane complained that African coaches never got jobs in Europe. He gestured toward the bar: "The coach of Egypt, who won the African Cup of Nations. Don't you think he could at least coach a team in the English first division?" Then Mosimane went off for a prematch practice at Griffin Park.

Minutes later he was back at the table. "That was quick," someone remarked. "No, we didn't train!" Mosimane said. Nobody had bothered telling Brentford the Bafana were coming, and so the field wasn't ready for them. Now they would have to play the African champions without having trained on the field. "And I'm carrying players who play for Blackburn Rovers and Borussia Dortmund, and you know? We're laughing about it." Mosimane jerked a thumb toward four men in suits drinking at the next table: "The organizers. It is the biggest problem. This wouldn't happen with any other national team."

He was wrong. Organizational mishaps are always happening to national teams from poor countries. Senegal, for instance, clean forgot to enter the World Cup of 1994. On most sub-Saharan African national teams that do make it to a World Cup, players and officials have a ritual dispute over pay about a week before the tournament. In 2002 Cameroon's dispute got out of hand, whereupon the squad made a brief airplane odyssey through Ethiopia, India, and Thailand before finally landing in Japan four days late. Jet-lagged and confused, the Indomitable Lions were knocked out in the first round. In 2006, Togo's players spent much of their brief stay at the country's first ever World Cup threatening to go on strike because of their pay dispute. They worried that after the tournament was over, Togo's federation might never get around to paying them. Eventually, FIFA sidestepped the federation, paid the players' bonuses directly, and told them to play or else, but it is little wonder that the team lost three matches out of three.

To win at sports, you need to find, develop, and nurture talent. Doing that requires money, know-how, and some kind of administrative infrastructure. Few African countries have enough of any.

"COLOURED" BEATS "BLACK": THE CAPE FLATS

If you stand on Table Mountain at night and look down at Cape Town, you will see a city of lights. Next to the lights are the railway tracks. And on the far side of the tracks are "black spots": Coloured townships without lights. These are the rainy, murderous Cape Flats where most of South Africa's best soccer players grew up.

Benni McCarthy of Blackburn is from the Cape Flats. So is his friend Quinton Fortune, for years a loyal reserve at Manchester United. So is Shaun Bartlett, the most capped player in South African history.

The key point is that according to the racial classifications of apartheid, still tacitly used by South Africans today, none of these players are "black." They are "Coloured": a group of generally lighter-skinned people, mostly derived from the lighter African tribes of the Cape, though some descend from Asian slaves and mixed white-black liaisons. Less than 10 percent of South Africans are Coloured, while about three-quarters are black. However, Coloureds often make up as much as half of the Bafana team. Pienaar and striker Delron Buckley, for instance, are from Coloured townships in other parts of South Africa. This density of Coloured talent is a legacy of apartheid.

Under apartheid, the Coloureds were slightly better off than the blacks. They had more to eat and more opportunities to organize themselves. In the Coloured Cape Flats, for instance, there were amateur soccer clubs with proper coaches like you might find in Europe. Not so in black townships, where a boys' team would typically be run by a local gangster or the shebeen owner, who seldom bothered much with training.

At the World Cup of 2010, to the irritation of many South African blacks, the Bafana will still be a largely "Coloured" team. The blacks are simply too poor to compete within their own country, let alone with Europeans. Even in the simplest game, the poor are excluded by malnutrition, disease, and disorganization.

That leaves one thing unexplained. Why is it that so many of the best European soccer players—Zidane, Drogba (officially an Ivorian but raised in France), Ibrahimovic, Wayne Rooney, Cristiano Ronaldo—come from the poorest neighborhoods in Europe?

It cannot be that boys from the ghetto have an unquenchable hunger to succeed. If that were so, they would do better at school and in jobs outside soccer. There must be something about their childhoods that makes them particularly well suited to soccer. That reason is practice.

Malcolm Gladwell, in his book *Outliers: The Story of Success,* popularized the "ten-thousand-hour rule." This is a notion from psychology, which says that to achieve expertise in any field you need at least ten thousand hours of practice. "In study after study, of composers, basketball players, fiction writers, ice-skaters, concert pianists, chess players, master criminals," says neurologist Daniel Levitin in *Outliers,* "this number comes up again and again. . . . No one has yet found a case in which true world-class expertise was accomplished in less time."

In soccer, it is the poorest European boys who are most likely to reach the ten-thousand-hour mark. They tend to live in small apartments, which forces them to spend time outdoors. There they meet a ready supply of local boys equally keen to get out of their apartments and play soccer. Their parents are less likely than middle-class parents to force them to waste precious time doing homework. And they have less money for other leisure pursuits. A constant in soccer players' ghosted autobiographies is the monomaniacal childhood spent playing nonstop soccer and, in a classic story, sleeping with a ball. Here, for instance, is Nourdin Boukhari, a Dutch-Moroccan soccer player who grew up in an immigrant neighborhood of Rotterdam, recalling his childhood for a Dutch magazine:

> I grew up in a family of eight children. . . . There was no chance of pocket money. . . . I lived more on the street than at home. . . . And look at Robin van Persie, Mounir El Hamdaoui and Said Boutahar. And I'm forgetting Youssef El-Akchaoui. [Like the other players Boukhari mentions, El-Akchaoui is a current professional soccer player.] Those boys and I played on the street in Rotterdam to-

gether. We never forget where we came from and that we used to have nothing except for one thing: the ball. . . .

What we have in common is that we were on the street every minute playing soccer, day and night. We were always busy, games, juggling, shooting at the crossbar. The ball was everything for me, for us. We'd meet on squares.

By the time these boys were fifteen, they were much better players than suburban kids. The ten-thousand-hour rule also explains why blacks raised in American ghettoes are overrepresented in basketball and football.

But it would be misleading to say these European soccer players grew up "poor." By global standards, they were rich. Even in Cristiano Ronaldo's Madeira, Rooney's Croxteth, or Zidane's La Castellane, children generally got enough to eat and decent medical care. It is true that Cristiano Ronaldo grew up in a house so small that they kept the washing machine on the roof, but in black South Africa, that washing machine would have marked the family as rich. Besides the ten-thousand-hour rule, there is another rule that explains sporting success: the fifteen-thousand-dollar rule. That's the minimum average income per person that a country needs to win anything. There is only one way around this: be Brazil.

14

TOM THUMB

The Best Little Soccer Country on Earth

In 1970, when Brazil won its third World Cup, it got to keep the Jules Rimet trophy. The little statuette of Nike, then still known mainly as the Greek goddess of victory, ended up in a glass case in the Brazilian federation's offices in Rio de Janeiro. One night in 1983 the trophy was stolen and was never seen again.

However, the point is that everyone agrees that Brazil deserves the Jules Rimet. The fivefold world champion is undoubtedly the best country in soccer history. Our question here is a different one: which country is best after taking into account its population, experience, and income per capita? If Brazil is the absolute world champion, who is the relative champion, the biggest overperformer? That overachieving country deserves its own version of the Jules Rimet trophy—call it the Tom Thumb. And which countries are the worst underachievers relative to their resources? Along the way we will have to consider several impressive candidates and make some judgment calls before coming up with our winner and loser.

First of all, if we are dealing with statistics, we have to construct our arguments on the basis of large numbers of games played. There have only been eighteen World Cups, and most of these involved hardly any countries from outside Europe and Latin America. So crunching the numbers from World Cups might at best tell us something about the pecking order among the long-established large soccer nations. But when the difference between, say, Argentina's two victories and England's one comes down to as little as Diego Maradona's "hand of God" goal, or the difference between Italy's four and France's one to a prematch pep talk given by Benito Mussolini to the referee in 1934 and a comment by Marco Materazzi about Zidane's parentage in 2006, then the statistician needs to look elsewhere. Happily, since national teams play a lot of games, we have plenty of data. As in chapter 2, we will rely on the remarkable database of 22,130 matches accumulated by math professor Russell Gerrard.

The number of international matches has soared over time. Between the foundation of FIFA in 1904 and the First World War the number rose quickly to 50 per year. After 1918 growth resumed. By the eve of the Second World War, there were more than 100 international matches a year. But this was still a world dominated by colonial powers, and only with the independence movement after the war did international competition mushroom. In 1947 there were 107 international matches; by 1957 there were 203; by 1967, 308. Few new countries were founded in the next two decades, but the number of international matches continued to rise thanks to the jet plane, which made travel less of a pain and more financially worthwhile. In 1977 there were 368 international matches; in 1987 there were 393. At that point the world seems to have reached some sort of stable equilibrium.

But then the Soviet Union broke up into fifteen separate states, and Yugoslavia collapsed. The new countries flocked into FIFA. At the same time the commercial development of soccer meant that cash-hungry national associations were eager to play lucrative friendlies. In 1997 there were 850 international games, more than double the figure of a decade before.

If we concentrate on just the past twenty years or so of Russell's database, from 1980 through 2001, a list of the most successful teams

FIGURE 14.1 The top ten national teams by win percentage, 1980–2001

Team	Played	Won	Tied	Win percentage	Goal difference
Brazil	285	0.625	0.235	0.742	1.29
Germany (united)	128	0.609	0.219	0.719	0.97
France	188	0.590	0.239	0.710	0.98
Italy	203	0.557	0.276	0.695	0.78
Iraq	146	0.548	0.288	0.692	1.13
Czech Republic	83	0.554	0.217	0.663	0.88
Yugoslavia (Serbia and Montenegro)	65	0.523	0.277	0.662	0.78
Spain	198	0.520	0.273	0.657	0.88
West Germany	102	0.520	0.265	0.652	0.76
England	228	0.491	0.320	0.651	0.84

features the usual suspects. Let's rank the top ten countries by the percentage of games won, or, given that around one-third of matches are ties, by the "win percentage" statistic calculated by valuing a tie as worth half a win.

The top four are exactly as you would expect. Even in a twenty-two-year period when Brazil won just one World Cup and tried to reinvent its national style of soccer, its win percentage was almost 75 percent. That equates to bookmakers' odds of 3 to 1, or about as close as you can get to a sure thing in a two-horse race.

Strangely, the old West Germany appears only near the bottom of the top ten, alongside England with a win percentage of around 65 percent. Moreover, England's average goal difference was actually slightly higher than West Germany's. It's just that West Germany had a knack of winning the matches that counted.

Only in fifth place do we find our first big surprise: Saddam Hussein's Iraq. It was the only country other than Brazil in this period to win its matches by an average of more than a goal a game. Of course, the Iraqis' presence illustrates the problem of ranking national teams absent a league format. It is hard to imagine that they would have done all that well against the other teams in the top ten. In fact, they did not meet any of them in full internationals during this period (Saddam's boys didn't get many invitations to friendlies at Wembley). Mostly, Iraq beat Middle Eastern and Asian countries.

Yet whatever their route to the top ten, getting there was some achievement. The years from 1980 through 2001—wars, massacres, sanctions, Saddam—were not happy ones for Iraq. Nonetheless, the country produced a "golden generation" of soccer players.

It did so under the thumb of the ruling family, which loved sports. Each April Baghdad celebrated Saddam's birthday by hosting the "Saddam Olympics." You may not have caught these on ESPN, but as late as 2002, with Baghdad's Russian-Iraqi Friendship Society as sponsor, these Games attracted athletes from seventy-two countries. And not many people know that Baghdad was also bidding to host the real Olympics in 2012 before events intervened.

Saddam left control of the soccer team to his bestial son Uday. A playboy and pervert, paralyzed from the waist down in an assassination attempt, Uday motivated his players by threatening to amputate their legs if they lost. One former international reported being beaten on the soles of his feet, dragged on his bare back through gravel, and then dipped in raw sewage so that his wounds would be infected. Some players spent time in Abu Ghraib prison. After Kuwait came to Baghdad in 1981 and won, one of the ruling family's helpers beat up the referee, who was then "driven hurriedly to the airport and put bleeding on a plane out of the country," writes Declan Hill in his book on global match fixing, *The Fix*.

Stories like these from Iraqi defectors prompted FIFA to send a committee to Iraq to investigate. The Iraqis produced players and coaches who swore blind that it was all lies. FIFA believed them, and so the Lions of Mesopotamia were allowed to keep on collecting prizes.

Only when American troops entered Baghdad in 2003 did they find the prison Uday maintained in the basement of Iraq's Olympic headquarters. It featured "a rack and a medieval torture device used to rip open a man's anus," writes James Montague in his *When Friday Comes: Football in the War Zone*.

But despite everything, under Saddam the Lions of Mesopotamia were the strongest team in the world's largest continent. Though they had to play on neutral ground for much of Saddam's reign due to the war with Iran, they qualified for the World Cup of 1986 and for three Olympics. They won the 1982 Asian Games, four Arab Nations Cups, three Gulf Cups of Nations, and the 1985 Pan Arab Games despite fielding a B team. As Iraqi supporters used to chant (often while firing bullets into the air): "Here we are Sunni—yah! Here we are Shiite—yah! Bring us happiness, sons of Iraq!" Even Kurds supported the Lions. Montague calls the team "arguably the last symbol of national unity left in Iraq." Only in the 1990s, as Saddam's regime became even more isolated and brutal, did Iraqi soccer decline.

All this may be a case of people immersing themselves in soccer because it was their only form of public expression. Huthyfa Zahra, an Iraqi artist who now produces soccer-themed "pop art" from the safety of nearby Abu Dhabi, says, "Even during the wars, in the nineties, there were bombs above us, and we were playing in the streets. Because we didn't have anything to do."

Why were the Lions so good under Saddam? Zahra is surprised to hear that they were. "We are much better now," he replies. "Because the players play without fear now. If you don't feel comfortable, you can't play." He points out that since the fall of Saddam and Uday, Iraq's Lions have finished fourth in the Athens Olympics and won the Asian Cup of 2007. If Iraq ever experiences normality, then watch out Brazil.

Also in our top ten of most successful soccer countries, the new Czech and Serbian republics inherited proud soccer traditions. Even so, their performances are remarkable: each country has only about 10 million inhabitants, compared to the 40–80 million of the large European nations and Brazil's 178 million.

Some readers may be surprised to see Spain and England complete the top ten, given that both countries are often described as "notorious underachievers"—meaning that they don't win as many championships as the very best teams.

Pace Brazil and Iraq, one thing the table tells us is that Europeans dominate world soccer. The continent has eight countries in the top ten. The most obvious explanation for that is tradition: European nations are generally older, and have played international soccer for longer, than the rest of the world. It may also help that control of global soccer has largely remained in Europe. FIFA makes the rules of the game from a posh suburb of Zurich, and although western Europe has only 6 percent of the world's population, it has hosted ten out of eighteen World Cups.

But tradition does not in itself secure dominance. If it did, then British companies would still dominate industries like textiles, ship-building, and car making. Dominance is transitory unless producers have the resources to stay ahead of the competition. The key resource in soccer is talent. Generally speaking, the more populous countries are more likely to have the largest supply of talented people. We have also seen that rich countries are best at finding, training, and developing talent. In short, it takes experience, population, and wealth to make a successful soccer nation.

The easy bit is recognizing this. The hard work is assembling the data to answer our question: which countries do best relative to their resources of experience, population, and wealth?

Thankfully, Russell's data can help us with the issue of experience. He has a complete list of every single international game in history. With it, we can measure the cumulative number of games a country had played up to any given date. Sweden is the most experienced nation in soccer, with 802 internationals played through 2001, while England had played 790, Argentina 770, Hungary 752, Brazil 715, and Germany (including West but not East Germany) 713. Pedants might dispute some of these numbers—identifying international games is often a judgment call if we go back more than fifty years, when arrangements could be quite informal—but even if these figures were off by 5 percent, it wouldn't significantly affect the statistical analysis.

We also have data on each country's income. The measure typically used is gross domestic product. GDP is the total value of all goods and services bought and sold within an economy. (It includes imports and exports, but excludes income from assets owned overseas and profits repatriated to foreign countries.) The best source for GDP figures are the Penn World Tables, produced by the Center for International Comparisons at the University of Pennsylvania. The center has estimates of GDP for 188 countries between 1950 and 2004. To measure the economic resources available to each person, it divides GDP by population. Admittedly, there are all sorts of finicky issues involved in making comparisons across countries and across time, not to mention worries about measurement error and statistical reliability. Nonetheless, these data are the best we've got.

Now we run the multiple regressions we described in chapter 2. Our aim is to find the connection between goal difference per game and our three key inputs—population, wealth, and experience—while also allowing for home advantage.

After all these pyrotechnics, we can make another ranking. But this time, we can compensate all the world's national teams for that trio of factors beyond their control: experience, population, and income per head.

Oddly, if we rank every team no matter how few international matches they have played, it is the "Stans" of central Asia that emerge as the world's leading overperformers relative to their experience, income, and populations. Uzbekistan, Tajikistan, Turkmenistan, and Kazakhstan all feature in our first draft of a top ten of overachieving countries. All the Stans are poor in experience and income, while Tajikistan and Turkmenistan are short of inhabitants, too. Most of the Stans have a negative goal difference, but they do not lose as badly as they have reason to fear. Even so, their high rankings feel counterintuitive: name five great Uzbek soccer players. The fact is that these countries do well not because they are particularly good at soccer but because they have exploited a geographical loophole.

When the Stans were still Soviet republics, they were a part—albeit a distant part—of European soccer. Their clubs played in Soviet leagues, and their best players dreamed of playing in all-Soviet "national" teams for their age groups. That means their benchmark was Europe, where the world's best soccer was played. They were learning soccer in the top school. They became pretty decent at it.

Then, after the Soviet Union broke up, the Stans joined the Asian Soccer Confederation. (Kazakhstan switched to the UEFA only in

FIGURE 14.2 The top ten national teams in the world, allowing for population, wealth, and experience, all games 1980–2001 (teams playing more than 100 games)

Team	Played	Won	Tied	Win percentage	Goal difference	Overperformance[a]
Honduras	167	0.491	0.275	0.629	0.84	0.978
Iraq	146	0.548	0.288	0.692	1.13	0.882
Syria	104	0.375	0.269	0.510	0.54	0.852
Iran	163	0.515	0.264	0.647	1.10	0.730
New Zealand	124	0.379	0.210	0.484	0.37	0.691
South Africa	111	0.450	0.261	0.581	0.23	0.673
Brazil	285	0.625	0.235	0.742	1.29	0.665
Spain	198	0.520	0.273	0.657	0.88	0.585
Australia	162	0.475	0.235	0.593	0.90	0.569
Ireland	172	0.395	0.308	0.549	0.34	0.547

[a]Overperformance is defined as the expected goal difference minus the actual goal difference.

2002, after the period covered by our database.) Suddenly, they could flaunt their European know-how against much weaker Asian countries. Of course they did well. But the Stans have played too few matches to accumulate much of a sample size. Here we will concentrate on the teams that play more often. Figure 14.2 is our "efficiency table" of the ten best countries in the world relative to their resources, including only those that played more than 100 games in the period.

The final column of the table is the one to notice. It shows what you might call each country's "overperformance," the gap between the goal difference they "should" have achieved against opponents—given their national resources and experience—and what they actually did achieve (listed in the penultimate column). Honduras, the most overachieving country in soccer according to this table, score 0.978 goals per game more than you would have expected judging by their resources. All our top ten scored on average between half and one goal per game more than their resources would predict. Of our original "absolute" top ten, only Iraq, Brazil, and Spain survive in this "relative" top ten. It turns out that "notorious underachiever" Spain has in fact long been an over-achiever. Everyone instinctively benchmarks the Spanish team against Germany, Italy, and France, but that is unfair. Spain is a much smaller country, and though its economy has been catching up fast, it's still significantly poorer. Consider, for instance, Spain's record against Italy in these twenty-two years. Over the period Spain's population, income per head, and international experience were on average about 30 percent inferior to Italy's. Given that, we would have expected Spain's goal difference to be about minus two over its four games against Italy. Instead Spain overachieved, notching a win, two ties, and a defeat with a goal difference of zero.

The only other European team in the top ten of overachievers is the Irish Republic. Ireland performed brilliantly between 1980 and 2001 despite having only 4 million inhabitants and, for most of this period, relatively low income per capita. Not until 1994 did an economist from the Morgan Stanley bank coin the phrase "Celtic Tiger."

However, once again we have the difficulty that many of the teams in our top ten compete almost exclusively against weak opponents. Syria and Iran played much the same easy schedule as Iraq did. Honduras is a titan of central America. Australia and New Zealand spent much of their time thrashing tiny Pacific islands. South Africa makes the top ten largely because it has so little experience: it rejoined FIFA only in 1992. Furthermore, GDP statistics for poorer countries outside Europe tend to be notoriously unreliable. In general, there is more "noise" in all the data for countries outside Europe, meaning that we struggle to pick up the influence of the factors we are interested in. It's like listening to a radio with poor reception: the meaning of the words becomes hard to make out.

It therefore makes more sense to focus on Europe alone. Europe is a more homogeneous place than the world as a whole, meaning that differences, especially in incomes and experience, tend to be smaller. Second, the data are better: Europeans have been collecting them for longer, and they have a relatively long history of transparent record keeping (though there are some very suspicious European statistics). Last, most of the world's dominant teams are grouped together in Europe, playing against pretty much the same set of opponents. It all adds up to a fairly accurate picture of how well each European team performs.

FIGURE 14.3 Top ten European teams by win percentage, games between European countries, 1980–2001

Team	Played	Won	Tied	Win percentage	Goal difference
Germany (united)	97	0.608	0.227	0.722	0.98
West Germany	81	0.580	0.259	0.710	0.98
France	160	0.581	0.238	0.700	0.94
Italy	170	0.565	0.253	0.691	0.78
Czech Republic	70	0.557	0.200	0.657	0.91
Spain	172	0.529	0.256	0.657	0.91
Croatia	69	0.493	0.319	0.652	0.65
England	172	0.483	0.320	0.642	0.87
Netherlands	156	0.494	0.282	0.635	0.92
Russia	75	0.493	0.280	0.633	0.69

Let's first rank the best European teams on their absolute performance, without taking into account their population, experience, or GDP. Taking only those games played between European teams (that is, eliminating games where at least one team comes from outside Europe), figure 14.3 presents the "absolute" top ten ranked by win percentage.

Crowded at the top, with almost indistinguishable records, are Germany (West and united), France, and Italy. This trio is a clear notch ahead of the Czech Republic, Spain, Croatia, England, Holland, and Russia. None of this is very surprising.

However, things become more interesting after we correct for population, experience, and GDP. Now a new picture emerges. We find that in Europe, home advantage boosts the home team by a little under half a goal per game, compared with two-thirds of a goal in global soccer. Experience also counts for less in Europe than in the world in general, though it remains the most important of our key variables in winning soccer matches. Having twice the experience of your opponent gives you an advantage of about 30 percent of a goal per game. By contrast, population and GDP count for more in European soccer than they do in global soccer. Having twice the population as the other team is worth a quarter of a goal per game in Europe. Having twice the opponent's income per capita is worth about one goal every six games. So the factors in order of importance are (1) playing at home, (2) experience, (3) population, and (4) GDP.

Figure 14.4, the European efficiency table (the first of its kind, as far as we know), may be the most telling we have, so we have ranked every team for which we have data.

FIGURE 14.4 Overachievers: Ranking of European national teams, correcting for population, wealth, and experience, all games between two European opponents, 1980–2001

Rank	Team	Played	Won	Tied	Win Percentage	Average goal difference per game	Overachievement[a]
1	Georgia	61	0.361	0.164	0.443	-0.11	1.167
2	Yugoslavia (Serbia and Montenegro)	42	0.452	0.333	0.619	0.74	1.099
3	Croatia	69	0.493	0.319	0.652	0.65	0.901
4	Iceland	113	0.274	0.195	0.372	-0.50	0.837
5	Irish Republic	144	0.410	0.306	0.563	0.42	0.702
6	Armenia	42	0.119	0.310	0.274	-1.10	0.629
7	Czech Republic	70	0.557	0.200	0.657	0.91	0.598
8	Portugal	151	0.483	0.285	0.626	0.51	0.550
9	Netherlands	156	0.494	0.282	0.635	0.92	0.486
10	Bulgaria	78	0.449	0.218	0.558	0.37	0.406
11	Denmark	181	0.508	0.188	0.602	0.44	0.400
12	Moldova	51	0.157	0.216	0.265	-1.25	0.359
13	Northern Ireland	128	0.305	0.266	0.438	-0.32	0.334
14	Belarus	47	0.170	0.298	0.319	-0.77	0.284
15	Spain	172	0.529	0.256	0.657	0.91	0.241
16	Sweden	178	0.506	0.236	0.624	0.63	0.238
17	Romania	179	0.441	0.302	0.592	0.44	0.225
18	Norway	162	0.383	0.340	0.552	0.33	0.211
19	West Germany	81	0.580	0.259	0.710	0.98	0.168
20	East Germany	57	0.491	0.193	0.588	0.46	0.096
21	Scotland	140	0.400	0.271	0.536	0.10	0.086
22	Albania	70	0.214	0.171	0.300	-0.83	0.063
23	England	172	0.483	0.320	0.642	0.87	0.051
24	France	160	0.581	0.238	0.700	0.94	0.029
25	Belgium	136	0.375	0.309	0.529	0.23	-0.004
26	Wales	114	0.325	0.211	0.430	-0.33	-0.023
27	Israel	126	0.294	0.254	0.421	-0.25	-0.073
28	Bosnia-Herzegovina	29	0.276	0.207	0.379	-0.48	-0.077

(continues)

FIGURE 14.4 (*continued*)

Rank	Team	Played	Won	Tied	Win Percentage	Average goal difference per game	Overachievement[a]
29	Lithuania	79	0.291	0.165	0.373	-0.68	-0.087
30	Italy	170	0.565	0.253	0.691	0.78	-0.119
31	Slovakia	67	0.388	0.254	0.515	-0.03	-0.136
32	Slovenia	64	0.297	0.281	0.438	-0.30	-0.157
33	Switzerland	149	0.329	0.302	0.480	-0.01	-0.171
34	Greece	169	0.349	0.266	0.482	-0.13	-0.198
35	Latvia	73	0.233	0.151	0.308	-0.64	-0.200
36	FYR Macedonia	51	0.275	0.275	0.412	-0.31	-0.212
37	Cyprus	121	0.174	0.182	0.264	-1.36	-0.217
38	Germany (united)	97	0.608	0.227	0.722	0.98	-0.224
39	Poland	174	0.391	0.282	0.532	0.13	-0.304
40	Hungary	168	0.339	0.292	0.485	-0.04	-0.374
41	Austria	125	0.344	0.248	0.468	-0.16	-0.384
42	Russia	75	0.493	0.280	0.633	0.69	-0.390
43	Azerbaijan	52	0.115	0.154	0.192	-1.75	-0.423
44	Finland	146	0.212	0.281	0.353	-0.73	-0.651
45	Ukraine	57	0.368	0.333	0.535	0.05	-0.748
46	Malta	139	0.072	0.144	0.144	-2.04	-0.807
47	Estonia	91	0.099	0.220	0.209	-1.57	-0.984
48	Turkey	130	0.300	0.223	0.412	-0.66	-1.044
49	Luxembourg	100	0.030	0.090	0.075	-2.27	-1.050

[a]Overachievement is defined as the actual minus the expected goal difference.

Again, the most important number is in the last column: each country's "relative goal difference." It turns out that the top ten of overachievers with the best relative goal difference is monopolized by small nations. The Netherlands with its 15 million inhabitants is the giant of the ten. The Portuguese, Serbs (and Montenegrins), and Czechs all have populations around the 10 million mark, while the Croats are at just 5 million.

This European top ten looks more credible than our global one featuring Honduras et al., because a number of the teams on the European list—chiefly, the Dutch, Czechs, Croats, and Portuguese—have achieved genuine success despite being small. However, one cannot but notice that at the very top of our table is a team whose win percentage is a mere 44 percent: Georgia.

Georgia comes at the top largely because its official soccer history is so short. Only on May 27, 1990, did the country play its first official international match. In truth it was a 2–2 tie between the Georgian club Dinamo Tblisi and the Lithuanian club Zalgiris Vilnius. Georgia and Lithuania did not exist as independent states at the time, and so couldn't very well play an international. But in 1991 both nations gained their independence from the USSR, and soon afterward they agreed to redefine the club friendly as their maiden international. By 2001 Georgia had still played only seventy-one internationals in its history, fewer than a tenth as many as England. Armenia, another surprise entrant in our top ten, had played just fifty-seven.

Of course, the notion that these nations started gaining experience in international soccer only in 1990 is a fiction. Georgia and Armenia, like the "Stans," had been learning the game for decades in the USSR. Yet for the purposes of our table, we have treated them almost as soccer virgins, and thanks to this statistical quirk they rocket to the top. If we credited these states with the experience of the hundreds of international matches played by the USSR, they would tumble down our rankings.

Nonetheless, Georgia clearly has potential. The country is small (5 million people), and horribly poor (even today, average income is below $4,000 per year). If the Georgians could just become as rich as Croatia, they too could start beating England at Wembley.

Perhaps the most surprising thing about our top ten is the countries that don't make it. Germany, France, and Italy—the dominant European nations—turn out to perform not much better or even a little worse against other Europeans than you would expect. We saw at the start of the book that these countries benefited from their location at the heart of western Europe, smack in the middle of the world's best knowledge network. Those networks correlate pretty well with high income and long experience in soccer. These are wealthy large nations that have been playing the game for more than a century. They *should* win prizes, and they do. In the decade from 1980 to 1990, West Germany reached three straight World Cup finals, winning one, and won a European championship. Yet its performance against European teams was only 0.15 goals per game better than you would have expected based on the country's vast population, experience, and income per capita. In fact, once you allow for these advantages, West Germany performed worse than Romania and only fractionally better than the improbable trio of East Germany, Scotland, and Albania.

France won two European championships and one World Cup between 1980 and 2001. Yet against fellow Europeans, it scored just one goal every thirty-four games more than it "should" have. England—which won nothing in the period—"outperformed" its population, experience, and income by more than France did.

Italy was world champion in 1982. Nonetheless, against fellow Europeans it was a goal every nine games *worse* than it should have been given its resources.

At the bottom of our rankings of relative performance, Turkey and Luxembourg are the shockers. The Turks clearly suffered from being so far adrift from the western European network of soccer know-how. As we will explain in the final chapter, they have recently rectified this defect and are now one of our countries of the future.

If you judge by the map, Luxembourg was smack in the middle of said western European network. But networks are never simply geographical. Nobody in soccer wanted to network with Luxembourg because the country of a little more than a half-million inhabitants was too small to support a decent league or to produce many good players. Top-class foreign coaches and players were never spotted at the Jeunesse Esch ground passing on their know-how. And so Luxembourg never gained any. It is so bad at soccer that it is even worse than it should be. Admittedly, its dry spell of fifteen years without a win ended with Paul Koch's legendary last-minute penalty save against Malta in 1995, but even after that it hardly hit the heights. In 2001, Joel Wolff, secretary-general of the country's FA, confessed to us in a world exclusive interview: "Let's say that we have arrived at a relative nadir." Whenever soccer managers invoked the verity, "There

FIGURE 14.5 Worst underperformers, 1980–2001, entire world

Team	Rank	Played	Won	Tied	Win Percentage	Goal difference per game	Underachievement[a]
Canada	88	174	0.339	0.259	0.468	-0.36	-0.535
Malaysia	89	146	0.384	0.219	0.493	0.13	-0.717
Ethiopia	90	106	0.302	0.274	0.439	-0.38	-0.721
US	91	276	0.384	0.272	0.520	0.17	-0.734
Finland	92	193	0.207	0.275	0.345	-0.73	-0.814
Indonesia	93	134	0.299	0.231	0.414	-0.22	-0.948
Malta	94	158	0.114	0.152	0.190	-1.79	-0.969
Venezuela	95	122	0.107	0.213	0.213	-1.73	-0.992
Estonia	96	105	0.124	0.238	0.243	-1.44	-1.021
India	97	110	0.318	0.273	0.455	-0.26	-1.364
Luxembourg	98	109	0.046	0.083	0.087	-2.17	-1.392

[a]Underachievement is defined as the actual minus the expected goal difference.

are no more minnows in international soccer," they were forgetting Luxembourg.

We award the country both our relative and our absolute prizes for worst soccer team in Europe. But the competition for the relatively worst team in the world is hotter. Of the ninety-eight teams with more than one hundred games in our database, figure 14.5 shows the worst underperformers relative to their population, income, and soccer experience.

We're sorry: the US doesn't do well at all. If only Americans took soccer seriously, the country's fabulous wealth and enormous population would translate into dominance. As it is the US wins or ties most of its games, but it "should" score nearly three-quarters of a goal more per game than it does. However, for once Canadians are in no position to smirk.

Luxembourg is an even worse underachiever. Yet it probably doesn't deserve the title of relatively worst soccer team on earth. Using a little bit of judgment, we reserve that honor for India. With a win percentage of just 46 percent, and a goal difference of -0.26 per game, the world's second-most-populous country really should be doing better. And it's a myth that India's 1.1 billion people are not interested in soccer. Their newspapers are almost as full of the carryings-on in the English Premier

League as they are of cricket matches. It's true that India's poverty makes it hard to convert all those budding Rooneys and Ronaldos in Rajasthan and Orissa into stars (though that hasn't stopped the Indian cricket team). Still, from our model we estimated that India should be outscoring its opponents by more than a goal a game.

Admittedly, the country ranks just above Luxembourg in our global efficiency table, but once you take into account that India plays most of its matches in weak Asia whereas Luxembourg plays its in strong Europe, the Indians have it by a nose. A good indication is India's FIFA ranking (at the time of writing) of 146th in the world, six whole spots behind the Pacific island of Vanuatu.

But who gets the Tom Thumb trophy—the poor, small, inexperienced man's Jules Rimet—for the relatively best team on earth? Which country does best allowing for experience, population, and income? Well, one day we'd like to see this played out on grass. Let's have a World Cup in which teams start with a handicap, settled by a panel of econometricians chaired by Professor Gerrard. But until that great day comes, all we have is our model. The best little country on earth might be Honduras or Georgia, but not even the authors believe that. A safer conclusion is that the Serbs, Croats, and Czechs do wonders with their modest resources. However, the country that stands out most given what it has to work with is Iraq, even taking into account its easy Asian schedule. If the country ever sorts itself out, then watch out, world.

15

CORE TO PERIPHERY
The Future Map of Global Soccer

On a snowy night in Amsterdam, a dozen or so Dutch soccer writers and ex-players have gathered in an apartment in the dinky city center. Guus Hiddink walks in and grabs someone's shoulders from behind by way of greeting. Growing up with five brothers gave him a knack for male bonding. (Hiddink appears to find women more exotic, and his cohabitation with his then mistress in Seoul shocked Koreans.)

The evening starts with a soccer quiz, at which the future manager of Chelsea and Russia performs indifferently. Then there is food and soccer talk until the early morning. Though Hiddink is the senior figure at the table, he never tries to dominate. He likes telling stories—about his former player Romario, or his old teammate at the San Jose Earthquakes, George Best—but when others interrupt he is just as happy to lean back in his chair and listen. He is a solid, soothing, jowly presence. "You can feel he's at ease," Boudewijn Zenden, one of his former players, told us, "so if he's at ease, the others are at ease. He creates this environment where you feel safe."

Hiddink has a special place in the latest stage of soccer's history. In the twenty-first century, he has been the world's leading exporter of soccer know-how from western Europe to the margins of the earth. We saw in chapter 2 that from about 1970 to 2000, the six founding members of the European Economic Community dominated soccer thinking and won almost all the game's prizes. These countries perfected what you might call the continental European style: a fast, physical, collectivist soccer.

But then these countries began exporting their expertise. Hiddink and other Dutch, German, French, and Italian expat managers established themselves in Hiltons and westerners' compounds around the planet. In the past few years they have helped several new soccer countries—Russia, Australia, South Korea, Turkey, and Greece, to name a few—overtake their own native countries. It's because of men like these that England will not be the best soccer country of the future. Hiddink's native Holland appears even more thoroughly doomed. On the new map of soccer, which Hiddink is helping to draw, his own country will shrink to a dot. We bet on the US to overtake it

FROM THE BACK CORNER TO THE WORLD

Born in 1946, Hiddink grew up close to what was then just becoming the epicenter of global soccer knowledge. He is the son of a village schoolteacher and Resistance hero from a small town in the Achterhoek, or "Back Corner," about five miles from the German border. The Back Corner is wooded and quiet, one of the few empty bits of the Netherlands, and on visits home from stints in Seoul or Moscow, Hiddink enjoys tooling along its back roads on his Harley-Davidson Fatboy. "Pom-pom-pom-pom-pom," he puffs out his cheeks to mimic the motor's roar.

He grew up milking cows, plowing behind two horses, and dreaming of becoming a farmer. But Dutch farms were already dying, and he became a soccer coach instead. At nineteen he took an assistant's job at the Back Corner's semiprofessional club, De Graafschap, where his father had played before him. He then made an unusual career move: from coach to player. The head coach, seeing that his young assistant could kick a ball, stuck him in the team, and thus began a sixteen-year playing career.

The handsome, round-faced, wavy-haired playmaker was too lazy and slow for the top, yet he was present at a golden age. The Dutch 1970s shaped Hiddink. Holland, playing what foreigners called "total soccer," a new kind of game in which players constantly swapped positions and thought for themselves, reached two World Cup finals. Dutch clubs won four European Cups. Off the field, Dutch players of Hiddink's generation would answer foreign journalists' questions with sophisticated discourses in several languages. For a keen observer like Hiddink, the players' constant squabbles provided object lessons in how to keep stars just about functioning within a collective.

Dutch soccer's renown at the time helped even a second-rate player like Hiddink find work abroad, with the Washington Diplomats and the San Jose Earthquakes. "I was Best's roommate," says Hiddink, enjoying the quirky American word, and he mimics himself fielding the phone calls from Best's groupies: "George is not here. George is sleeping."

It was the start of a world tour that culminated in a suite in a five-star hotel in Moscow where, according to the president of the Russian FA, he spent a fortune ordering cappuccinos from room service. At Euro 2008 Hiddink got Russia playing the best soccer in its history, just as he had previously gotten South Korea and Australia playing their best soccer in history. Hiddink has helped to draw the new map of soccer power.

1889–2002: OFF THE PLANE WITH A LEATHER SOCCER BALL

Soccer seems to have a quality that enables it eventually to conquer every known society. The first wave of exporters of the game were Victorian British sailors, businessmen, missionaries, and colonial officers. In 1889, to cite a typical story, twenty-one-year-old Englishman Frederick Rea disembarked on the island of South Uist off the west coast of Scotland to work as a headmaster. A couple of years later two of his brothers visited, carrying with them a leather soccer ball. Within two decades the game had conquered South Uist. Shinty, a stick sport that had been played there for fourteen hundred years, "was wiped like chalk from the face of the island," wrote Roger Hutchinson in the British soccer journal *Perfect Pitch* in 1998, "supplanted, like a thousand of its distant relatives from Buenos Aires to Smolensk, by a game almost as young and innocent as Frederick Rea himself." Today soccer is the dominant sport on South Uist. It conquered because of its magic.

Victorian Britons spread the game to continental Europe, Latin America, and bits of Africa. However, for a century Asia and North America remained almost immune. Contrary to myth, soccer took a long time to become a global game. What people called the "World Cup" should until the 1980s have been called "the Euro–Latin American Duopoly." Though most people on the planet lived in Asia, the continent's only representative at the World Cup of 1978 was Iran. Even in 1990 the British Isles had more teams at the World Cup (three) than all of Asia combined (two). Many Asian countries still barely knew about soccer. When that year's World Cup final was shown on Japanese television, there was a surprising studio guest: baseball player Sadaharu Oh. "Mr. Oh," he was asked during the match, "what is the difference between sliding in baseball and in soccer?" In Australia, too, soccer was then still marginal. Johnny Warren, an Australian international and later TV commentator on the game, called his memoirs *Sheilas, Wogs, and Poofters*, because according to Australian myth in the years before Hiddink landed there, those were the three core elements of the national soccer public: women, immigrants, and gays.

But by 1990 the so-called third wave of globalization was under way. Increased world trade, cable television, and finally the Internet brought soccer to new territories. Roberto Fontanarrosa, the late Argentine cartoonist, novelist, and soccer nut, said, "If TV were only an invention to broadcast soccer, it would be justified."

Suddenly, the Chinese, Japanese, Americans, and even some Indians could see soccer's magic. They saw it even more clearly than the people of Uist had a century before. Soccer by now had the prestige of being the world's biggest sport, and everyone wanted a piece of its fans' passion. Soccer is often mocked for its low scores, but precisely because goals are so scarce, the release of joy is greater than in other sports. When the former goalkeeper Osama bin Laden visited London in 1994, he watched four Arsenal matches, bought souvenirs for his sons in the club shop, and remarked that he had never seen as much passion as among soccer supporters.

Just then soccer was capturing the last holdouts. On May 15, 1993, Japan's J-League kicked off. The next year China acquired a national professional league, and in 1996 the US and India followed. The new marginal countries began to hire European coaches who could quickly teach them the latest in soccer.

By the turn of the millennium, Hiddink was an obvious candidate for export. He had won the European Cup with PSV Eindhoven, had managed clubs in Turkey and Spain, and had taken Holland to the World Cup semifinal in 1998. After he passed fifty, he felt his ambition begin to wane. Never a workaholic to start with, the boy from the Back Corner had by now proven himself. He had met with triumph and disaster and treated those two impostors just the same. He had gone from villager to cosmopolitan. He had fallen in love with golf. Soccer was becoming just a hobby.

He took a break and in 2001 popped up in his first missionary posting, as manager of South Korea. As part of the globalization of soccer, the country was due to cohost the 2002 World Cup with Japan. South Korea had played in several World Cups before, but had never won a single match, and in 1998 had lost 5–0 to Hiddink's Holland.

When Hiddink landed in Seoul, history was beginning to work in his favor. Like many emerging nations, the South Koreans were getting bigger. Thanks to increased wealth, the average height of a South Korean man had risen from five foot four in the 1930s to about five foot eight by 2002. That meant a bigger pool of men with the physique required to play international soccer. In an interview during a Korean training camp in the Back Corner, a year before the World Cup, Hiddink told us he'd caught Koreans using their smallness as an excuse in soccer. He added, "But I won't allow that. I won't let them say beforehand, 'They're a bit bigger and broader; we're small and sad.' And gradually, I notice that some of our players are big, too, and know how to look after themselves." The "height effect" was also quietly lifting many other emerging soccer countries, from China to Turkey.

But the Koreans had other problems. The Dutch psychological quirk had been squabbling. The Korean disease, as Hiddink soon discovered, was hierarchy. In Korean soccer, the older the player, the higher his status. A thirty-one-year-old veteran international was so respected he could coast. At meals, the group of older players would sit down at the table first, and the youngest last.

Whereas Dutch players talked too much, Koreans were practically mute. "*Slavishness* is a big word," Hiddink said that day in the Back Corner, "but they do have something like: if the commander says it, we'll follow it blindly. They are used to thinking, 'I'm a soldier. I'll do what's asked of me.' And you have to go a step further if you want to make a team really mature. You need people who can and will take the team in their hands." Hiddink wanted autonomous, thinking "Dutch," players: a center half who at a certain point in the game sees he should push into midfield, a striker who drops back a few yards. He was teaching the Koreans the Dutch variant of the continental European style.

Hiddink said of his players: "Commitment is not their problem. Almost too much. But if your commitment is too high, you often lose the strategic overview."

Hiddink had started out in Korea by kicking a couple of the older players out of his squad. He made a young man captain. He asked his players to make their own decisions on the field. "That makes them a bit freer, easier," he said. Shortly before the World Cup, he brought back the jilted older players, who by then were pretty motivated.

However, the educational process in Korea was always two-way. During his eighteen months in the country, Hiddink learned a few things himself. Already during his stints in Turkey and Spain, he had begun freeing himself from the national superiority complex that pervades Dutch soccer: the belief that the Dutch way is the only way. In Holland, soccer is a thinking man's game. When the Dutch talk about it, the concepts to which they always return are *techniek* and *tactiek*. *Passie*, or passion, was a quality they associated with unsophisticated soccer players from other countries. In Korea, Hiddink learned that it was actually pretty important. Even when speaking Dutch he tends to describe this quality with the English word *commitment*, perhaps because there is no obvious Dutch equivalent.

He had also learned what every successful missionary knows: respect the native way of life, or at least pretend to, because otherwise the natives won't listen to you. That afternoon in the Back Corner he said, "I don't go to work on the culture of the country. I just leave it; I respect it. I only do something about the conditions that they need to perform on the pitch. And of course there are a couple of things off the field that do influence that."

At the 2002 World Cup the Koreans played with a fervor rarely seen in soccer. Helped by bizarre refereeing decisions, the country from soccer's periphery reached the semifinal.

Korea had craved global recognition, and Hiddink achieved it. Korean cities planned statues in his honor, and a caricature of his face appeared on Korean stamps. Hiddink's autobiography appeared in a Korean print run of a half million, despite having to compete with an estimated sixteen Hiddink biographies. In the Back Corner, Korean tour buses made pilgrimages to the Hiddink ancestral home. Soon after the World Cup, the man himself dropped by to visit his octogenarian parents. "Well, it wasn't bad," admitted his father. "Coffee?"

2002–2004: THE PERIPHERY
TAKES OVER INTERNATIONAL SOCCER

During that World Cup of 2002, other peripheral soccer countries were emerging, too. Japan reached the second round, the US got to the quarters, and Korea's conqueror in the match for third place was Turkey, which hadn't even played in a World Cup since 1954.

We said at the start of this book that a country's success in soccer correlates strongly with three variables: its population, its income per capita, and its experience in soccer. For Turkey as for many other emerging countries, all three variables were improving fast.

We have seen that from 1980 through 2001, Turkey was the second-worst underperformer in European soccer. It scored a full goal per game fewer than it should have done given its vast population, decent experience in international soccer, and admittedly low incomes.

But just as the period we measured was ending, the Turks were beginning their rise. It is no coincidence that the country went from being a pathetic soccer team to one of the best in Europe at the same time as it grew from a midsize European state into the continent's third-most-populous nation. Turkey had 19 million inhabitants in 1945, double that by 1973, and about 72 million by 2008. In Europe, only Russia and Germany have more. While Turkey's population grows, most European countries are losing people. Add several million Turks in the diaspora, and the youth of most Turks, and the country starts to rival even Germany in its soccer potential. And Turkey is just one of many developing countries whose population is fast outstripping that of rich countries.

At the same time Turkey's economy was booming, and it was using some of the new money to import soccer knowledge. In that early chapter, we had measured a country's soccer experience by how many matches its national team had played. However, there is a shortcut to gaining experience: import it. This process began for Turkey in June 1984, when West Germany got knocked out of the European championship. The Germans sacked their coach, Jupp Derwall. That year he joined Galatasaray and began to import the continental European style of soccer into Turkey.

Derwall and other German coaches (as well as the Englishman Gordon Milne at Besiktas) got Turkish players actually working. They also introduced the novel idea of training on grass. Turkish television began showing foreign matches, which introduced some Turkish viewers to the concept of the pass.

Before Derwall's arrival, the average Turkish player had been a tiny, selfish dribbler. Derwall shipped German-born Turks into Galatasaray. The German Turks were bigger than Turkish Turks thanks to a better diet, and they trained like Germans. Admittedly, soon after arrival in Istanbul they were exposed to the sultanesque harem lifestyle of many Turkish players and their game deteriorated, but it was a start. Diaspora Turks—mostly from Germany—have continued to give Turkey a fast track to European soccer know-how. No other national team in Europe includes as many players who grew up in other European countries.

In 1996, Turkey qualified for its first major tournament since 1954. Though it didn't score a goal or register a point at Euro '96, it was judged to have done quite well. It has since reached two semis and a quarter-final at major tournaments.

In short, globalization saved Turkish soccer. Turks came to the realization that every marginal country needs: there is only one way to play good soccer—you combine Italian defending with German work ethic and Dutch passing into the European style. ("Industrial soccer," some Turks sulkily call it.) In soccer, national styles don't work. You have to have all the different elements. You cannot win international matches playing traditional Turkish soccer. You need to play continental European soccer.

Both Hiddink's and Turkey's experiences point to an important truth: in soccer, "culture" doesn't matter much. Perhaps, as the former French president Giscard d'Estaing said when he drafted the European Union's failed constitution, Turkey had "a different culture, a different approach, a different way of life," but it didn't stop the Turks in soccer. Cultures are not eternal and unalterable. When they have an incentive to change—like the prospect of winning more soccer matches, or perhaps the prospect of getting richer—they can change.

Turkey was one of the first countries brave enough to jettison its traditional soccer culture. Most countries on the fringes of Europe had dysfunctional indigenous playing styles. The ones on the southern fringe—Greece, Turkey, Portugal—favored pointless dribbling, while the British and Scandinavians played kick-and-rush. Gradually, they came to accept that these styles didn't work.

Nobody did better out of abandoning their roots and adopting continental European soccer than Turkey's friends across the water, the

Greeks. The Greek national team had traditionally played terrible soccer in front of a couple of thousand spectators. During foreign trips, their camp followers—friends, journalists, and miscellaneous—would hang around the team hotel drinking espressos with players until the early morning. When Greece somehow made it to the World Cup of 1994, it ended up regretting it. At the team's training sessions outside Boston, an outfield player would stand in the goal while the others blasted shots into the bushes. They spent most of the tournament traveling the East Coast to receptions with Greek Americans, though they did find time to be thrashed in three matches. In 2002, Greece gave up on the Greek style and imported a vast chunk of experience in the person of an aging German manager, Otto Rehhagel.

The Rhinelander was the prototypical postwar West German collectivist. He had grown up a short drive across the border from Hiddink, amid the ruins of postwar western Germany. An apprentice housepainter and bone-hard defender, Rehhagel was brought up on the "German virtues" of hard work and discipline. As a coach in Germany for decades, he aimed to sign only collectivist European-type players whose personality had been vetted by his wife over dinner in the Rehhagel home. Everywhere he tried to build an organization. Sacked as manager of Arminia Bielefeld, he sighed, "At least thanks to me there is now a toilet at the training ground." On later visits to Bielefeld with other clubs, he always inquired about his toilet.

Rehhagel quickly rooted out Greece's cult of the soloist, introduced core European soccer, and took the team to Euro 2004 in Portugal. There he went around saying things like, "Now that I am coaching Greece, I want to make one philosophical statement. Please write it down: man needs nothing more than other people." Banal as this sounded, it must have resonated in postwar West Germany. Certainly, the Greek players, who pre-Rehhagel never seemed to have heard of collective spirit, had begun preaching the notion in many languages. "We was very good organized," said Zisis Vryzas after Greece beat France in the quarter-finals. Andreas Charisteas, the reserve at Werder Bremen who would become highest scorer of Euro 2004, eulogized, "We have a German coach, he has a German mentality, and we play like a German team." In fact, Greece had made the same journey as Turkey: from midget dribblers to boring European soccer thanks to German coaching.

Rehhagel himself called it "learning from European soccer." Becoming "European"—code for becoming organized—is the aspiration of many marginal European countries, in soccer and outside. Just as these countries were joining the European Union, they were absorbing European soccer. The final of Euro 2004 pitted Greece against another recently marginal country. The Greeks beat the Portuguese 1–0 thanks to another header from Charisteas, who soon afterward would be a reserve again at Ajax. It turned out that with merely half-decent players, a good continental European coach, and time to prepare, almost any marginal country could do well.

2005–2006: EVEN AUSTRALIA

In this new climate, the best continental European coaches could pick their posts. Hiddink received many offers to take teams to the World Cup of 2006, but he chose the most marginal country of all: Australia.

In 1974, while Hiddink was still absorbing total soccer in the Back Corner, Australia had qualified for its first World Cup as Asia's sole representatives. The Socceroos of the day were part-timers, and some had to give up their jobs to go to Germany. The German press was particularly interested in the milkman-cum-defender Manfred Schaefer, who had been born in Hitler's Reich in 1943 and emigrated to Australia as a child refugee after the war. At one point in the tournament West Germany's striker Gerd Müller asked him if he really was an amateur. Well, Schaefer proudly replied, he had earned forty-six hundred dollars by qualifying for the World Cup. "That's what I earn a week," said Müller.

The Australians achieved one tie in three matches at the World Cup. "However," writes Matthew Hall in his excellent book about

Australian soccer, *The Away Game*, "their thongs, super-tight Aussie Rules–style shorts and marsupial mascots endeared them to the German public."

In the next thirty years, soccer sank so low in Australia that the country's soccer federation was sometimes reduced to filming its own matches and giving them to TV channels for free. Australian club soccer was punctuated by weird vendettas between Balkan ethnic groups. Only in 1997, during the new wave of globalization, were the Socceroos of 1974 publicly honored in their own country.

Then, in 2005, Hiddink landed with a mission to teach European soccer. First, he gathered the Australian team in a training camp in his native Back Corner. His first impression: "What a bunch of vagabonds. Everyone came in wearing a cap, or flip-flops. One had on long trousers, another shorts, and another Bermuda shorts. I said, 'What is this?' 'Well, that's how we live.' 'Hello, but you probably play like that, too.'"

Hiddink spent Australia's first training session in the Back Corner watching his new charges fly into each other like Kamikaze pilots. "You don't have to chase these guys up," he remarked. After a half hour he stopped the game. When the players' cries of "Come on, Emmo!" "Hold the ball, Johnno!" "Let's go!" and the streams of "Fucking" had finally faded, Hiddink asked them to shout only when a teammate was in trouble and needed coaching. That would improve everyone's vision of play, he said. The game resumed in near silence. It was Australia's first baby step toward continental European soccer.

Just as he had with the Koreans, Hiddink was turning the Australians into Dutch soccer players. That meant giving them the intellectual discipline needed for the World Cup. The Australian way was to train hard, play hard, but then relax with late-night beers in the hotel bar. Hiddink wanted the players thinking on their own about their jobs. Working hard wasn't enough. Since the Australians already had "commitment" and *passie*, Hiddink was teaching them to think like Dutchmen. The Socceroos tended to run to wherever the ball was. Hiddink forbade them from entering certain zones. In core

European soccer, doing the right things is always better than doing a lot of things.

He had noticed that at the Confederations Cup of 2005, shortly before he took over, where the Socceroos had lost all their three games and conceded ten goals, all four Australian defenders would often stay back to mark a single forward. That left them short elsewhere on the field. No semiprofessional Dutch team would be so naive.

Hiddink was surprised that the Australians were so willing to listen to him. They understood that they had a chance to learn the European style from the man himself. Hiddink had always excelled in dealing with difficult characters: Romario, Edgar Davids, or the Korean Ahn Jung-Hwan. He knew just how to touch them. But the Australians, he admitted, were "zero difficult."

Except perhaps Mark Viduka, Australia's best but not its most committed player. Hiddink recalled later, "He came in with, 'Oh, I'd like to go to a World Cup, but it's going to be difficult. We've never made it, and I'm not fit.'" Hiddink sent the Socceroos' physiotherapist to work with Viduka at his club, Middlesbrough. This didn't merely get the player fit. It made him feel wanted. Hiddink also made Viduka his captain, to make sure he would be inside the tent pissing out rather than outside pissing in.

It was striking how quickly the Socceroos learned core European soccer. Once again, "culture" seemed to be no obstacle. In November 2005, only a couple of months after Hiddink had started part-time work with them (he was also coaching PSV at the other end of the globe), they beat Uruguay in a playoff to qualify for the World Cup. Suddenly, the *Melbourne Herald Sun* found itself wondering whether the "Aussie Rules" version of football could survive as the dominant sport in Australia's southern states. Already more Australian children played soccer than Aussie Rules and both rugby codes combined.

The newspaper's worries appeared justified when a few months later, just before the World Cup of 2006, an Australia-Greece friendly drew ninety-five thousand people to the Melbourne Cricket Ground. In no city in Europe or Latin America could such a game have drawn such a crowd. Australia had also just become approximately the last country on earth to acquire a national professional soccer league.

And then Hiddink led the Socceroos to the second round of the World Cup of 2006. Great crowds of Australians set their alarm clocks to watch at unearthly hours. What had happened on Uist more than a century before was now threatening to happen in Oz. A century from now, Aussie Rules might exist only at subsidized folklore festivals.

2006–2009: HIDDINK TO GHIDDINK IN A MOSCOW HOTEL SUITE

After Australia, Hiddink could have had almost any job in soccer. In an ideal world, he would have liked to manage England. Of all the world's marginal soccer countries, England had the most potential because it was rich and large and had recently rejoined the network of core countries.

Hiddink also relished the specific challenges of managing England. He had the psychological expertise to inspire tired multimillionaires. He loved dealing with difficult characters; Wayne Rooney would be a cinch for him. And he would have improved the thinking of a team that had everything but intellect. As a lover of the bohemian life, he would have been happy in London, and his girlfriend would have been an hour from her beloved Amsterdam. But Hiddink couldn't bear the thought of British tabloids crawling over his family, and so he decided to spread his continental European know-how to Russia instead.

Admittedly, Russia's population was collapsing rather than growing, as Russian men drank themselves to death. However, when he took the job, the country's economy was moving the right way. In the decade from 1998, Russian income per capita nearly doubled. The country's new oil money bought Hiddink's brain.

As in Korea, Hiddink's job was to force his players to be free. Traditionally, Russian soccer players had the "I only work here" demeanor of *Homo sovieticus*. They feared their coaches as much as they feared the mafiosi who stole their jeeps. They shoved safe sideways passes into each other's feet, because that way nobody could ever shout at them. There was *zaorganizovannost*, overorganization.

Ghiddink, as the Russians call him, joked with his players, relaxed them. As a "punishment" in training, a player might have a ball kicked at his backside, while the rest of the squad stood around laughing. The times helped: this generation of Russian players could not remember the USSR. Armed with iPhones and SUVs, they had left the periphery and joined the global mainstream.

As he had in Korea, Hiddink practically ordered his players to think for themselves, to give riskier passes, to move into new positions without his telling them to. Marc Bennetts, author of *Football Dynamo: Modern Russia and the People's Game*, said, "It's as if he's beaten the Marxism-Leninism out of them." At Euro 2008, Russia's hammering of Ghiddink's native Holland was the ultimate triumph of a marginal country over a core one. It also provided the almost unprecedented sight of Russian soccer players having fun. They swapped positions and dribbled, knowing that if they lost the ball no one would scream at them. After the game, their best player, Andrei Arshavin, muttered something about "a wise Dutch coach" and cried.

Russia lost in the semis of Euro 2008 to another former marginal country, Spain. By then, after twenty-two years in the European Union, Spain was so networked that it didn't even need a foreign coach to win the Euro.

Spain, Russia, and Turkey, another semifinalist at Euro 2008, were all beneficiaries of the spread of soccer know-how to marginal countries. When all countries have about the same soccer information, and converging incomes, the countries with the most inhabitants usually win. Three of the four semifinalists at Euro 2008 (Russia, Germany, and Turkey) had the largest populations in Europe. This was bad news for small core countries like Holland, Denmark, and the Czech Republic. Their populations and economies are almost static, and they have exported their soccer knowledge. What made them unique between 1970 and 2000 was their networks. Now that the networks have expanded to include much of the world, they are probably doomed.

2009–? THE PERIPHERY WINS THE WORLD CUP

Until the late 1990s the cliché in soccer was that an African country would "soon" win the World Cup. Everyone said it, from England's manager Walter Winterbottom to Pelé. But it turned out not to be true, mostly because although African populations were growing, their incomes remained too low to import much good soccer experience. A better tip for future World Cups might be Iraq. If the country remains halfway stable, it's likely to do even better than it did in its years of madness. However, the best bets for the future are probably Japan, the US, or China: the three largest economies on earth, which can afford coaches like Hiddink, where potential soccer players have enough to eat and don't get terrible diseases. There are already omens of their rise: the US has the most young soccer players of any country, and has reached a World Cup quarter-final; Japan says it aims to host the World Cup again by 2050 and win it; China topped the medals table at the last Olympics. These countries will get to the top sooner than the Africans. In the new world, distance no longer separates a country from the best soccer. Only poverty does.

ACKNOWLEDGMENTS

Dozens of people helped make this book possible. We received great help from Peter Allden, Dave Berri, Joe Boyle, Dennis Coates, Rod Fort, Bernd Frick, Brian Goff, Jahn Hakes, Pauline Harris, Brad Humphreys, Paul Husbands, Kai Konrad, Dan Kuper, Markus Kurscheidt, Mike Leeds, Wolfgang Maennig, John McMillan, Roger Noll, Andrew Oswald, Holger Preuss, Skip Sauer, and Lia Na'ama ten Brink for all their help.

We got ideas and information from Kevin Alavy, Rob Baade, Vendeline von Bredow, Carl Bromley, Tunde Buraimo, Pamela Druckerman, Russell Gerrard, Matti Goksøyr, Adam Kuper, Hannah Kuper, Kaz Mochlinski, Ignacio Palacios-Huerta, Ian Preston, Andreas Selliaas, and Paul in 't Hout; from Benjamin Cohen, Jonathan Hill, Mark O'Keefe, and Alex Phillips at UEFA; and from David O'Connor and Andrew Walsh at Sport+Markt.

The following were fantastic collaborators: Kevin Alavy, Wladimir Andreff, Giles Atkinson, Tunde Buraimo, Luigi Buzzacchi, Filippo dell'Osso, David Forrest, Pedro Garcia-del-Barrio, Steve Hall, David Harbord, Takeo Hirata, Tom Hoehn, Georgios Kavetsos, Stefan Késenne, Tim Kuypers, Umberto Lago, Stephanie Leach, Neil Longley, Susana Mourato, Susanne Parlasca, Ian Preston, Steve Ross, Rob Simmons, Ron Smith, Tommaso Valletti, and Andy Zimbalist.

Gordon Wise was a hardworking and imaginative agent. Carl Bromley thought from the start that this book should appear in the US, and he, Sandra Beris, and Annette Wenda helped make the American edition much better than it could have been without them.

We also want to thank all the interviewees quoted in the text.

SELECT BIBLIOGRAPHY

BOOKS

Andreff, Wladimir, and Stefan Szymanski, eds. *Handbook on the Economics of Sport.* Cheltenham: Edward Elgar, 2006.

Andrews, David L. *Manchester United: A Thematic Study.* London: Routledge, 2004.

Bellos, Alex. *Futebol: The Brazilian Way of Life.* London: Bloomsbury, 2002.

Bennetts, Marc. *Football Dynamo: Modern Russia and the People's Game.* London: Virgin Books, 2008.

Burns, Jimmy. *Hand of God: The Life of Diego Maradona.* London: Bloomsbury, 1996.

———. *When Beckham Went to Spain: Power, Stardom, and Real Madrid.* London: Penguin, 2004.

Dobson, Stephen, and John Goddard. *The Economics of Football.* Cambridge: Cambridge University Press, 2001.

Drogba, Didier. *"C'était pas gagné . . ."* Issy-les-Moulineaux: Éditions Prolongations, 2008.

Exley, Frederick. *A Fan's Notes.* London: Yellow Jersey Press, 1999.

Ferguson, Alex. *Managing My Life: My Autobiography.* London: Hodder and Stoughton, 2000.

Foot, John. *Calcio: A History of Italian Football.* London: Fourth Estate, 2006.

Ginsborg, Paul. *A History of Contemporary Italy.* London: Penguin, 1990.

Gladwell, Malcolm. *Outliers: The Story of Success.* London: Allen Lane, 2008.

Gopnik, Adam. *Paris to the Moon.* New York: Random House, 2000.

Hall, Matthew. *The Away Game*. Sydney: HarperSports, 2000.

Hamilton, Aidan. *An Entirely Different Game: The British Influence on Brazilian Football*. Edinburgh: Mainstream Publishing, 1998.

Hill, Declan. *The Fix: Soccer and Organized Crime*. Toronto: McClelland and Stewart, 2008.

Holt, Richard, and Tony Mason. *Sport in Britain, 1945–2000*. London: Wiley-Blackwell, 2000.

Hornby, Nick. *Fever Pitch*. London: Indigo, 1996.

Kapuściński, Ryszard. *The Soccer War*. New York: Vintage International, 1992.

Kok, Auke. *1974: Wij waren de besten*. Amsterdam: Thomas Rap, 2004.

Kolfschooten, Frank van. *De bal is niet rond*. Amsterdam and Antwerp: L. J. Veen, 1998.

Lever, Janet. *Soccer Madness*. Chicago: University of Chicago Press, 1983.

Lewis, Michael. *Moneyball*. New York: W. W. Norton, 2004.

Mandela, Nelson. *The Long Walk to Freedom*. London: Abacus, 1995.

Montague, James. *When Friday Comes: Football in the War Zone*. Edinburgh: Mainstream Publishing, 2008.

Mora y Araujo, Marcela, and Simon Kuper, eds. *Perfect Pitch 3: Men and Women*. London: Headline Book, 1998.

Nieuwenhof, Frans van de. *Hiddink, Dit is mijn wereld*. Eindhoven: De Boekenmakers, 2006.

Norridge, Julian. *Can We Have Our Balls Back, Please? How the British Invented Sport and Then Almost Forgot How to Play It*. London: Penguin, 2008.

Oliver and Ohlbaum Associates and Fletcher Research. *Net Profits: How to Make Money Out of Football*. London: Fletcher Research, 1997.

Orakwue, Stella. *Pitch Invaders: The Modern Black Football Revolution*. London: Victor Gollancz, 1998.

Peace, David. *The Damned United*. London: Faber and Faber, 2006.

Simons, Rowan. *Bamboo Goalposts: One Man's Quest to Teach the People's Republic of China to Love Football*. London: Macmillan, 2008.

Szymanski, Stefan. *Playbooks and Checkbooks: An Introduction to the Economics of Modern Sports*. Princeton: Princeton University Press, 2009.

Szymanski, Stefan, and Tim Kuypers. *Winners and Losers: The Business Strategy of Football*. London: Penguin Group, 1999.

Szymanski, Stefan, and Andrew Zimbalist. *National Pastime: How Americans Play Baseball and the Rest of the World Plays Soccer*. Washington, DC: Brookings Institution, 2005.

Taylor, Peter. *With Clough by Taylor.* London: Sidgwick and Jackson, 1980.

Turnbull, John, Thom Satterlee, and Alon Raab, eds. *The Global Game: Writers on Soccer.* Lincoln: University of Nebraska Press, 2008.

Varley, Nick. *Parklife: A Search for the Heart of Football.* London: Penguin, 1999.

Vergouw, Gyuri. *De Strafschop: Zoektocht naar de ultieme penalty.* Antwerp: Uitgeverij Funsultancy, 2000.

When Saturday Comes. *Power Corruption and Pies: A Decade of the Best Football Writing from "When Saturday Comes."* London: Two Heads Publishing, 1997.

White, Jim. *Manchester United: The Biography.* London: Sphere, 2008.

Zirin, Dave. *A People's History of Sports in the United States.* New York: New Press, 2008.

ARTICLES AND RESEARCH PAPERS

Baade, R. "Professional Sports as Catalysts for Metropolitan Economic Development." *Journal of Urban Affairs* 18, no. 1 (1996): 1–17.

Gabaix, Xavier. "Zipf's Law for Cities: An Explanation." *Quarterly Journal of Economics* (MIT Press) 114, no. 3 (August 1999): 739–767.

Hicks, Joe, and Grahame Allen. *A Century of Change: Trends in UK Statistics Since 1900.* House of Commons Library Research Paper 99/111. London: House of Commons Library, December 1999.

Hirshleifer, J. "The Paradox of Power." *Economics and Politics* 3 (1991): 177–200.

Kavetsos, Georgios, and Stefan Szymanski. "National Wellbeing and International Sports Events." *Journal of Economic Psychology* (forthcoming).

McGrath, Ben. "The Sporting Scene: The Professor of Baseball." *New Yorker,* July 7, 2003.

Palacios-Huerta, Ignacio. "Professionals Play Minimax." *Review of Economic Studies* 70, no. 2 (2003): 395–415.

Szymanski, Stefan. "Income Inequality, Competitive Balance, and the Attractiveness of Team Sports: Some Evidence and a Natural Experiment from English Soccer." *Economic Journal* 111 (2001): F69–F84.

———. "A Market Test for Discrimination in the English Professional Soccer Leagues." *Journal of Political Economy* 108, no. 3 (2000): 590–603.

Tapp, A. "The Loyalty of Football Fans—We'll Support You Evermore?" *Journal of Database Marketing and Customer Strategy Management* 11, no. 3 (April 1, 2004).

Tapp, A., and J. Clowes. "From 'Carefree Casuals' to 'Professional Wanderers': Segmentation Possibilities for Football Supporters." *European Journal of Marketing* 36, no. 11 (2002).

MAGAZINES

Hard Gras (Netherlands)
Johan (Netherlands, now defunct)
So Foot (France)
Voetbal International (Netherlands)

INDEX

Abidal, Eric, 71
Abrahams, Mike, 161
Abramovich, Roman, 154, 207
AC Milan, 6, 16–17, 27, 47, 60, 62, 84, 133, 139(fig.),140(fig.), 155, 175
Adams, Tony, 19(fig.), 20, 58, 84
Addicted (Adams), 84
Addictions, 58
Adidas, 78–79
Adu, Freddy, 70
Age
    flame-out in younger players, 69–70
    happiness and, 246
    Korea's hierarchy impeding success, 296
    Milan Lab, 6
    overvaluing older players, 57–58
Ajax Amsterdam, 62–63, 80, 135–136, 139(fig.), 145(fig.), 301
Alavy, Kevin, 190–193, 197–200
Albania, 285(fig.)
Alcohol use and abuse, 21, 58
Aldershot FC, 90–91
All Played Out: The Full Story of Italia '90 (Davies), 5
Amazulu team, 267–268
Amokachi, Daniel, 107
Anderson, Sonny, 71
Anderson, Viv, 100
Anderton, Darren, 19(fig.), 20
Anelka, Nicolas, 60–61, 126–127

Apartheid, 266–267, 271
Argentina
    England's World Cup loss, 8, 11, 25, 37
    goal performance measures, 38
    international experience, 36
    penalty kick behavior, 122–124
    soccer couch potatoes, 197(fig.)
    top teams by experience, 280
Armenia, 285(fig.), 287
Arshavin, Andrei, 305
Asian Soccer Confederation, 281–282
Athletes' Performance, 30–31
Atkinson, Ron, 106
Aulas, Jean-Michel, 65–68, 71–72, 140
Aussie Rules, 262–263, 303
Australia, 162, 199(fig.), 262–263, 282(fig.), 283, 294, 301–304
Austria, 183–184, 230(fig.),231(fig.), 286(fig.)
Auto racing, 260
Auzout, Adrien, 26
The Away Game (Hall), 301–302
Azerbaijan, 38, 286(fig.)

Baade, Rob, 238–241
Bacon, Francis, 26
Bafana Bafana, 266–271

Balance, competitive, 166–172,
175–177
Ballack, Michael, 125
Bamboo Goalposts (Simons), 206
Bangladesh, 222
Banks, Gordon, 9
Barcelona, 31, 52, 59, 85,
139(fig.),140(fig.), 143–144, 155,
175
Barnes, John, 47, 100–101, 110
Bartlett, Shaun, 271
Baseball, 2–4, 40, 42, 58, 66, 68, 85–86,
109–110, 115, 224, 232, 237,
257–258, 294
Baseball Abstracts (James), 3
Basketball, 109, 258
Batistuta, Gabriel, 148
Batty, David, 19(fig.), 20
Bayern Leverkusen, 146
Bayern Munich, 140(fig.), 147, 155,
175–176
Beane, Billy, 3, 40, 53, 57, 66, 69–70
Beckenbauer, Franz, 133
Beckham. David, 9, 11, 19(fig.), 20,
164
Belarus, 285(fig.)
Belgium, 28, 247, 285(fig.)
Belletti, Juliano, 125
Bellos, Alex, 4, 52–53
Benfica, 122, 134
Bennetts, Marc, 305
Bergkamp, Dennis, 57–58
Berlusconi, Silvio, 148
Best, George, 293
Big Count, 181–182
Bin Laden, Osama, 295
BIRGing (basking in reflected glory),
210–212, 217
Birmingham City, 56
Birtles, Gary, 55
Black players
America's dearth of, 165
black managers, 110–112

clichés of athletic excellence,
255–256
countries' wealth and sporting
success, 265
econometrics determining presence
of discrimination, 101–109
history of England's black and
immigrant population, 99–101
import substitution in English
soccer, 15–16
overt racism and discrimination,
97–99
public perception of "blackness," 105
South Africa's "Coloured" players,
271
See also Poverty
*The Black Swan: The Impact of the
Highly Improbable* (Taleb), 44
Blatter, Sepp, 14
Blissett, Luther, 47, 59, 110
Blond players, 53
Bolaños, Amelia, 222
Bonetti, Peter, 9, 11
Bonhof, Rainer, 145
*Book of Numbers: Everything You Need
to Know About Simple Math*
(Bellos), 4
Borussia Mönchengladbach, 145–146,
145(fig.), 147
Bosnia-Herzegovina, 285(fig.)
Boukhari, Nourdin, 272–273
Bowles, Stan, 58
Boyle, Joe, 18
Brady, Chris, 83
Bramcote, 133–134
Brazil
Brazilian players adjusting to
English soccer, 62
England's World Cup loss, 9, 11
fan suicides, 221
global ranking in sporting success,
262–263
goal performance measures, 38

inevitable victory at 2008 World
  Cup, 41–42
international experience, 36
Jules Rimet trophy, 275
origins of soccer in, 159
overvaluing Brazilian players, 52–53
top teams, 277(fig.), 280, 282,
  282(fig.)
win percentage, 12
Brentford, 98
Bridgewater, Sue, 83
Bristol City, 211–212
Bristol Rovers, 91
Bronckhorst, Giovanni van, 52
Brown, Gordon, 249
Bruges, 145(fig.)
Buckley, Delron, 271
Bulgaria, 285(fig.)
Bundesliga, 94, 136, 175–176, 184
Bungs, 54
Buraimo, Tunde, 116–117
Burnham, Andy, 166
Burns, Jimmy, 135
Burns, Kenny, 56–57
Bush, George W., 237
Business, soccer as a
  big business, 75–78
  failure of business strategies, 91–95
  hiring a manager, 81–84
  incompetent staff hirings, 84–88
  stupidity and bad business, 78–80
  surviving economic downturn,
    88–91
Butcher, Terry, 14

Cambiasso, Esteban, 123–124
Cameron, David, 249–250
Cameroon, 222, 270
Campbell, Sol, 19(fig.), 20
Canada, 199(fig.), 223, 289(fig.)
Cantona, Eric, 55
Capello, Fabian, 31
Carragher, Jamie, 19(fig.), 20

Carvalho, Ricardo, 9
Castiella, Maria, 135
Cecchi Gori, Vittorio, 148
Cech, Petr, 125
Celtic, 80
Center for International Comparisons,
  280–281
Champions League, 2, 27–28, 31, 48,
  67, 124–127, 133. See also
  European Cup
Charisteas, Andreas, 300–301
Charlton, 90–91
Chelsea, 60, 63, 76, 78, 113–114,
  124–127, 139(fig.), 140, 154, 176,
  190, 207–208
Cheltenham Town, 143
Chess, 259
China, 182, 206, 265, 295, 306
Clarkebury Institute, 157
Clough, Brian, 40, 54–58, 133–134,
  147, 185
Clowes, Jeff, 214, 218
Cole, Ashley, 19(fig.), 20, 126
Cole, Joe, 19(fig.), 20
Colombia, 37
Commitment, 296–297
Communist regimes, 134–135
Confederation Cup (2005), 303
Congress, U.S., 241
Constantinou, Demitri, 267–268
Copenhagen, 63–64
Copernicus, 26
Cragnotti, Sergio, 86–87
Crick, Michael, 104–109
Cricket, 23, 257, 266
Croatia, 13, 196, 197(fig.), 284,
  284(fig.),285(fig.), 287
Crooks, Garth, 98
Crouch, Peter, 19(fig.), 20
Cruijff, Johan, 22, 31
Culture, 59, 161, 297, 299
Cycling, 259–260
Cyprus, 188–189, 286(fig.)

Czech Republic, 35, 230(fig.),231(fig.), 277(fig.), 279, 284, 284(fig.),285(fig.), 286, 305

The Damned United (Peace), 55
Davies, Pete, 5
De Oliveira, William, 69
De Zeeuw, Demy, 77–78
Dearnaley, George, 267–268
Defoe, Jermaine, 51
Deisler, Sebastian, 147
Denmark, 28, 197, 197(fig.), 229, 230(fig.),231(fig.), 285(fig.), 305
Derwall, Jupp, 298
Dessypris, Nick, 228
Development economics, 14–15, 24–25
Discrimination. *See* Black players
Dobson, Stephen, 171
Domenech, Raymond, 65
Downing, Stewart, 19(fig.), 20
Draper, Peter, 160–161
Drogba, Didier, 63, 71–72, 255, 271–272
Durkheim, Émile, 223
Dyer, Kieron, 19(fig.), 20
Dynamo Berlin, 135
Dynamo Kiev, 51
Dynamo Moscow, 139(fig.)

East Germany, 135, 261(fig.), 262, 285(fig.). *See also* Germany (united); West Germany
Econometrics, 101–102, 116
Economic crisis, 88–89
Economic performance, 298
Education: England's exclusion of middle-class players, 20–23
Edworthy, Niall, 9
Eggers, Dave, 164
Egypt, 269–270
El Salvador, 222
Engels, Friedrich, 137

England
  armchair fans, 208–209
  bad business, soccer as, 78–80
  blaming foreign players for World Cup losses, 14–18
  colonial spread of soccer, 157–161, 293–294
  competitive balance, 176
  demise of midsize-town teams, 149
  econometric demonstration of discrimination, 101–109
  economic impact of Euro '96, 242
  employment of World Cup fathers, 19(fig.)
  exclusion of the middle classes, 18–23
  fan behavior, 207, 213–220, 225
  favorite team rankings, 140(fig.)
  freakish bad luck causing World Cup losses, 8–9
  Gerrard's international soccer database, 34–39
  global ranking in sporting success, 262
  goal performance measures, 38
  happiness, national, 247, 249–251
  Hiddink's desire to manage, 304
  incompetent staff, 85
  Industrial Revolution and the rise of soccer, 137–144
  international experience measures, 36
  large-city dominance of soccer, 153–155
  manager hirings, 81–84
  Nelson Mandela Challenge, 269–270
  networking, 23–26, 28–32
  Norway's support of English teams, 200–201
  pacing the game, 31–32
  qualifying records, 40–44
  racism, 97–101

ranking European teams, 285(fig.)
relocating foreign players, 62
stadium attendance figures, 184–188
statistical predictions of World Cup
     losses, 12–14
surviving economic downturn, 90
televised sports, 190, 194
top European and national teams,
     277, 277(fig.), 279–280, 284,
     284(fig.)
transfer fees, 48–50
underperformance myth, 32–34,
     36–39
wages and league position, 49(fig.)
wartime enemies, 8
World Cup victory prediction, 7–8
English Football League, 90–91, 138
Epstein, Theo, 3–4
Eriksson, Sven Goran, 8, 17, 30, 86–88
Essien, Michael, 71–72
Estonia, 185, 286(fig.), 289(fig.)
Ethiopia, 289(fig.)
Eto'o, Samuel, 256
Eulberg, Frank, 266
Euro '80, 247
Euro '84, 247–248
Euro '88, 40, 247–248
Euro '96, 39, 127, 242, 247, 298
Euro 2000, 247–248
Euro 2004, 191, 202, 300–301
Euro 2008, 13–14, 30, 41, 198, 293,
     305
Euro 2012, 244
Eurobarometer, 245–246
European Cup, 133–134
     democratic regimes, 135–137
     industrialized provinces, 137–144
     lack of competitive balance, 176
     provincial-city teams, 149–150
     small-town teams, 144–147
     totalitarian regimes, 134–135
Everton, 97–98, 104–105, 107, 144,
     266

Exley, Frederick, 226–227, 234
Experience, importance in team
     statistics
England, 44
European and global team
     comparisons, 39, 284–285,
     284(fig.)
former Soviet nations, 287
ranking European teams by
     population, wealth, and
     experience, 285–286(fig.)
regression method, 35–37
top national teams, 280, 282–283,
     282(fig.)

Fans
     armchair-and hard-core fans,
          208–209
     English fans supporting foreign
          players, 17–18
     Europe's favorite clubs, 139(fig.)
     global market for, 177–178
     Hornbyesque Fan, 203–205
     loyalty of foreign fans to English
          clubs, 206–208
     penalties, 114
     racism among, 100–101
     shifting relationships with team
          loyalty, 217–218
     shopping for teams, 66–67
     spectator information, 209–213
     Tapp and Clowes' fan loyalty study,
          213–216
     ties that bind, 218–220
     See also Suicide
A Fan's Notes (Exley), 226–227
Faroe Islands, 182, 184, 189
Fascist regimes, 134–135
Al Fayed, Mohamed, 154
Fear and Loathing on the Campaign
     Trail '72 (Thompson), 225
Fenerbahce, 139(fig.), 143
Ferdinand, Rio, 19(fig.), 20, 125

Ferguson, Alex, 14, 21, 111, 127
Fernquist, Robert, 224
Fever Pitch (Hornby), 98, 100,
    203–205, 207–208, 217–218,
    226
Field of Dreams (film), 236
Finland, 286(fig.), 289(fig.)
Fiorentina, 90, 147–149
The Fix (Hill), 278
Fofi, Goffredo, 141–142
Fontanarrosa, Roberto, 294
Football, American, 158, 163–167,
    224–227
Ford, Stuart, 22–23
Forrest, David, 169–170
Fortune, Quinton, 271
Fowler, Robbie, 15, 19(fig.), 20
France
    black players, 108
    collectivized western European
        soccer, 28
    fan suicides, 230(fig.),231(fig.)
    favorite team rankings, 140(fig.)
    global ranking in sporting success,
        263
    goal performance measures,
        38–39
    happiness of hosting a tournament,
        247–248
    industrial migration, 142
    large-city dominance of soccer, 153
    Olympique Lyon, 64–73
    performance relative to smaller
        nations, 287–288
    population statistics, 36
    ranking European teams, 285(fig.)
    Ribéry's penalty kick strategy, 131
    stadium attendance figures, 185
    television viewers, 199
    top European and national teams by
        win percentage, 277(fig.), 284,
        284(fig.)
Francis, Trevor, 56, 146–147

Fulham, 154
Futebol: The Brazilian Way of Life
    (Bellos), 4, 52–53
Futures Sport & Entertainment,
    191–192

Gabaix, Xavier, 151–152
Gaetjens, Joe, 8–9
Galatasary, 139(fig.), 143, 298–299
Galileo, 26
Game theory, 119–122, 127–131
Gauss, Carl Friedrich, 34–35
Gemmill, Archie, 56
George, Ricky, 78–79
Georgia, 285(fig.), 287
Germany (united)
    collectivized western European
        soccer, 28
    competitive balance, 176
    economic impact of the World Cup,
        242–243
    exporting soccer expertise to Turkey
        and Greece, 298–301
    fan suicides, 228–229,
        230(fig.),231(fig.)
    favorite team rankings, 140(fig.)
    global ranking in sporting success,
        262
    goal performance measures, 38–39
    happiness factor, 246–247
    industrial migrants, 141
    international experience, 36
    penalty kick behavior, 122–124
    performance relative to smaller
        nations, 287–288
    population statistics, 36
    ranking European teams,
        285(fig.),286(fig.)
    small-town teams, 145–146
    sport participation by country,
        183–184
    stadium attendance figures, 185
    suicide figures, 223

televised sports, 190, 192–193,
  197–198
top European and national teams by
  win percentage, 277(fig.), 284,
  284(fig.)
2006 World Cup, 25
World Cup victory over England, 8,
  10
See also East Germany; West
  Germany
Gerrard, Russell, 33–39, 276, 280
Gerrard, Steven, 14, 19(fig.), 20
Giants, Zipf's law and, 152
Giggs, Ryan, 105
Ginsborg, Paul, 141
Gladwell, Malcolm, 272
Globalization, 294–295, 299
Goal difference measures, 34–38, 281,
  282(fig.), 285–286(fig.),
  286–287
Goddard, John, 171
Goksøyr, Matti, 199–200
Gopnik, Adam, 114–115
Graham, George, 51
Grant, Avram, 114, 124–125
Gray, John, 161–162
Greece, 28, 230(fig.),231(fig.),
  286(fig.), 299–300, 303–304
Greenwood, Ron, 8
Gullit, Ruud, 60, 110

Hall, John, 80
Hall, Matthew, 301–302
Happiness: Lessons from a New Science
  (Layard), 245–246
Happiness, politics of, 245–247,
  249–250
Harald, King of Sweden, 201
Haynes, Johnny, 8
Health issues, 266–268
Height effect, 295–296
Helder, Glenn, 108–109
Helland, Knut, 265

Hembert, Emmanuel, 69, 85–86, 94
Henry, Thierry, 58, 154
Hereford, 78
Heskey, Emile, 19(fig.), 20
Hiddink, Guus, 30, 291–293, 295–297,
  301–305
Hill, Dave, 11, 97, 107
Hill, Declan, 278
Hirshleifer, Jack, 174–175
HIV/AIDS, 268
Hockey, 163, 223
Hoddle, Glenn, 8, 51, 84
Holland. *See* Netherlands
Home-field advantage, 35–36, 39, 44,
  117, 281, 284–285, 284(fig.)
Honduras, 222, 282, 282(fig.), 283
Hooke, Robert, 26
Hooper, Tom, 55
Hornby, Nick, 98, 100–101, 189,
  203–205, 207–208, 217–218,
  226
Houllier, Gerard, 69, 71
Human development index, 264
Humphreys, Brad, 244
Hungary, 263, 280, 286(fig.)
Hussein, Saddam, 277–279
Hussein, Uday, 278
Hutchinson, Roger, 294
Hutton, Alexander Watson, 160
Huygens, Christiaan, 26

Ibrahimovic, Zlatan, 256, 272
Iceland, 188–189, 200, 264, 285(fig.)
Import substitution, 15, 17–18
In 't Hout, Paul, 184–186, 188, 209
Ince, Paul, 19(fig.), 20, 110
Income, team performance and, 35,
  37–38, 264–266, 280–283,
  282(fig.), 284–285, 284(fig.),
  285–286(fig.)
Income from soccer. *See* Business,
  soccer as a
India, 199(fig.), 289(fig.), 290, 295

Indonesia, 197(fig.), 198, 289(fig.)
Industrial Revolution, 138–140, 142–143
Industrial soccer, 299
Inequality, 166–172, 175–177
Inter Milan, 86–87
Internet, 24–25, 80, 184, 294
Inzaghi, Filippo, 6
Iran, 282(fig.), 283
Iraq, 161–162, 277–279, 277(fig.), 282, 282(fig.), 290, 306
Ireland, 182, 184, 230(fig.),231(fig.)
Irish Republic, 282(fig.), 283, 285(fig.)
Island countries, 182
Isolationism, 29–30
Israel, 285(fig.)
Italy
    collectivized western European soccer, 28
    competitive balance, 175
    European Cup wins, 136
    favorite team rankings, 140(fig.)
    Fiorentina's demise, 147–149
    global ranking in sporting success, 263
    goal performance measures, 38–39
    happiness of hosting a tournament, 247–248
    industrial migrants, 141–142
    pacing the game, 31–32
    performance relative to smaller nations, 287–288
    population statistics, 36
    ranking European teams, 286(fig.)
    Spain's overperformance, 283
    stadium attendance figures, 184–186
    surviving economic downturn, 90
    televised viewing, 197(fig.)
    top European and national teams by win percentage, 277(fig.), 284, 284(fig.)
Ivory Coast, 38

James, Bill, 3, 58, 69
James, David, 19(fig.), 20
Japan
    import substitution, 15
    launching professional league, 295
    potential for World Cup win, 306
    2002 World Cup, 242, 297
    2006 World Cup, 25–26
Jenas, Jermaine, 19(fig.), 20
Johansson, Bjørn, 81
Joiner, Thomas, 232–234
Jordaan, Danny, 268
Juventus, 48, 94, 139(fig.), 141–142, 144, 175, 185, 213

Kahn, Lawrence, 109
Karate, 257
al-Kathiri, Mohammed, 70
Katz, Michael, 244
Kavetsos, Georgios, 247
Kazakhstan, 281–282
Keane, Robbie, 51
Keane, Roy, 55
Keller, Kasey, 52
Kennedy, John F., 233
Kennedy, Robert, 249
Kenyon, Peter, 78, 86
Kirkwood, Alistair, 163
Klein, Stefan, 10
Klinsmann, Jürgen, 30
Koch, Paul, 288
Köpke, Andreas, 123
Korea, 198, 242, 295–297
Kuper, Dan, 18
Kuwait, 278
Kwok Tong Soo, 151

Lacombe, Bernard, 67–68
Lake Forest College, Illinois, 239, 241
Lampard, Frank, 19(fig.), 20
Lamptey, Nii, 69
Language issues, 60
Latin, 26

Latvia, 199(fig.), 286(fig.)
Layard, Richard, 245–246
Lazio, 86–88
Le Saux, Graeme, 19(fig.), 20
Lebanon, 197
Lee, Rob, 19(fig.), 20
Leeds United, 91, 149, 190, 213
Lehmann, Jens, 122–123, 128
Lens grinder, 26
Lever, Janet, 221
Levitin, Daniel, 272
Levitt, Steve, 119, 127–128, 130
Lewis, Michael, 3, 5, 40, 42, 70, 85–86
Leyton Orient, 201
Lineker, Gary, 23
Lithuania, 199(fig.), 223, 286(fig.), 287
Liverpool FC, 23, 51, 57, 80, 97–98,
    104–105, 133, 139(fig.), 145(fig.),
    155, 176
Livingstone, Ken, 250
Lobanovski, Valeri, 29
Luck, role in winning, 41–43, 114
Luxembourg, 286(fig.), 288–289,
    289(fig.)

Macedonia, 286(fig.)
Malaysia, 289(fig.)
Maldini, Paolo, 6
Mali, 182
Malmö, 145(fig.), 147
Malnutrition and body size, 266–267
Malouda, Florent, 71
Malta, 286(fig.), 289(fig.)
Managers
    as market inefficiencies, 50–51
    discrimination against blacks,
        110–112
    hiring strategy, 81–84
    penalties, 114–115
Manchester City, 176–178, 210
Manchester United, 2, 55, 76, 85, 88,
    92–93, 104, 111, 124–127,
    137–139, 139(fig.), 155, 172, 206

Manchester United: The Biography
    (White), 137
Mandela, Nelson, 157–158
Mander, Anthony J., 231–232
Maradona, Diego, 9, 222, 256
Marini, Valeria, 148
Markovits, Andrei, 164
Masterton, George, 231–232
Matheson, Victor, 241
Matthäus, Lothar, 147
McCarthy, Benni, 271
McClaren, Steve, 30, 84
McCulloch, Robert, 247
McLeod, Ally, 231
McManaman, Steve, 19(fig.), 20
Mears, Joe, 11
Mears, Tyrone, 61
Media coverage
    England's underachiever status,
        13–14
    English from the cradle to the
        shame, 30
    global spread of soccer, 163
    Murdoch's television rights, 79–80
    penalty coverage, 115
    soccer as a business, 2, 77–78
    When Saturday Comes fanzine, 107,
        174
Meerseman, Jean-Pierre, 6
Merson, Paul, 19(fig.), 20, 58
Merthyr Town, 91
Mexico, 9, 25, 199(fig.)
Michels, Rinus, 31
Microscope, 26
Middle class players, England's
    exclusion of, 18–23
Middlesbrough, 84
Middleton, John, 56
Mielke, Erich, 135
Milan Lab, 6, 16–17
Miller, Charles, 158
Mills, Danny, 19(fig.), 20
Milne, Gordon, 298

Mittal, Lakshmi, 154
Mixed strategies, 128–131
Moldova, 285(fig.)
Moneyball (Lewis), 3, 40, 42, 52, 66, 70, 85–86
Montague, James, 278–279
Moore, Bobby, 79
Moray, Robert, 26
Morocco, 38
Mosimane, Pitso, 270
Mozambique, 38
Mulier, Pim, 160
Mulier Instituut, 182–183
Müller, Gerd, 301
Multiple regression technique, 34–35, 106, 108, 193–199, 281
Murdoch, Rupert, 79–80
"Must-win" concept, 13

Ndlovu, Peter, 268
Nelson Mandela Challenge, 269–270
Netherlands
    Amsterdam's European Cup wins, 135–136
    black managers, 110
    collectivized western European soccer, 28
    colonial spread of soccer, 160
    fan suicides, 228–229, 230(fig.),231(fig.)
    happiness of hosting a tournament, 247–248
    national superiority complex, 296–297
    overperformance, 286
    overvaluing Dutch players, 52
    penalty kick behavior, 122
    ranking European teams, 284, 284(fig.),285(fig.)
    sport participation by country, 183–184
    spread of soccer to marginalized countries, 305
    squabbling, 296
    stadium attendance figures, 185, 189
    television viewers, 197
    2006 World Cup, 25
    See also Hiddink, Guus
Networks, 23–24, 268, 288–289, 305
Netzer, Gunter, 145–146
Neville, Gary, 23
New York Giants, 226–227
New Zealand, 199(fig.), 263, 282(fig.), 283
Newcastle United, 51–52, 76, 78, 92, 210
Newton Heath, 137. *See also* Manchester United
NFL (National Football League), 165–169, 173, 177, 241
Nixon, Richard, 225
Noades, Ron, 97–98, 106
Northern Ireland, 285(fig.)
Norway, 182, 184, 188–189, 197, 199–202, 229, 230(fig.),231(fig.), 263–265, 285(fig.)
Nottingham Forest, 40, 54–55, 57–58, 145(fig.), 147, 176, 225

Oakland A's, 68
Oh, Sadaharu, 294
Olav, King of Sweden, 201
Olympic games, 190, 250–251, 260–261, 263–264
Olympique Lyon, 40, 139(fig.),140(fig.)
Olympique Marseille, 63, 67, 136, 139(fig.)
Orakwue, Stella, 110
Osundo, Philip, 69
Outliers: The Story of Success (Gladwell), 272
Overmars, Marc, 58
Overperformance, 282, 282(fig.), 284–285, 285(fig.),286(fig.)
Owen, Michael, 19(fig.), 20, 52

Pace, 31–32
Paisley, Bob, 57
Palacios-Huerta, Ignacio, 124–127, 129–130
Panathinaikos, 134
Papadapoulos, Fotis, 228
Paradox of power, 174–175
Parasuicide, 231
Paris St. Germain, 137
Parma, 149
Parry, Rick, 214
Passion, 297
Peace, David, 55
Penalty kicks
    assessing the unfairness of, 114–119
    England's loss to Argentina, 37
    England's World Cup losses, 9
    kick strategies, 119–122
    perceived unfairness of, 113–114
    pure and mixed strategies, 127–131
    tracking player behavior, 122–127
Penn World Tables, 280–281
People meter data, 191–192
People's History of Sports in the United States (Zirin), 238
Pérez Cutiño, Francisco, 52
Perfect Pitch (Hutchinson), 294
Peri, Scott, 30
Perry, William "the Refrigerator," 163
Peters, Martin, 9
Petit, Emmanuel, 58
Petridou, Eleni, 228
Phillips, Trevor, 109–110
Pienaar, Steven, 62–63, 266, 271
Pitch Invaders (Orakwue), 110
Platini, Michel, 14–16, 133, 166, 173, 176
Playing for Profits report, 86
Plenderleith, Ian, 174
Poland
    economic impact of Euro 2012, 244
    England's 1998 World Cup match, 37–38

favorite team rankings, 140(fig.)
ranking European teams, 286(fig.)
2006 World Cup, 25
World Cup victory over England, 9
Population statistics
    assessing England's performance, 34–39
    European and global team comparisons, 284–285, 284(fig.)
    importance of, 36–37
    ranking European teams by population, wealth, and experience, 285–286(fig.)
    spread of soccer to marginalized countries, 305–306
    top European and national teams, 279–280, 282–283, 282(fig.)
    Turkey's improving performance, 297–298
    Zipf's law, 150–151
Portsmouth, 51
Portugal
    Euro 2004, 301
    European Cup wins, 136
    overperformance, 286
    ranking European teams, 285(fig.)
    television viewers, 199
    2006 World Cup, 25
Poverty
    clichés of athletic excellence, 255–256
    health issues depleting player pool, 267–268
    hosting a World Cup, 235–236, 241–242, 244–245
    malnutrition and body size, 266–267
    politics of happiness, 246
    poor countries' exclusion from sporting success, 256–266
    potential for future World Cup wins, 306
    South Africa's black and coloured players, 271–273

Poverty (*continued*)
  South Africa's political and
    socioeconomic isolation, 267–268
Premier League (EPL), 14–18, 48, 52,
    76–77, 93(fig.), 94, 105–106,
    116–119, 138–139, 165–173, 184,
    208–209
Primera Liga, 16
Prokopowicz, Szymon, 244
Proportionate growth, law of, 152
Provincial teams, 138–144
Pure strategies, 127–128

Queens Park Rangers, 154

Rachman, Gideon, 205, 217
Racism, 97–101. *See also* Black players
Ramsey, Alf, 7
Randomness, 44
Rausch, Friedel, 146
Rea, Frederick, 293
Reading, 76
Real Madrid, 60–61, 76, 88, 134–135,
    139(fig.), 150, 160–161, 175, 206
Rebrov, Sergei, 51
Red Sox (Boston), 3–4
Red Star Belgrade, 134–135
Redgrave, Steve, 250
Redknapp, Harry, 17, 51
Referees, 9–10, 114–115, 297
Rehhagel, Otto, 300–301
Reker, Jan, 122
Relative performance, 38
Relocation problems, 59–64, 71–72
Ribéry, Franck, 131
Rice Krispies, 47, 59
Rickey, Branch, 109
Robinson, Jackie, 109–110
Romania, 37, 185, 197, 197(fig.),
    285(fig.)
Ronaldinho, 9
Ronaldo, Cristiano, 9, 11, 124–126,
    272–273

Rooney, Wayne, 9, 19(fig.), 20, 272
Rugby, 23, 115, 257, 266
Rush, Ian, 60
Russia
  Euro 2008, 13
  favorite team rankings, 140(fig.)
  global ranking in sporting success,
    262
  Hiddink's management of, 293,
    304–305
  large-city dominance of soccer, 153
  moderate overachievement, 38
  ranking European teams, 286(fig.)
  stadium attendance figures, 185–186
  top European teams by win
    percentage, 284, 284(fig.)

Sabermetricians, 3
Sacchi, Arrigo, 27, 84
Saint-Étienne, 65, 145(fig.)
Salaries, 48, 49(fig.), 52, 103–109, 111,
    146–147. *See also* Transfers
Sanchez, Jose Angel, 206–207
Santini, Jacques, 69, 154
Scapegoats, 11, 14–18
Schaefer, Manfred, 301
Scholes, Paul, 19(fig.), 20
Scientific revolution, 26
Scolari, Luiz Felipe, 42
Scotland, 188–189, 231, 285(fig.)
Seaman, David, 19(fig.), 20
The Second Most Important Job in the
    Country (Edworthy), 9
Senegal, 270
Serbia, 35, 197, 197(fig.), 277(fig.),
    279, 285(fig.), 286
Shearer, Alan, 19(fig.), 20, 92
Shearman, Montague, 138
Sheilas, Wogs, and Poofters (Warren),
    294
Sheringham, Teddy, 19(fig.), 20
Shilton, Peter, 56
Shinty, 294

Simeone, Diego, 9
Simmons, Robert, 169–170
Simonsen, Alan, 145
Singapore, 197(fig.), 198
Size of players: Korea, 295–296
Slovakia, 184, 286(fig.)
Slovenia, 286(fig.)
Small-town teams, 144–147
Smith, David, 104
Smith, Ron, 101–102
Soccer Dynamo: Modern Russia and the People's Game (Bennetts), 305
Soccer Madness (Lever), 221
Soccer Money League, 76
Social cohesion, 232–233
Soriano, Osvaldo, 120
South Africa
    apartheid's impact on South African soccer, 265–266
    black versus coloured players, 271–273
    British colonialism, 157–158, 161–162
    malnutrition and body size, 266–267
    Nelson Mandela Challenge, 269–270
    political and socioeconomic isolation, 267–268
    television viewers, 193
    top ten national teams, 282(fig.), 283
    2010 World Cup, 235–236, 241–242, 244–245
South Uist, 293–294
Southgate, Gareth, 19(fig.), 20, 39, 127
Soviet Union, 120, 262, 281, 287
Spain
    competitive balance, 175
    demise of midsize-town teams, 149
    Euro 2008 victory, 31, 305
    fan suicides, 230(fig.),231(fig.)
    fascist regime, 134–135
    favorite team rankings, 140(fig.)

importance of networks, 29
industrial migrants, 141–142
population statistics, 36
provincial-city teams, 150
ranking European teams, 285(fig.)
spread of soccer to marginalized countries, 305
television viewers, 199
top European teams, 277(fig.), 279, 282–283, 282(fig.), 284, 284(fig.)
Sport participation by country, 182–184
Sport+Markt, 67, 139–142, 206–207
Stadium finance, 236–241
Staff, 84–88
Stark, Steven, 160
Statistics
    assessing the unfairness of penalty kicks, 115–119
    econometrics demonstrating discrimination, 101–109
    England's qualifying record, 40–44
    fans' team loyalty, 206–207
    game theory applied to penalty kicks, 119–122
    Gerrard's international database, 33–39, 276–277, 280
    happiness of hosting a World Cup, 247–249
    increasing value and popularity of sports statistics, 4–6
    most enthusiastic spectators by country, 199–202
    NFL win percentage, 167–168
    poor countries' exclusion from sporting success, 256–266
    predicting England's World Cup losses, 12–14
    relative and absolute achievement, 275–276
    soccer players worldwide, 181–184
    spectator information, 184–189, 209–213

Statistics (*continued*)
   stadium finance, 240–241
   suicide, 228
   team experience, 280
   top national teams by win
      percentage, 1980–2001, 277(fig.)
   TV viewers, 189–199
   underperformance, 289–290,
      289(fig.)
   upsetting traditional beliefs, 2–3
   Wenger's reliance on, 57–58
   "wisdom of crowds" method of
      choosing players, 68
Steaua Bucharest, 134
Steels, Mark, 225
Strachan, J.A., 231
Sugar, Alan, 51, 54, 92
Suicide
   correlating with sports, 225–232
   risks, rates, and reasons for,
      222–225
   social cohesion preventing, 232–234
   World Cup loss, 221–222
Sunderland, 49(fig.), 80, 173, 201, 203,
   210
Super Bowl, 191
Sweden
   fan suicides, 230(fig.),231(fig.)
   international experience, 35–36
   most enthusiastic soccer countries,
      183–184
   national team performance per
      capita, 263
   ranking European teams, 285(fig.)
   top teams by experience, 280
   2006 World Cup, 25
Switzerland, 230(fig.),231(fig.),
   286(fig.)
Syria, 282(fig.), 283

Tagliabue, Paul, 177, 241
Taiwan, 198
Tajikistan, 281

Taleb, Nick, 44
Tapp, Alan, 213–216, 218
Taylor, Graham, 118–119
Taylor, Peter, 40, 54–58
Taylor, Rogan, 91
Taylor Report, 80
Tekle, Stephanus, 206–207
Television spectator figures, 189–200
Tennis, 259
Ten-thousand-hour rule, 272
Terry, John, 19(fig.), 20, 113–114,
   125–126
Tevez, Carlos, 125
Texas Rangers, 237
"The Longest Penalty Ever" (short
   story), 120–121
Thinking game, soccer as, 296–297,
   302–303
Thompson, Hunter S., 224–225
"Three Lions," 12
Thuram, Lilian, 108
Tigana, Jean, 110
Titanium Metals corporation
   (TIMET), 75–76
Tognaccini, Daniele, 16–17
Togo, 270
Tomaszewski, Jan, 9
Totalitarian Europe, 134–135
Tottenham Hotspur, 51, 92, 94, 201
Traditional beliefs, 2–3
Transfers
   Blissett's transfer mistake, 47
   blond players, 53
   new managers' inefficiencies
      through, 50–51
   Olympique Lyon strategy, 66–73
   overvaluing specific nationalities,
      52–53
   overvaluing star players, 51–52
   relocation problems, 59–64, 71–72
   Taylor–Clough partnership, 54–58
   transfer fees, 47–50
   See also Salaries

Trapattoni, Giovanni, 148
Troubled players, 58
Trovato, Frank, 223
Tunisia, 36–37
Turkey, 30–31, 142–143, 286(fig.), 288, 297–299, 305
Turkmenistan, 281

Ukraine, 199(fig.), 286(fig.)
Umbro, 78
Underperformance, 289–290, 289(fig.)
United States
    American football, 158
    baseball ranking, 257–258
    cultural reach, 161–162
    England's World Cup defeat, 10
    fan suicides, 221, 224
    global ranking in sporting success, 262
    international experience, 35
    launching professional league, 295
    1950 World Cup, 8–9
    number of soccer players, 182
    potential for World Cup win, 306
    social cohesion preventing suicide, 233
    spread of soccer to, 162–165
    stadium finance, 236–241
    Super Bowl viewer data, 191
    televised sports, 190, 193, 198–199
    2002 World Cup, 297
    2006 World Cup, 25
    underperformance, 289
Uruguay, 197(fig.), 303
Uzbekistan, 281

Van Breukelen, Hans, 122
Van der Sar, Edwin, 113–114, 124–127
Vassell, Darius, 19(fig.), 20
Veenhoven, Ruut, 246
Venables, Terry, 54
Venezuela, 289(fig.)

Viduka, Mark, 303
Vieira, Patrick, 58
Vieri, Christian, 86–87
Vogts, Berti, 145–146
Vryzas, Zisis, 300

Wagg, Stephen, 8
Walcott, Theo, 19(fig.), 20
Wales, 285(fig.)
Warren, Johnny, 294
Watford, 47, 49(fig.), 76
Weisweiler, Hennes, 146
Wenger, Arsène, 5–6, 40, 42, 57, 84, 115, 131, 218
Werder Bremen, 300–301
West Bromwich Albion, 49(fig.), 106
West Germany
    European Cup wins, 136
    fan suicides, 221
    goal performance measures, 38–39
    happiness of hosting a tournament, 247
    ranking European teams, 285(fig.)
    top European and national teams, 277, 277(fig.), 280, 284, 284(fig.)
    Turkey's 1984 victory, 298
    World Cup 1974, 301
    See also Germany (united)
West Ham, 51
West Indies, 263
Wharton, Arthur, 99
When Beckham Went to Spain (Burns), 135
When Friday Comes: Football in the War Zone (Montague), 278–279
When Saturday Comes fanzine, 107, 174
White, Jim, 137
Why People Die by Suicide (Joiner), 232–233
Wigan Borough, 91
Will, James, 70
Wimmer, Hacki, 146

Win percentage
  England, 12–14, 34, 40–44
  NFL, 167–168
  top European teams by win
    percentage, 284(fig.)
  top national teams by win
    percentage, 1980–2001, 277–278,
    277(fig.)
"Wisdom of crowds" method of
  choosing players, 68
With Clough by Taylor (Taylor), 55–57
Wolff, Joel, 288
Women
  as managers, 84
  fan suicides, 231(fig.)
  happiness and, 246
  Norwegian players and fans,
    201–202
  suicide attempts, 223
  television spectatorship, 190
  World Cup rankings, 258
Working class, 18–23, 137–138
World Cup
  collectivized western European
    soccer, 28
  economic impact of hosting, 242
  employment of English team
    members' fathers, 19(fig.)
  England's colonial spread of soccer,
    294
  England's conviction of win
    followed by surprise at loss, 7–12
  England's history of qualification, 40
  fan suicides, 221, 228–229

  global rankings, 261–262
  happiness of hosting, 245–250
  overvaluing star players, 51–52
  potential for future wins, 306
  statistical evaluation of achievement,
    275–276
  win percentage predicting qualifying,
    12–14
World Cup (1966), 44
World Cup (1970), 275
World Cup (1974), 231, 301
World Cup (1978), 231
World Cup (1982), 231
World Cup (1986), 231, 279
World Cup (1994), 241, 270, 300
World Cup (1998), 36–37
World Cup (2002), 41–42, 242, 244,
    295, 297
World Cup (2006), 25, 122–124, 164,
    190, 198, 242–243, 246–247,
    303–304
World Cup (2010), 193, 205, 235–236,
    241–242, 244–245, 268, 271
Wortmann, Sönke, 123
Wright, Billy, 10–11
Wright, Ian, 108–109

Yugoslavia, 134–135

Zahra, Huthyfa, 279
Zenden, Boudewijn, 59–61, 63, 291
Zidane, Dinedine, 256, 271–272
Zipf's law, 150–155
Zirin, Dave, 238